Curriculum Design

Principles and practice for modern education

David Hall

Curriculum Design
© DHP 2025. All rights reserved.
First edition.

No part of this publication may be reproduced, distributed, or transmitted in any form or by any means, including photocopying, recording, or other electronic or mechanical methods, without the prior written permission of the publisher, except in the case of brief quotations embodied in critical reviews and certain other non-commercial uses permitted by copyright law.

For permission requests, write to the publisher, addressed "Attention: Permissions Coordinator", at the address below:

David Hall Publishing (DHP)
Carlisle, Cumbria
Email: dhp@davidhall.uk
Website: davidhall.uk/dhp

This book is a work of nonfiction. The events, situations, and dialogue described are based on the author's experiences, and while the intent is to provide accurate and reliable information, the author and publisher make no representations or warranties with respect to the completeness, accuracy, or timeliness of the content within this book.

Published by David Hall Publishing (DHP)
Printed in the United Kingdom

ISBN: 978-1-917541-12-1

Cover design by DHP / Perplexity

First Printing, 2025

 DHP Books

CONTENTS

List of illustrations	vi
Acknowledgments	vii
Foreword	viii
Chapter 1 - Foundations of curriculum studies	1
Curriculum as a field of study	1
The concept of curriculum	3
The components of curriculum	6
Formal and informal curriculum	10
Product and process models of curriculum	14
Pedagogy	18
Curriculum planning as targets	21
Historical foundations and societal needs	22
Chapter 2 - Curriculum design	26
Fundamentals of curriculum design	26
The Tyler Rationale	30
Other design rationales	35
Taba Model	35
Wiggins & McTighe's Backward Design	35
Spiral Curriculum (Bruner)	36
Stenhouse's Process Model	36
Wheeler Model	36
Kerr Model	37
Eisner's Connoisseurship	37
Ornstein and Hunkins Framework	37
Freire's Critical Pedagogy	37
Curriculum frameworks	38
Common pitfalls and challenges of curriculum design	43
Learning outcomes, objectives and standards	47
Establishing the need for a curriculum	52
Chapter 3 - Organising the curriculum	62
What is curriculum organisation?	62
Criteria for effective organisation	65
Taxonomic levels	69
The Gronlund classification	70
Subject-based vs. integrated curricula	74

Modularisation and credit transfer	79
Accreditation for prior learning and experience	84

Chapter 4 - External influences on curriculum — 89

Agencies for UK curriculum development	90
Principles underpinning a national curriculum	93
Problems with a national curriculum	97
Balancing the curriculum	101
The political influence on the national curriculum	105
Who designs the national curriculum	109

Chapter 5 - Articulating curriculum intent — 115

What is curriculum intent?	115
Theoretical foundations of curriculum intent	121
Ofsted's inspection framework: Intent explained	125
Developing a school's curriculum intent	129

Chapter 6 - Curriculum implementation — 135

What is curriculum implementation?	136
Influences on curriculum implementation	139
Creating learning experiences	144
The importance of the teacher	148
Measuring implementation	152
What do Ofsted say about implementation?	158

Chapter 7 - Curriculum evaluation — 164

Measuring impact	164
Summative and formative evaluation	168
Evaluation models	171
Tyler's objectives model	172
Stake's countenance model	173
Stufflebeam's CIPP model	176
The Kirkpatrick model	178
Eisner's educational connoisseurship	182
Phases of evaluation	186
Evaluation documents	187
Ofsted's role in curriculum evaluation	191

Chapter 8 - Designing online learning — 197

Introduction to online learning	197
Key principles of online course design	200
Defining learning outcomes and objectives	204

Course structuring	206
Learner engagement strategies	209
Use of multimedia and interactive content	214
Assessment and feedback in online learning	218
Technology platforms and learning management systems	222

Chapter 9 - Assessment, grading and reporting — 226

The principles of assessment	227
The assessment cycle	231
Assessment design	233
Designing fit-for-purpose assessments	236
Assessment formats	241
Grading and feedback	246
Technology-enhanced assessment	252
Future trends in assessment	254

Chapter 10 - Managing the curriculum — 258

Planning curriculum change	258
Reasons for curriculum change	261
Leaders of curriculum change	263
Curriculum management roles	266

Appendix 1 - Action verbs for learning outcomes — 275

Appendix 2 - Learning taxonomies — 276

Appendix 3 - Sample programme specification — 280

Appendix 4 - Sample module specification — 283

Appendix 5 - Sample scheme of work — 285

Appendix 6 - Sample lesson plan — 287

Appendix 7 - Statements of intent — 290

Appendix 8 - Sample assessment rubric — 292

References — 296

Index — 314

LIST OF ILLUSTRATIONS

Figures

Figure 1.1	-	The total curriculum	6
Figure 2.1	-	Tyler's 4-stage rationale	31
Figure 2.2	-	Curriculum design example	38
Figure 3.1	-	Subject-based curricula	75
Figure 3.2	-	Interdisciplinary integrated curricula	77
Figure 3.3	-	Key skills competencies (English National Curriculum)	83
Figure 4.1	-	Curriculum re-contextualisation	110
Figure 6.1	-	Curriculum implementation	136
Figure 7.1	-	Summative curriculum evaluation	169
Figure 7.2	-	Formative curriculum evaluation	170
Figure 7.3	-	Stufflebeam's curriculum evaluation model	176
Figure 7.4	-	Kirkpatrick's four level approach	179
Figure 7.5	-	Five phases of evaluation	186
Figure 8.1	-	ADDIE model for digital learning	201
Figure 9.1	-	Curriculum and assessment interconnected	228
Figure 9.2	-	The assessment cycle	232
Figure 9.3	-	Observation rubric	242
Figure 10.1	-	Curriculum change	259

Tables

Table 1.1	-	Comparison of the product and process models	17
Table 2.1	-	Composition and use of frameworks	42
Table 2.2	-	Global comparisons of curriculum frameworks	43
Table 2.3	-	Needs analysis in major curriculum rationales	53
Table 2.4	-	Implications of curriculum review	59
Table 3.1	-	European credit transfer and accumulation system	81
Table 3.2	-	Modularisation and key skills integration	83
Table 4.1	-	Selected comparative models	112
Table 6.1	-	Stages of Concern (SoC)	155
Table 7.1	-	Stake's judgmental matrix	174
Table 7.2	-	Comparison of evaluation models	185
Table 9.1	-	Assessment types	230
Table 9.2	-	Bloom's taxonomy and associated question types	243
Table 10.1	-	Comparison of drivers of change	262
Table 10.2	-	Practical strategies for fostering leadership	268

ACKNOWLEDGMENTS

I would like to express my sincere gratitude to the many educators, leaders, and institutions whose experiences have informed the case studies and insights presented in this book. While their identities remain anonymous to respect their privacy, their real-world contributions have been invaluable in shaping the content and providing practical relevance. Their willingness to share their experiences has greatly enriched this work, and I am deeply appreciative of their support and cooperation.

A particular mention goes to Perplexity, whose creative assistance in the generation of the book's images, helps to catch people's attention and visualise the book's content.

FOREWORD

The landscape of education is in a period of profound transformation - a fact that makes the challenges and opportunities of curriculum design more relevant than ever. In an age marked by rapid technological advancement, shifting societal needs, and increasingly complex policy demands, educators must be prepared not only to deliver quality content but to shape and lead dynamic learning experiences that meet the needs of diverse learners.

Curriculum Design: Principles and practice for modern education is written in direct response to these complexities and guides readers through the foundational theories that underpin curriculum design. With practical chapters devoted to effective curriculum implementation, evaluation methods, and innovation, the book equips educators with tools to critically assess both the internal and external influences - policy, research, and reflective practice - that shape today's educational programmes.

Beyond theory, the book addresses the "how" of curriculum: how leadership and collaborative practice drive curriculum change; how educators can create and adapt curricula for specific contexts; and how technology and research support continual improvement. By intentionally weaving together historical context, policy analysis, educational research, and practical reflection, this work provides a holistic approach essential for those aiming to develop high-quality, inclusive programmes.

Through discussion prompts, practical scenarios, and reflective activities, readers will deepen their understanding of curriculum as both an academic field and a pathway to meaningful educational transformation. Whether you are an aspiring curriculum leader, a practicing educator, or a policy maker, this book will support you in addressing contemporary educational challenges and improving the quality and relevance of curriculum in your own setting.

Chapter 1 - Foundations of curriculum studies: Curriculum lies at the heart of educational practice, shaping both what is taught and how learning is experienced across all phases of education. This chapter invites readers to engage with the evolving field of curriculum studies, tracing its emergence as a cornerstone of modern education. By exploring foundational theories, diverse curricular models, and the vital interplay between policy, society, and classroom realities, the discussion uncovers why a dynamic and responsive curriculum is essential for meeting contemporary educational needs and preparing learners for an ever-changing world.

Chapter 2 - Curriculum design: In navigating the changing landscape of education, the significance of effective curriculum design has never been greater. This chapter invites readers to critically engage with the ever-evolving principles that shape curriculum development, blending historical insight with practical models suited for contemporary learning environments. Drawing on global perspectives, leading theories, and real-world examples from primary, secondary, further, and higher education, it provides a robust foundation for professional reflection and action. Beyond technical frameworks, the text champions the creative and ethical dimensions of curriculum leadership and classroom innovation. Whether you are a teacher, leader, or curriculum designer, this chapter will equip you to shape learning programmes that are rigorous, inclusive, and responsive to the needs of diverse learners in a rapidly transforming world.

Chapter 3 - Organising the curriculum: How knowledge is selected, sequenced, and experienced is as important as what is taught. This chapter guides educators, leaders, and curriculum designers through the foundational principles and practical strategies for structuring meaningful, coherent educational programmes across all phases - primary, secondary, further, and higher education. Drawing on both traditional and contemporary models, the discussion explores the relationship between curriculum structure, pedagogy, and policy, while highlighting the potential of modularisation, technology, and evidence-based frameworks to enhance flexibility, progression, and learner engagement.

Chapter 4 - External influences on curriculum: In a globalised and rapidly evolving society, educational curricula do not develop in isolation. This chapter explores the powerful external influences that shape curriculum content, design, and implementation in the UK and internationally. From national government agencies and international organisations, to political ideologies, public policy, and shifting societal expectations, these influences set the direction and constraints for what is taught in schools, colleges, and universities. Understanding the drivers, tensions, and debates that underpin curriculum reform is essential for educators, leaders, and policy-makers tasked with shaping learning for future generations. As educational provision becomes increasingly subject to close scrutiny, comparison, and policy intervention, this chapter invites readers to critically analyse the external factors that continually impact curriculum choices and outcomes.

Chapter 5 - Articulating curriculum intent: In recent years, curriculum intent has emerged as a critical focus in curriculum theory, policy, and practice - particularly following reforms to Ofsted's Inspection Framework (2019) in England. Alongside traditional curriculum development methods, intent challenges educators to articulate more clearly what the curriculum is designed to achieve and why. This shift invites reflection on how educational values, knowledge, learner needs, and long-term societal purposes are embedded into planning and design. Across all sectors - primary, secondary, further education (FE), and higher education (HE) - curriculum intent now shapes how institutions define ambitions, structure progression, and respond to context. By exploring historical developments and current frameworks, this chapter helps educators and curriculum leaders position intent as the foundation for effective, inclusive, and future-focused curriculum development.

Chapter 6 - Curriculum implementation: While curriculum intent provides the vision and rationale for what should be learned, implementation concerns itself with how this vision becomes reality for learners. No matter how carefully designed, a curriculum's true value is determined by its enactment - in the daily interactions, tasks, and adaptations made by teachers and learners across diverse contexts. This chapter explores the crucial, multi-faceted process of curriculum implementation, highlighting the factors, challenges, and opportunities that shape effective delivery in the real world.

Chapter 7 - Curriculum evaluation: Curriculum evaluation stands as the essential final stage in the curriculum cycle, measuring the impact on learners and bridging design and implementation with sustained, effective educational improvement. In a landscape of increasing accountability, evolving learner needs, and frequent policy reform, institutions cannot afford to leave curriculum impact unmeasured or unexplored. Rigorous evaluation provides the evidence and insight needed for meaningful, evidence-informed change, ensuring that curriculum serves its intended purpose for all learners. This chapter introduces the principles, models, and practicalities of curriculum evaluation, offering a critical foundation for leaders, teachers, and policymakers committed to achieving excellence and equity in education.

Chapter 8 - Designing online learning: The shift towards online learning continues to reshape the educational landscape, presenting significant opportunities for flexibility, accessibility, and personalisation across all levels of teaching and learning. Effective online course design demands the thoughtful integration of sound pedagogical principles, appropriate technological tools, and learner-centred approaches to ensure engagement and inclusivity for diverse populations. This process involves creating clear course structures, fostering active learner interaction, and delivering timely, meaningful feedback to support progress. As online environments pose unique challenges, best practices emphasise structured navigation, transparent expectations, and strong instructor presence. Notably, emerging trends such as AI-assisted content creation and activity-led module development now enable adaptive, continually improving digital courses. These innovations enhance both customisation and responsiveness, supporting deeper learning outcomes and redefining what is possible in twenty-first-century education.

Chapter 9 - Assessment, grading and reporting: Assessment is a deeply embedded element of the curriculum. It influences learners' experiences, progress, and the validity of reported achievement. When aligned explicitly with curriculum intent, assessment acts as the vital link between planned aims and actual learning, ensuring purposeful, coherent teaching and outcomes. This chapter explores assessment, grading, and reporting through a curriculum lens, highlighting how they inform and are shaped by curriculum structure and progression. Embedding assessment thoughtfully within curriculum design transforms it from a mere measure of results into a tool that deepens understanding, promotes equity, and drives improvement. Clear assessment practices and meaningful reporting foster transparency and shared understanding among learners, educators, leaders, and families, making assessment central to guiding, valuing, and advancing learning.

Chapter 10 - Managing the curriculum: Effective curriculum management demands vision, strategy, and a tenacious focus on relevance, coherence, and learner achievement. Strong curriculum leadership drives the entire process - from design to delivery and review - ensuring that the curriculum adapts to changing needs while holding true to the institution's values and goals. The leadership role extends beyond individuals, encompassing the contributions of principals, middle leaders, and teams working collaboratively to interpret and enact the curriculum in diverse settings. Success in this area hinges on aligning curriculum decisions with wider institutional priorities, navigating the challenges of shared responsibility, and building a culture in which every member of staff understands and contributes to the ongoing evolution of the curriculum.

Case Study — Case studies, drawn from real-life experiences in educational institutions, provide practical insights and illustrate key leadership and management concepts in action.

Activity — Activities encourage readers to apply their learning in practical contexts, promoting critical thinking and skill development. They help bridge theory and practice.

Information — Factual information boxes present clear, concise summaries of key theories and research. They serve as quick reference points and ground broader discussions in concrete evidence.

 **Question** Question boxes prompt deeper thinking, reflection and self-assessment, helping readers connect theory with their own experiences and contexts.

 Example boxes highlight instances of specific theories and concepts in action in educational institutes.

1 FOUNDATIONS OF CURRICULUM STUDIES

Introduction

Curriculum forms the core of all educational practice, fundamentally shaping what students learn and how learning takes place in every educational sector. This chapter explores the dynamic field of curriculum studies, tracing its development as an essential element within modern education. Readers will encounter key theories, varied curricular models, and the crucial relationships between policy, societal expectations, and daily classroom experiences. Through this examination, the chapter highlights the importance of a responsive and evolving curriculum in addressing today's educational demands and equipping learners for a rapidly changing global context.

This chapter:

- Examines the emergence and development of curriculum as an independent field of study.
- Investigates key historical milestones in UK curriculum planning and policy.
- Explores foundational definitions and components of curriculum across educational sectors.
- Considers the relationship between curriculum and societal change.
- Discusses curriculum challenges in primary, secondary, further, and higher education settings.
- Analyses the evolving role of curriculum in responding to learner needs and future demands.
- Highlights tensions between centralised control and professional autonomy in curriculum development.

Curriculum as a field of study

Curriculum studies has emerged over the past century as a distinct and essential domain within the educational landscape, driven by the recognition that purposeful planning and systematic organisation of educational content are fundamental to effective learning. The development of curriculum studies as an academic discipline is relatively recent but has been profoundly influenced by ongoing social, technological, and political changes. These forces have significantly raised expectations for educational systems, both nationally and internationally, demanding a more reflective, responsive, and research-informed approach to the questions of what, how, and why students learn (Kelly, 2009).

In the UK, the post-World War II era marked a turning point. The expansion of state education and growing awareness of the role of schooling in social change led to heightened attention to curriculum planning and evaluation. Prior to this, curriculum development was largely uncoordinated - best characterised as a 'haphazard drift' - with individual teachers or schools making ad hoc decisions about content and pedagogy (Gillard, 2011). As society progressed, it became increasingly clear that a structured and flexible approach was necessary if education was to keep pace with societal change, particularly technological advances.

This realisation prompted a series of policy responses, including the UK Ministry of Education's formation of the Curriculum Study Group and the Secondary Schools Examination Council in the mid-twentieth century. The establishment of the Schools Council in 1964 reflected a shift towards more formalised, research-informed curriculum development and oversight in England and Wales (Gillard, 2011). Although subsequent reorganisations have occurred, this development marked the beginning of curriculum as an independent field of research and practice in the UK.

The rise of curriculum studies is closely linked to the challenge of ensuring education meets both current and future learner needs. This requires curricula to evolve in anticipation of social and economic change, rather than reacting only after such shifts have occurred (Priestley & Biesta, 2013). The tension between centralised, politically driven curriculum reforms and the professional autonomy required to adapt curricula to local contexts remains a fundamental issue, explored extensively throughout both research and practice (Young et al., 2014).

Curriculum studies considers not just what is taught, but how learning is organised across diverse educational sectors. In primary education, the curriculum tends to be broad and integrated, designed around the holistic development of children and connecting subject areas to everyday life. Teachers are frequently generalists, responsible for delivering most or all subject content, which positions them as central architects of curriculum enactment (Alexander, 2021). In contrast, secondary education sees a shift towards much greater subject specialisation and compartmentalisation. Here, curriculum studies interrogate questions of subject balance, progression, and assessment, alongside the pressures of external examination systems and league tables (Pring, 2013).

Further education (FE) presents its own distinctive curriculum challenges. Programmes at this level are often tailored to vocational, personal development, or access needs. Curriculum studies in FE have prioritised the need for flexible, learner-centred design, recognising diverse student cohorts including adult returners, apprentices, and those seeking professional qualifications. The tension between sector requirements (such as employability) and wider educational aims brings curriculum as a field of study into active debate in FE settings.

In higher education (HE), the curriculum has traditionally been shaped by disciplinary norms and academic autonomy. However, increasing policy pressure for graduate employability, widening participation, and integration of digital technologies has led universities to rethink curriculum models. Contemporary studies focus on interdisciplinarity, student voice, and internationalisation, reflecting the fluid demands placed upon HE institutions in an era of global competition and technological innovation (Barnett & Coate, 2005). Here, curriculum is not simply a list of modules or units, but a dynamic process involving the co-construction of knowledge between students and academics.

Across all these sectors, curriculum studies as a field equips educators, leaders, and policymakers with tools to analyse, design, and implement educational programmes suited to changing personal, social, and economic needs. As education systems become increasingly complex, curriculum as a field of study plays a vital role in democratising learning and ensuring that schools, colleges, and universities are prepared for the challenges ahead.

The concept of curriculum

The term 'curriculum' is multifaceted and has been defined in numerous ways by educators, theorists, and policymakers, reflecting its complex role within education. At its most fundamental, curriculum refers to the planned sequence of learning experiences that an educational institution offers to learners. However, this simple description conceals the breadth of meanings, interpretations, and applications that exist across different educational contexts including primary, secondary, further education (FE), and higher education (HE) (Kelly, 2009).

One influential definition comes from Tanner & Tanner (1995), who describe curriculum as both a product - a specific set of subjects or content to be taught - and a process - the dynamic interactions between teachers, learners, and the contexts in which learning takes place. This dual perspective emphasises that curriculum is not merely a static document but an evolving experience shaped by numerous factors including pedagogy, learner needs, societal expectations, and policy directives.

In primary education, the curriculum is often broad, integrative, and child-centred, aiming to promote holistic development. Here, curriculum embodies essential knowledge, skills, and attitudes across numerous subject areas, but it also prioritises the integration of learning experiences to make connections between different domains (Alexander, 2021). This approach recognises early childhood as a critical period for developing cognitive, social, and emotional foundations. For example, the UK's Early Years Foundation Stage (EYFS) curriculum exemplifies this broad-based conception, focusing on communication, physical development, and personal, social, and emotional growth alongside emergent literacy and numeracy (GOV.UK, 2025).

By contrast, secondary education increasingly emphasises subject specialisation, preparing learners for national examinations and further study. The curriculum concept here includes the organisation of subjects into specific disciplines such as English, mathematics, sciences, humanities, and arts, each with detailed content specifications and standards. At this stage, the curriculum is often designed to balance breadth with depth, providing learners with a coherent progression while maintaining flexibility. However, questions around the 'hidden curriculum' - the implicit values, norms, and behaviours conveyed in schooling - also emerge, highlighting that curriculum extends beyond formal subject matter alone (Kelly, 2009; Apple & Apple, 2004).

In FE, the curriculum must accommodate diverse learner profiles, from young people transitioning out of secondary education to adults engaging in lifelong learning or specific vocational training. The concept of curriculum in FE is therefore often characterised by flexibility and responsiveness. Programmes may range from academic qualifications to technical and professional certifications, prioritising employability alongside personal development. FE curricula also tend to spotlight partnership with employers and community organisations, indicating a shift from knowledge transmission towards practical application and skills development.

Higher education presents a further evolution in curriculum conceptions. Traditionally, HE curriculum has been shaped by disciplinary traditions, academic inquiry, and knowledge advancement. It emphasises intellectual rigour, critical thinking, and research skills (Barnett & Coate, 2005). However, contemporary HE curricula increasingly reflect broader educational goals including employability, global citizenship, and digital literacies. The curriculum here is often structured around modular programmes with learning outcomes, credit accumulation, and pathways that enable student choice and interdisciplinarity (Knight & Yorke, 2003). University curricula also centre on the co-construction of knowledge through active student engagement, research-led teaching, and diverse learning methods.

Despite these sectoral differences, some core conceptual elements unify curriculum across contexts. Bobbit (1918), often credited as an early curriculum theorist, described curriculum as a means to prepare learners for future roles in society, linking educational objectives to social functions. More recent critiques have emphasised curriculum as a site of power and ideology, shaping not only knowledge but also identities and social relations (Apple & Apple, 2004; Young et al., 2014). This critical lens underscores curriculum's role in cultural reproduction and transformation, challenging educators to think reflexively about whose knowledge is included or excluded.

Curriculum can also be conceptualised as a framework comprising several interrelated components (Ornstein & Hunkins, 2016):

- Objectives or aims: What the curriculum intends learners to know, understand, or be able to do.

- Content: The subject matter, themes, or knowledge areas included.

- Learning experiences: The activities, interactions, and pedagogical strategies employed.

- Evaluation and assessment: Methods to determine whether learning objectives have been met.

These components interact in complex ways, influenced by contextual factors such as policy environments, community expectations, and resource availability. For example, policy-driven national curricula enforce standardised content and assessment methods, while local or institutional curricula may adapt aims and content to meet specific learner needs and identities (Priestley & Biesta, 2013).

Contemporary curriculum concepts emphasise the importance of flexibility and responsiveness to change. As societal, technological, and economic landscapes evolve, curricula must adapt to prepare learners for uncertain futures. The concept of 'curriculum as praxis' highlights this dynamic, positioning curriculum development as an ongoing, reflective practice involving dialogue among educators, learners, and stakeholders (Schwab, 1969; Pinar, 2019). It challenges static, one-size-fits-all models and supports curricula that are culturally relevant, inclusive, and oriented towards social justice.

In summary, the concept of curriculum is complex and context-dependent, encompassing a broad range of theoretical perspectives and practical applications. Whether in primary schools fostering holistic growth, secondary institutions balancing specialisation and cohesion, FE colleges accommodating diverse learner pathways, or universities nurturing scholarly inquiry and transferable skills, curriculum remains a critical tool for shaping educational experiences and outcomes.

The components of curriculum

Curriculum, as experienced by learners and operationalised by educators, comprises several interlinked components that together form the "total curriculum" of an institution (Kelly, 2009) (Fig 1.1). Understanding these components allows teachers, curriculum leaders and policymakers to appreciate how complex forces and decisions shape educational experiences across all sectors. Although the basic elements may seem constant in definition, their expression and impact vary considerably across primary, secondary, further education (FE), and higher education (HE) contexts.

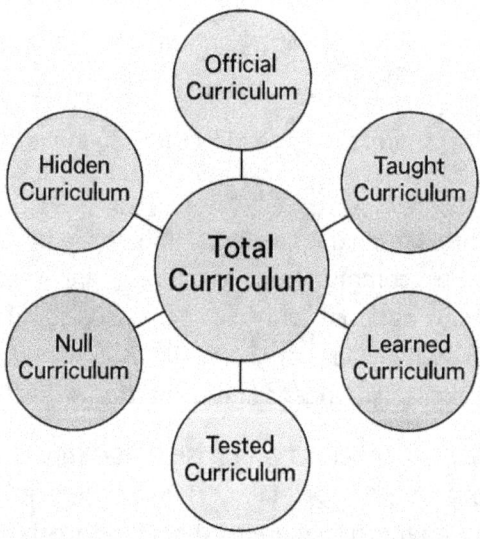

Figure 1.1 - The Total Curriculum

Official curriculum

The official curriculum represents the intended, planned, or prescribed curriculum that is devised by curriculum authorities and institutional leaders. In England, for example, the Department for Education and related agencies set the National Curriculum for maintained schools, providing a formal framework covering subjects, content, attainment targets, and assessment standards (DfE, 2014). At the FE level, regulators such as Ofqual specify qualifications and associated curricula, while in HE, the Quality Assurance Agency (QAA) provides benchmarks and subject statements, but greater autonomy is reserved for universities to shape their offerings.

In primary schools, the official curriculum tends to lay down what is to be taught in core and foundation subjects, aiming for entitlement and consistency for pupils nationally. In secondary education, subject syllabuses and examination specifications become more formalised, often narrowing curricular breadth in the senior years due to pressures from league tables and accountability frameworks (Whitty, 2010). FE and HE curricula, while influenced by official bodies, also respond to sector legislation, funding priorities and the demands of professional/accrediting organisations.

Year 4 maths curriculum

The UK National Curriculum outlines that in Year 4 mathematics, pupils should learn multiplication and division facts for multiplication tables up to 12×12, as well as developing efficient written methods for calculations. This ensures all primary pupils across the country are provided with similar learning opportunities and content, aiming for both entitlement and consistency, regardless of the school's location or individual teaching style.

Despite the detailed nature of official curricula, they cannot perfectly dictate what is actually encountered by learners - a phenomenon that leads onto the next component.

Taught curriculum

The taught curriculum refers to what teachers actually deliver in the classroom, workshop, lecture theatre or online. While official curricula act as guides, the taught curriculum is contextual, shaped by teachers' professional judgement, available resources, time limitations, local priorities, and the needs of learners (Yates, 2017). This lived reality is rarely identical to policy intentions (Stenhouse, 1975).

At primary level, much depends on individual teachers' interpretation and delivery, as they adapt content to the developmental needs of their pupils and respond to local circumstances. In secondary schools, subject teachers may exercise more autonomy within the constraints of externally imposed specifications, resulting in considerable variation in emphasis, depth, and pedagogy between different contexts. In FE, tutors may tailor the taught curriculum to meet the needs of adult learners or specific industries, while in HE, lecturers have substantial freedom to reinterpret curriculum aims, often integrating research-led content and diverse learning approaches (Barnett & Coate, 2005).

The disparity between the official and taught curriculum may sometimes be unintentional, arising from practical constraints or misunderstandings, but it can also be a deliberate and considered response to the inadequacy or inappropriateness of the prescribed content for particular groups of learners (Kelly, 2009). Such flexibility - or deviation - plays a crucial role in promoting inclusive education, allowing educators to tailor learning to diverse needs. However, this adaptability also introduces challenges, particularly in maintaining equity and consistency across educational settings, as variations in delivery may lead to unequal learning experiences for different student cohorts.

Learned curriculum

The learned curriculum is what students actually absorb, retain and are able to transfer into new contexts from what they have been taught. This component recognises that not all that is taught is learned; factors such as individual differences, teaching methods, motivations, and contextual influences all shape what remains in the learner's knowledge and skills repertoire (Biggs, 2022).

In primary education, the interplay between the taught and learned curriculum is significant, given young learners' varying rates of development. Teachers use formative assessment to adapt instruction, aiming to ensure key concepts and skills are truly grasped. In secondary and FE settings, external assessments may only capture surface-level understanding, whereas deeper or "unintended" learning may arise from projects, extra-curricular work, or peer collaboration (Black & Wiliam, 2009). Universities often explicitly confront the gap between teaching and learning by encouraging meta-cognitive strategies and self-directed learning, but the variability in what students learn - even within a single course - remains pronounced (Entwistle, 2017).

Understanding this component reminds educators to value evidence-informed, reflective practice and to seek continuous feedback on curricular and pedagogical effectiveness.

Tested curriculum

The tested curriculum is that subset of the official or taught curriculum that is formally assessed through examinations, coursework, or other mechanisms (Popham, 2001). Deciding what to test inevitably prioritises some aspects of a curriculum over others and may distort classroom priorities, especially where high-stakes testing exerts significant influence.

In primary and secondary phases, the dominance of standardised assessments can result in an emphasis on what is "testable" and neglect of the broader aims of education, such as creative thinking or social skills (Alexander, 2021). Teachers may be compelled to "teach to the test", narrowing the curriculum and potentially reducing engagement for students who benefit from a more holistic experience (Biesta, 2015). In FE, external examinations, apprenticeships, and competency-based frameworks each carry their own tested curriculum imperatives; some offer authentic assessment, while others risk excluding valuable professional qualities or tacit knowledge. In HE, assessment is often diversified but can still leave aspects of the broader curriculum unsupported, especially in modular, examination-focused programmes (Knight & Yorke, 2003).

Hidden curriculum

The hidden curriculum encompasses the implicit messages, values, and social norms that students absorb through their educational experience, apart from what is explicitly intended or taught (Apple & Apple, 2004). This includes institutional routines, classroom relationships, disciplinary regimes, and broader societal expectations. Hidden curriculum may reinforce the status quo or serve as a vehicle for social justice, often without conscious design.

In primary settings, classroom management routines, gender expectations, and modes of communication implicitly teach young children "how to be" within a school community (Skelton, 2003). Secondary education often witnesses the reproduction of class, gender, or ethnic stereotypes through streaming, discipline, or extra-curricular exclusion (Arnot & Dillabough, 2000). In FE, the hidden curriculum may play out in the values embedded in workplace placements or the modelling of professionalism. For HE students, the university environment communicates messages about academic hierarchy, independence, and cultural capital - sometimes privileging those whose backgrounds already align with institutional values (Reay et al., 2009).

Null curriculum

The null curriculum refers to what is left out - content, skills, or values that are omitted, whether deliberately or unintentionally (Eisner, 1985). These gaps may result from time constraints, lack of teacher expertise, resource limitations, policy decisions, or political expediency.

For example, the absence of comprehensive sex and relationships education in some primary or secondary schools, or the marginalisation of non-Western perspectives in literature courses, can profoundly influence what learners come to understand and value, significantly shaping their worldview and cultural awareness (Priestley & Biesta, 2015). In further education, rapidly changing workforce requirements can cause curricula to become outdated, omitting vital skills such as advanced digital literacy and environmental sustainability. In higher education, academic freedom can sometimes result in inconsistent coverage of foundational content, leading to knowledge gaps at graduation that impact graduates' readiness for both professional and societal roles.

Interaction and context

These six components are neither discrete nor static. Their relationships are dynamic and context-sensitive, shaped by the interplay of national policy, institutional leadership, teacher professionalism, learner diversity, and broader social trends. Curriculum decisions in each context - whether primary, secondary, FE, or HE - reflect unique priorities but are best understood as woven from these interdependent elements.

Question Reflect on your own educational context and consider which elements of the curriculum - official, taught, learned, tested, hidden, or null - are most evident and which are least visible or acknowledged. What might explain these patterns, and how do they shape the experiences and outcomes of learners?

Formal and informal curriculum

The concept of curriculum has traditionally been associated with formal, structured content delivered in classroom settings. However, contemporary educational discourse recognises a broader, more nuanced understanding of what constitutes meaningful learning. In this broader conception, curriculum includes not only what is officially planned and timetabled, but also what occurs through informal, voluntary, and co-curricular activities. Both formal and informal curricula contribute significantly to learners' development, often in complementary ways.

Formal curriculum

The formal curriculum refers to the structured, intentional learning programme officially sanctioned by educational authorities or institutions. It includes prescribed subjects, course content, instructional objectives, assessment methods, and scheduled teaching time. This aspect of curriculum is typically documented through national curriculum frameworks, institutional syllabuses, and qualification specifications (Kelly, 2009).

In primary education, the formal curriculum is largely determined by national initiatives such as the National Curriculum in England, which outlines core and foundation subjects including English, mathematics, science, and physical education (DfE, 2014). These subjects are clearly scheduled, assessed, and aligned to developmental milestones.

In secondary education, the formal curriculum becomes increasingly compartmentalised and subject-specific. It is structured around examination syllabuses, such as GCSEs or A-levels, with clearly delineated learning outcomes and content areas. The high level of external accountability and high-stakes testing can lead to a narrowing of curriculum focus, where educators feel pressure to prioritise examinable content, often at the expense of broader educational goals.

In further education (FE), formal curricula are designed around both academic and vocational pathways, including BTECs, T-Levels, apprenticeships, and Access programmes. The formal curriculum in FE must adapt to sector priorities and employer needs, which often results in competency-based frameworks with tightly defined outcomes. As a result, planning focuses on clear, measurable objectives but must also reflect diversity in learner need, age range, and career aspirations.

Within higher education (HE), the formal curriculum maintains a degree of autonomy through modular and credit-based systems. University departments design curricula in line with subject benchmarks published by the QAA (2024). Alongside discipline-specific knowledge, HE curricula are increasingly shaped by institutional strategies for graduate employability, internationalisation, and digital capability (Barnett & Coate, 2005). Teaching and learning are structured through lectures, tutorials, laboratory work, and assessments - all of which may carry formal weight.

Despite its structured nature, the formal curriculum alone does not encompass the full spectrum of learning experiences. To understand the broader educational process, attention must also be given to informal or co-curricular elements.

Informal curriculum

The informal curriculum encompasses the range of voluntary, unaccredited activities that fall outside the central timetable yet play a vital role in fostering skills, values, and dispositions. This includes breakfast clubs, after-school sports, school trips, lunch-time societies, peer mentoring schemes, creative workshops, and student-led organisations. These activities are often labelled 'extra-curricular', suggesting separation from the formal curriculum, but as Kelly (2009) and others argue, they are inseparable in practice and essential to holistic education.

In primary schools, informal learning commonly happens through structured play-based environments, outdoor learning, and enrichment activities. Forest schools, for instance, offer experiential education aimed at developing problem-solving, resilience, and teamwork - qualities not explicitly tested but essential for whole-child development (Waite, 2017). Many primary schools also run informal literacy or numeracy sessions before or after school, which, despite lacking formal assessment, are vital in supporting disadvantaged learners.

In the secondary sector, informal curriculum often assumes critical importance during adolescence - a stage when learners seek autonomy, community, and identity. Participation in sports teams, music ensembles, debate clubs, or volunteering schemes can develop leadership, collaboration, and emotional intelligence. Often guided by staff input but not formally assessed, these experiences shape learners' character and broaden their life chances. School ethos and house systems also promote a sense of belonging and shared values, even if not explicitly documented in formal curricula.

In FE colleges, informal curricula emerge through partnerships with local employers, enrichment weeks, career fairs, and student societies that reflect the diversity and maturity of the learner cohort. While often under-resourced or voluntary, these aspects foster civic responsibility, soft skills, and networking opportunities that formal vocational qualifications alone cannot deliver (Simmons, 2009). Importantly, the informal curriculum in FE provides routes for learners who may not have thrived in traditional academic settings to explore new ambitions.

In HE, the informal curriculum is deeply embedded in the wider student experience: residence life, student unions, study abroad schemes, and involvement in clubs and causes contribute to transformative learning far beyond lecture halls. These contexts offer opportunities for identity development, peer learning, and intercultural competence (Leask, 2009). Universities increasingly acknowledge the impact of such experiences through graduate attribute frameworks and co-curricular transcripts, recognising that learning also occurs through social engagement and self-directed exploration.

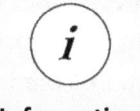
Information The informal curriculum - often dismissed as 'extra-curricular' - plays a vital role in fostering learners' skills, identities, and wellbeing. When formally recognised and integrated into curriculum planning, it enhances inclusion, engagement, and educational equity across all settings.

Combining formal and informal

Some theorists advocate for expanding curriculum definitions explicitly to include both formal and informal learning. Dewey (1938) long argued that education must be rooted in experience, and contemporary curriculum theorists view informal learning not as ancillary, but as integral to personal and social development. Indeed, research suggests that informal curricula can have significant impact on inclusion, wellbeing, and motivation - particularly for marginalised groups (James & Biesta, 2007).

Educators' attitudes towards informal learning are critical. Where informal activities are seen as peripheral, they risk being underfunded or sidelined. However, when integrated into broader curriculum planning - as seen with cross-curricular themes, first-hand experiences, or project-based learning - the boundaries between formal and informal begin to dissolve, resulting in more engaging and authentic education (Beane, 1997).

An academically rigorous yet inclusive curriculum must make deliberate space for informal learning. Not only do these experiences build cultural capital, they provide routes for students to express agency, build peer relationships, and apply classroom knowledge in lived contexts. In curriculum reform processes, particularly in response to calls for greater equity and diversity, informal learning environments are increasingly being seen as avenues for democratising access and enriching mainstream provision (Lumby & Coleman, 2007).

Curriculum as process and value

Kelly (2009) makes a distinction between a curriculum focused entirely on content transmission - more typical of formal syllabuses - and one that emphasises process and experience. When curriculum is viewed narrowly as a syllabus - a checklist of content - a focus emerges on extrinsic purposes such as examination success or vocational training. However, education in a truer sense is concerned with intrinsic values: enquiry, discovery, growth, and ethical understanding.

Informal elements offer fertile ground for learning that is intrinsically motivated and shaped by student input, often allowing learners to explore their interests, identities, and social relationships in meaningful contexts. These experiences empower educators to move beyond rigid, instrumental targets associated with formal assessment and instead nurture values such as empathy, collaboration, creativity, and democratic participation. As a result, the informal curriculum acquires a central role, not simply as a supplementary activity, but as a legitimate and essential site of educational practice, planning, and personal development.

Product and process models of curriculum

This section introduces two influential approaches to curriculum design - the product model and the process model - examining their theoretical foundations, practical applications, and relevance across educational sectors.

The product model

The product model, often called the *objective* or *behavioural* model, prioritises clarity, measurability, and standardisation in curriculum design. This model emerged in the early twentieth century, gaining prominence through the work of Franklin Bobbitt and Ralph W. Tyler. Both theorists saw education as a purposeful activity geared towards defined outcomes, with the curriculum engineered to produce specific competencies in learners (Tyler, 1949; Bobbitt, 1918).

In this approach, the curriculum is conceived as a set of objectives, which are then broken down into learning experiences and ultimately evaluated to determine whether the intended outcomes - 'products' - have been achieved. Tyler's rationale set out a series of systematic steps for curriculum development: diagnosing learner needs, formulating objectives (expressed as desired changes in behaviour), selecting relevant content, organising content and learning experiences, and, finally, evaluating attainment (Tyler, 1949).

In primary and secondary education, the product model underpins much official curriculum documentation. National guidelines in England, for example, provide detailed programmes of study and attainment targets for each subject, with assessment frameworks designed to measure progress towards these endpoints (DfE, 2014). The impact is visible in key stages, SATs, and GCSEs, where learning is codified through specifications and measurable outputs. Teachers are expected to align teaching and assessment closely with pre-defined objectives, making this model particularly compatible with high-stakes testing environments (Whitty, 2010; Kelly, 2009).

In further education (FE), product model logic is crystallised in vocational and apprenticeship programmes oriented around detailed lists of competencies, prescribed performance criteria, and summative assessment regimes set by awarding bodies or sector skills councils. The explicitness of objectives supports consistency, external accountability, and transferability of qualifications, important in a sector serving diverse industry needs. Within higher education (HE), the product model is evident in learning outcomes-based curriculum frameworks. These define what students should know or be able to do at the end of a module or programme, guided by benchmarks from national agencies such as the Quality Assurance Agency (QAA, 2024). Course handbooks map content, skills, and assessment tasks onto these outcomes, which facilitates credit accumulation and transfer (Knight & Yorke, 2003).

> **BTEC Level 3 National Diploma**
>
> An example of the product model in FE is the Pearson BTEC Level 3 National Extended Diploma in Health and Social Care. This vocational qualification is structured around very detailed unit specifications that include clearly defined learning aims, assessment criteria, and guided learning hours. Each unit outlines specific knowledge and skills that students must demonstrate - such as understanding human growth and development, or demonstrating effective communication in health and social care settings.

While the product model brings strengths - clarity of expectations, accountability, and comparability - critiques are also apparent. Critics argue that it can marginalise teacher autonomy, student voice, and deeper forms of engagement (Kelly, 2009). In schools, concerns have been raised that excessive instrumentalism leads to surface learning, narrowing of curriculum breadth, and limited innovation (Biesta, 2010). The emphasis on predetermined outcomes may provide little scope for emergent or unexpected learning, especially where learners' interests and experiences are diverse.

The process model

In contrast, the process model - sometimes called the *developmental* or *progressive* model - emphasises the lived experience of learning rather than predetermined ends. This tradition owes much to the work of Lawrence Stenhouse, who advocated for curricula designed not as lists of factual content or objectives but as frameworks for exploratory inquiry and reflective practice (Stenhouse, 1975).

The process model views curriculum as "an attempt to communicate the essential principles and features of an educational proposal in such a form that it is open to critical scrutiny and capable of effective translation into practice" (Stenhouse, 1975, p. 4). Here, learning is seen as a dynamic interaction among teacher, learner, and context. The teacher's role shifts: rather than acting as the transmitter of fixed content, the teacher becomes a facilitator, co-learner, and guide in open-ended, dialogic processes (Apple & Apple, 2004).

In primary education, process-led approaches emerge in enquiry-based learning, cross-curricular projects, and 'child-centred' pedagogy. For example, creative curricula or forest schools prioritise learning through activity, play, and investigation, valuing children's questions and interests as much as the content to be covered (Waite, 2017). In secondary schools, process models are visible in approaches such as project-based learning, the International Baccalaureate, or citizenship education - areas where curricula emphasise skills like critical thinking, collaboration, and ethical reasoning rather than solely prescribed knowledge (James & Biesta, 2007). In FE, process models are evident in learner-driven projects, reflective portfolios, and personal and social development programmes, where the process of enquiry, collaboration, and adapting to real-world contexts is as important as mastery of pre-determined outcomes (Edwards & Usher, 2008). In HE, the process tradition appears through problem-based learning, seminar discussion, and research-led teaching - modes which cultivate not only disciplinary knowledge but the skills and dispositions for independent enquiry. Within these frameworks, assessment is formative and ongoing (Knight, 2002).

Key strengths of the process model are its focus on teacher and student agency, the development of transferable skills, and responsiveness to learners' interests, experiences, and the broader socio-cultural context of learning. It prioritises meaningful engagement over the delivery of fixed content, allowing for more personalised and dialogic approaches to education. Assessment in this model is typically diagnostic and formative, integrated throughout the learning process to support continuous adaptation, feedback, and reflection (Black & Wiliam, 2009).

However, the process model faces its own hurdles. Critics point to difficulties in ensuring appropriate coverage of essential content and achieving reliable comparability between learners and institutions (Wiliam, 2011). In policy contexts driven by accountability and performance data, process-led curricula may struggle to gain systemic recognition or support. The inherent flexibility and openness of this model, while enabling personalisation, can also lead to inconsistencies across classrooms and sectors, raising concerns among policymakers regarding quality assurance, standardisation, and measurable outcomes.

The key aspects of the product and process models are compared in Table 1.1

Aspect	Product model	Process model
Foundations	Tyler, Bobbitt; behaviourism, objectives	Stenhouse; constructivism, inquiry
Main focus	Outcomes, objectives, content	Experiences, processes, interaction
Curriculum	Fixed endpoints, sequential planning	Flexible frameworks, emergent content
Assessment	Summative, end-point evaluation	Continuous, formative, diagnostic
Teacher role	Deliverer of content, implementer	Facilitator, co-learner, guide
Student role	Receiver, performer of outcomes	Agent, participant in knowledge creation
Typical sectors	Vocational, high-stakes test contexts	Enquiry-led, social and life skills

Table 1.1 - Comparison of the product and process models

Contemporary developments and integration

In practice, few curricula are wholly product or process oriented. Many sectors blend the two, seeking to combine the strengths of both approaches. Recent reform agendas in English primary and secondary settings, for instance, have attempted to specify core knowledge while encouraging deeper understanding through active, interactive methods (DfE, 2014).

In FE, there is a growing recognition that while clear outcomes are needed, the capacity to adapt and learn 'how to learn' is crucial for lifelong employability. In HE, the move towards constructive alignment - where outcomes, teaching, and assessment are deliberately synchronised - embodies elements of both traditions (Biggs, 2022).

The ongoing challenge for curriculum designers and educators is to negotiate the demands for accountability, comparability, and skill development without losing sight of education's broader purposes: fostering curiosity, autonomy, and capacity for informed participation in society.

Pedagogy

Pedagogy is frequently described as the art and science of teaching, encompassing the theories, methods, and practices that underpin effective learning experiences. The concept is at the heart of all educational activity - shaping what happens in classrooms, lecture halls, and training workshops across all educational sectors. While closely linked to curriculum, pedagogy is broader: it not only concerns what is taught, but fundamentally addresses how, why, and with what impact education takes place (Alexander, 2020).

Pedagogy and its theoretical foundations

The evolution of pedagogical theory has produced a diverse range of perspectives, each offering insights into how teachers can best support learning. Early behaviourist models - exemplified by Skinner's focus on stimulus and response - prioritised direct instruction and repetition, whereas constructivist theorists such as Piaget and Vygotsky highlighted the importance of active engagement, social context, and the construction of meaning. More recent socio-cultural views emphasise the importance of dialogue, collaboration, and culturally responsive teaching (Alexander, 2020).

Hilda Taba, a prominent curriculum and pedagogical theorist, stressed that effective teaching methods are essential for developing skills such as critical thinking and collaboration. She argued: "How you teach is more important than what you teach" (Taba, 1962, p.131), emphasising that the way learning experiences are organised directly shapes learners' cognitive and social development.

Pedagogy in primary education

Pedagogical approaches in primary settings are deeply influenced by developmental psychology, with a strong emphasis on holistic, child-centred learning. Teachers often act as facilitators, nurturing curiosity and adapting methods to suit diverse needs. Play-based learning, inquiry methods, and mixed-ability group work are prevalent strategies for promoting engagement and foundational skills (Burnett & Cremin, 2018). Formative assessment and feedback are integral, allowing learning to be adapted responsively.

The primary classroom is often rich with talk, demonstration, and modelling, engaging children in purposeful dialogue to develop language, reasoning, and socio-emotional understanding (Alexander, 2020). Creative approaches, such as storytelling, art, and outdoor learning, further support the development of the 'whole child'. The teacher's role goes beyond delivering content; it involves building supportive relationships, scaffolding learning, and fostering positive attitudes towards learning.

Pedagogy in secondary education

In secondary education, teaching tends to focus on subject specialism and progresses towards greater content depth and conceptual challenge. Pedagogy here must balance direct instruction - necessary for building subject knowledge - with more interactive methods that encourage learner autonomy and critical engagement (Sherrington, 2019). Strategies include explicit teaching of complex concepts, guided practice, collaborative projects, and the use of technology.

The pedagogical demands of secondary education also include differentiation: teaching must address a range of abilities, backgrounds, and interests, often in large and diverse classes. Formative and summative assessments are influential, shaping the rhythm of teaching and learning but also inviting criticism of 'teaching to the test' at the expense of deeper learning (Biesta, 2015).

Dialogue remains essential, but classroom management and behavioural expectations gain prominence as adolescents seek independence and negotiate identity. Teachers are challenged to maintain high expectations, foster a sense of community, and provide pastoral support - each a component of effective pedagogical practice (DfE, 2014).

Pedagogy in further education (FE)

Pedagogy in the FE sector is shaped by its dual commitment to vocational and academic learning. Teachers must engage with adult learners as partners, recognising their prior experiences and varying motivations for study (James & Biesta, 2007). The adult learning tradition, or andragogy, complements pedagogy: here, learners are increasingly self-directed, goal-oriented, and contextually driven (Knowles et al., 2014).

FE settings are highly diverse, encompassing apprenticeships, vocational programmes, and access courses. Practical, hands-on learning - through workshops, work placements, and simulations - are dominant, linking theory with authentic contexts. Effective FE pedagogy often involves coaching, mentoring, dialogic assessment, and the integration of employability skills.

Teachers in FE are also required to be adaptable, as courses frequently serve a transient or part-time cohort. Inclusive practices - such as flexible timetabling, differentiated support, and culturally responsive materials - are pivotal in sustaining learner engagement and achievement, especially among those returning to education after significant gaps.

Pedagogy in higher education (HE)

In universities, pedagogy is strongly shaped by disciplinary cultures and the research-teaching nexus. While traditional lecturing remains a feature, there has been significant movement towards active modes of learning, such as seminars, problem-based learning, flipped classrooms, and blended learning. These approaches foster independence, critical thinking, and the ability to synthesise complex ideas.

Student-centred teaching is now mainstream in many institutions, with lecturers acting as facilitators who encourage debate, investigation, and reflective practice. Assessment for learning - involving peer review, self-assessment, and project work - aims to develop students as active participants in their own education (Barnett & Coate, 2005). Digital technologies and AI are increasingly embedded, extending the reach and personalisation of pedagogical practice.

HE pedagogy faces particular challenges around inclusivity and retention, as cohorts become more diverse and expectations shift towards employability and life-wide learning. Tutors must balance the knowledge demands of their subject with the fostering of transferable skills, digital literacy, and civic responsibility (Knight & Yorke, 2003).

Pedagogy, curriculum, and teacher agency

Across all settings, the interplay between pedagogy and curriculum is critical. Hilda Taba's influence is still notable. She contended that teachers should play a central role in curriculum development, as they are best placed to design meaningful, contextually relevant learning experiences (Taba, 1962). Her eight-step process advocated for the inductive development of curriculum, starting with the specific needs and contexts of learners, and building out to generalisable principles.

Pedagogy, then, is not simply the implementation of external directives; it is an act of professional judgement, creativity, and reflective practice. Teachers must adapt their methods continually - responding to student feedback, classroom dynamics, and emerging research. Teacher agency, therefore, is a defining feature of effective pedagogy, as educators draw upon theory, evidence, and their own expertise to inform practice.

Emerging trends in pedagogy

Recent educational research has accentuated principles such as metacognition, or the explicit teaching of how to learn, as well as oracy, feedback, and collaborative learning as key levers for progress (EEF, 2025). The rise of digital technologies has introduced new modalities - online learning, adaptive systems, and rich multimedia resources - requiring teachers to develop new strategies for engagement and differentiation. Culturally responsive pedagogy is also gaining traction, focusing on inclusivity, representation, and meaningful connections to students' lived experiences (Ladson-Billings, 2021).

Professional development and learning communities now underpin sustained pedagogical improvement across sectors, with research-informed practice, mentoring, and reflective enquiry increasingly valued.

Curriculum planning as targets

Since the early 1990s, curriculum planning in schools has increasingly been shaped by performance targets, particularly following the introduction of school league tables in 1992. Framed initially as tools for accountability and parental choice, these rankings effectively compelled schools to set internal achievement targets to maintain or improve their public standing (West & Pennell, 2000). While the strategic use of targets can support clarity and motivation - especially when devised collaboratively by teachers and students - in this policy environment they are often externally imposed, prioritising quantifiable outcomes over the quality of educational experiences (Ball, 2003).

The emphasis on achieving numerical benchmarks risks narrowing pedagogical focus. Rather than encouraging deep learning or creative exploration, educators may instead concentrate on ensuring students meet the arbitrary criteria linked to high-stakes assessment and national performance measures. As a result, pedagogy becomes driven by what is measured, not necessarily by what is valued educationally (Alexander, 2020).

Such practices can lead to *curriculum distortion*, where subjects not included in accountability frameworks receive reduced attention or funding. For example, vocational programmes such as agricultural or horticultural studies - vital for a minority of learners - have historically been marginalised because their outcomes were not counted in official performance tables. This has resulted in the scaling back of practical learning environments like school farms in favour of more classroom-based approaches, despite the pedagogical value of experiential and hands-on learning (Whitty, 2010).

Ultimately, planning curriculum around government-imposed targets shifts the emphasis from educational purpose to statistical performance. This can undermine both curriculum breadth and the role of teacher agency, limiting the flexibility to design learning experiences that are responsive, inclusive, and rooted in pedagogical integrity.

Historical foundations and societal needs

The development of curriculum as both a concept and a practice has deep historical and philosophical roots. Historically, the evolution of curriculum reflects changes in society's purposes for education, and each era generates new debates about what knowledge is valuable and for whom. For centuries, Western education focused on classical knowledge: the study of grammar, rhetoric, logic, and later the natural sciences and literature - reflecting the values of the elite and preparing students for leadership roles (Hamilton, 1999). In the UK, the 19th century expansion of state education marked a pragmatic shift toward broader access, linking curriculum more tightly to economic utility and nation-building (McCulloch, 2011).

Philosophical foundations lie in perennial tensions: education as transmission of fixed knowledge versus as preparation for participation in democratic life, and the relative importance of the individual versus society. Essentialists argue for a curriculum based on enduring intellectual disciplines, whereas progressivists emphasise the needs and experiences of the learner. For example, John Dewey's influence is seen in efforts to democratise curricula by advocating learning through experience and reflection rather than rote transmission (Dewey, 1938). Reconstructionism, meanwhile, emphasises curriculum's potential to address social injustices and adapt to future challenges, shaping much contemporary practice (Young & Muller, 2016). These legacies persist in today's arguments about what - and whose - knowledge ought to be privileged in primary, secondary, further education (FE), and higher education (HE).

Influences shaping curriculum design and theory

Curriculum theory is continually shaped by a blend of intellectual, practical, and social forces. In primary education, psychological theories of child development - especially those of Piaget and Vygotsky - have prompted a focus on spiral curricula, scaffolding, and play-based approaches (Bruner, 2009). Subject content and sequencing are adapted to children's readiness to learn, underpinned by ideas from Rousseau and Froebel.

In secondary education, discipline-centred models have dominated, reinforced by public examination systems and subject associations. Curriculum is shaped by scholarship, specialist teacher expertise, and a tradition of academic rigour (Priestley & Biesta, 2013). In further education, theories of vocational learning and adult education exert unique influence, positioning learning as a means of personal and professional transformation. Practical competence, workplace skills, and lifelong learning are foregrounded.

HE curriculum design is often driven by disciplinary norms, research cultures, and, increasingly, employability agendas and international benchmarking (Barnett & Coate, 2005). Models such as constructive alignment - where teaching, assessment, and intended learning outcomes are planned holistically - are widely implemented (Biggs, 2022). Across all sectors, theories of inclusion and social justice prompt ongoing curriculum scrutiny to ensure access, equity, and cultural relevance (Apple & Apple, 2004).

Societal needs

Societal needs have always been a core driver of curriculum reform. The earliest curricula in state systems reflected industrial and imperial goals, equipping learners with the skills, values, and knowledge demanded by employers and governments (Hamilton, 1999). Over time, priorities have shifted: post-war Britain saw the rise of welfare-state values in education, while the late 20th century questioned whose interests curricula should serve and how best to address pluralism and inequality (Whitty, 2010).

In contemporary contexts, new societal challenges - globalisation, migration, digital transformation, climate change - demand curricula that are responsive and anticipatory. In primary schools, this is seen in a greater emphasis on digital literacy, citizenship, and sustainability education. Secondary education has begun to move beyond narrow academic subjects to embrace interdisciplinary learning and social responsibility, while in FE and HE, employability, entrepreneurship, and community engagement have become prominent goals (Barnett & Coate, 2005).

Community and parental voices, alongside youth activism, are increasingly calling for curricula that reflect a broad spectrum of histories, cultures, identities, and ambitions. This trend underscores the need for ongoing dialogue, adaptation, and meaningful contributions from a wide array of stakeholders to ensure education remains relevant, inclusive, and responsive to societal change (Priestley & Biesta, 2013).

How changing societal demands inform curricular priorities

Curricular priorities have never remained static, but recent decades have seen especially rapid evolution. Technological innovation has triggered new emphases on coding, computational thinking, and media literacy across all sectors. Environmental challenges have spurred education for sustainability, concluding in cross-curricular initiatives, outdoor education, and climate literacy. The mental health crisis has redirected priorities towards wellbeing, resilience, and social-emotional learning (OECD, 2020).

The rise of a knowledge economy is reflected in pressure for 'futureproof' skills: critical thinking, creativity, collaboration, and adaptability. This is visible in primary and secondary curricula through renewed focus on problem-solving and metacognition, as well as in FE and HE through work-integrated learning and enterprise modules (James & Biesta, 2007). Policy responses to inequality and social mobility, meanwhile, have pushed for inclusive, accessible curricula that challenge discrimination and open pathways for marginalised groups (Apple & Apple, 2004; Ladson-Billings, 2021).

Ultimately, curriculum construction across all educational sectors is a negotiation between historical legacies, philosophical aspirations, practical realities, and the fast-changing challenges facing society today.

Activity: Reflective curriculum analysis

This activity encourages you to consolidate and apply your understanding from the chapter by critically analysing the key concepts, essential components, and various influences shaping the curriculum in your own educational context. Engaging deeply with these foundational aspects will foster critical thinking about curriculum theory and practical application. This reflective process not only reinforces your learning but also prepares you to engage more confidently and thoughtfully with upcoming chapters on curriculum design, implementation, and evaluation.

1. Curriculum mapping and reflection
- Identify a curriculum you are familiar with (such as a subject, course, or programme in primary, secondary, FE, or HE).
- Using the models and definitions explored in this chapter, map out its main features under the following headings: Official curriculum; Taught curriculum; Learned curriculum; Tested curriculum; Hidden curriculum; Null curriculum.

> **2. Critical commentary**
> For each component:
> - Explain how it is visible (or not) in your chosen context.
> - Discuss at least one factor - historical, philosophical, pedagogical, or societal - that has influenced the curriculum's current form.
>
> **3. Discussion questions**
> After your mapping, respond briefly to the following:
> - In what ways does the formal or informal curriculum shape learners' experiences and outcomes in your context?
> - Which model - product or process or both - best represents the dominant approach in your context? Justify your answer with examples.
> - Identify one area where curriculum development could better respond to changing societal needs, and suggest how pedagogical choices might help achieve this.
>
> **Extension (optional):**
> Share your findings with peers or colleagues and discuss similarities and differences in curriculum experiences. Consider how the theoretical perspectives covered might influence your future approach to teaching or curriculum design.

Summary

This chapter has explored the multifaceted nature of curriculum as a field of study, tracing its historical and philosophical foundations and examining how theory, policy, and societal needs shape educational programmes across primary, secondary, further, and higher education contexts.

It dissected the core components of curriculum - official, taught, learned, tested, hidden, and null - and contrasted formal and informal curricular experiences. The discussion embraced key curriculum models, notably the product and process approaches, highlighting their varied influence on curriculum planning and classroom practice. Central to the chapter is the critical role of pedagogy in shaping what and how students learn.

The chapter concludes by emphasising that effective curriculum design is a dynamic, context-sensitive process, continually shaped by evolving disciplinary, societal, and cultural demands.

2 CURRICULUM DESIGN

Introduction

This chapter explores the essential concepts and frameworks that underpin curriculum design, from foundational rationales such as the Tyler model to contemporary approaches that prioritise learner needs, inclusion, and adaptability. Readers will encounter comparative analyses of national and international curriculum frameworks, as well as critical principles guiding effective design in diverse contexts - including primary, secondary, further education (FE), and higher education (HE).

The chapter also addresses common pitfalls and challenges - such as the so-called "twin sins" of curriculum planning - and examines methods for setting purposeful learning outcomes and standards. By engaging with different models and the broader context in which curricula are created, readers will be prepared to make informed, reflective decisions that shape impactful educational experiences for all learners.

This chapter

- Explores the fundamental principles and stages of curriculum design across educational contexts.
- Analyses the Tyler Curriculum Development Rationale.
- Compares diverse curriculum frameworks and models, considering both UK and international approaches.
- Investigates the theoretical foundations and practical considerations that underpin curriculum design decisions.
- Examines curriculum design challenges, including the "twin sins" of curriculum planning and their consequences for teaching and learning.
- Discusses strategies for establishing learner needs and formulating clear objectives, outcomes, and standards.
- Evaluates how curriculum theory is translated into practical frameworks that support meaningful, equitable learning experiences.

Fundamentals of curriculum design

Curriculum design is the intentional and systematic process of organising educational experiences to achieve purposeful and meaningful learning outcomes for all students. Its fundamentals are deeply informed by the aims of education, insights from theories of learning and instruction, evolving societal needs, and the changing landscape of educational policy and accountability. Effective curriculum design depends upon a balance of clear intention, evidence-based choices, and professional judgement that ensures curricular relevance and coherence across diverse educational contexts, including primary, secondary, further education (FE), and higher education (HE) (Kelly, 2009; Ambition Institute, 2023).

Defining curriculum design

At the heart of curriculum design lies a careful determination of what knowledge, skills, and values are most important for learners to acquire, as well as decisions about how and when this is best learned. The process encompasses setting educational purposes, selecting and sequencing content, choosing pedagogical approaches, and aligning assessment with intended outcomes (Biggs, 2022). The ultimate aim is a coherent educational experience that is meaningful, accessible, and responsive to all learners, regardless of background or context.

Guiding principles

Modern curriculum design is shaped by several universally recognised principles:

- **Purpose and values:** Curriculum development must be underpinned by a clear articulation of aims, informed by the broader values and mission of the educational setting, whether to foster personal growth, social responsibility, economic prospects, or critical citizenship (Kelly, 2009).

- **Coherence and progression:** Well-designed curricula logically sequence learning experiences so that each stage builds on previous knowledge, supporting both progression and continuity (Third Space Learning, 2024).

- **Breadth and balance:** A high-quality curriculum offers a wide range of knowledge and skills, allowing for both breadth (multiple subjects or topics) and depth (detailed study of important areas), preventing unnecessary narrowing of opportunities, especially under assessment pressures (Ofsted, 2019).

- **Relevance and context:** To motivate and engage learners, curriculum content and activities must connect to students' prior knowledge, everyday lives, and future aspirations (Barnett & Coate, 2005).

- **Equity and inclusion:** Curriculum design should ensure that all students, regardless of their background or abilities, can access, participate in, and achieve through the curriculum. This includes differentiation, adaptive resources, and flexible pathways (Advance HE, 2021).

- **Evidence and evaluation:** Effective curriculum is continuously refined through evidence - be it from student assessment data, research, or practitioner enquiry - ensuring learning remains rigorous and fit for purpose (Ambition Institute, 2023).

Application in primary education

In primary schools, curriculum design is usually guided by national frameworks but adapted to reflect local circumstances, values, and children's developmental needs (DfE, 2014). Key steps include:

- Defining curriculum intent, which articulates both statutory entitlement to essential knowledge and the school's particular aspirations for creativity, character development, and enrichment.
- Sequencing and spiralling of content, revisiting concepts across age groups to promote mastery and retention (Burnett & Cremin, 2018).
- Integrating subjects (cross-curricular approaches) to make learning more holistic and connected to real-life experiences.
- Embedding regular formative assessment, so teachers can identify gaps and adapt teaching accordingly.
- Ensuring that curriculum design reflects inclusivity, local priorities, and opportunities for culturally relevant enrichment (Kelly, 2009).

Application in secondary education

Secondary education brings increased subject specialisation and external accountability requirements (e.g., GCSEs and A-levels):

- Subject departments interpret and map out specifications, clearly sequencing "big ideas" and threshold concepts within years and across key stages (Ofsted, 2019).
- Curriculum design in this phase often balances compulsory core with elective options, allowing some individualisation within a clearly defined framework.
- Planning considers transition points (such as the move between Key Stages or from school to FE/HE), ensuring prior attainment supports future study.

- High-stakes assessment frameworks strongly influence what is prioritised, sometimes leading to curricular narrowing; effective design seeks to mitigate this and preserve a broad, balanced offer (Whitty, 2010; Kelly, 2009).
- Effective secondary curricula use regular assessment feedback - not only summative, but also formative and diagnostic - to adapt teaching and sequencing (Black & Wiliam, 2009).

Application in further education (FE)

The FE sector serves a diverse population, with learners ranging from 16-year-olds on career pathways to adult returners and apprentices:

- Curriculum design frequently starts with external qualifications or frameworks, such as BTEC, T Levels, or apprenticeship standards, but must be adapted to local employer needs and the interests of learners.
- FE curricula feature a mix of theoretical and practical learning, organised with clarity (typically into modules or units), and an emphasis on authentic, real-world outcomes.
- Design is flexible, enabling part-time study, credit accumulation, and progression routes into HE or skilled employment.
- Strong partnerships with employers and other stakeholders ensure relevance, and regular review keeps content up to date with labour market needs (Simmons, 2009).
- Adult learning principles ("andragogy") mean that learners' experiences and motivations are explicitly considered, with curricula emphasising self-direction and transferable skills (Knowles et al., 2014).

Application in higher education (HE)

Curriculum design in HE is marked by autonomy, innovation, and responsiveness to diverse student needs:

- Frameworks are shaped by national standards (e.g., QAA subject benchmarks in the UK), institutional strategies, and professional body requirements (QAA, 2024).
- Programmes are typically modular, with clear credit structures, enabling a combination of depth (specialisation) and breadth (elective pathways or interdisciplinary learning).

- Constructive alignment ensures teaching activities and assessments are designed to meet well-defined learning outcomes (Biggs, 2022).

- Inclusion and universal design principles mean curricula are increasingly expected to reflect diversity, accessibility, and anti-discriminatory practices (Advance HE, 2021).

- Ongoing evaluation - using student feedback, external examiners, and industry consultation - supports continual development and improvement (Barnett & Coate, 2005).

Shared steps and collaboration

Across all phases, curriculum design is a collaborative and iterative process that typically involves:

- Establishing aims and purposes based on institutional values and stakeholder input.
- Identifying and sequencing essential content and skills.
- Designing pedagogical approaches suited to learners' needs.
- Allocating time, resources, and clear structures for delivery.
- Building in formative and summative assessment to monitor progress and provide feedback.
- Undertaking regular review and renewal to keep the curriculum current and effective (Ambition Institute, 2023; SSAT, 2023).

Teachers, leaders, students, experts, and community partners often contribute to curriculum development and review, bringing diverse perspectives and expertise. Their collaboration ensures the curriculum remains relevant, inclusive, evidence-informed, and tailored to local contexts, while also aligning with national or institutional goals and evolving societal needs. A co-constructed, reflective approach helps build ownership, professional trust, innovation, and sustained curriculum quality across diverse educational settings and phases.

The Tyler rationale

The Tyler rationale, first articulated by Ralph W. Tyler in 1949, has long stood as a cornerstone in curriculum theory and practice across educational phases. It is regarded as a systematic, scientific approach to curriculum design, with distinct, procedural clarity that continues to influence international curriculum frameworks in primary, secondary, further education (FE), and higher education (HE) settings (Tyler, 2013).

Tyler's four fundamental questions

The basis of Tyler's model is a set of four guiding questions, providing both a logical sequence and an evaluative lens for curriculum designers:

1. What educational purposes should the institute seek to attain?
2. What educational learning experiences can be provided that are likely to attain these purposes?
3. How can these educational experiences be effectively organised?
4. How can we determine whether these purposes are being attained?

(Tyler, 2013)

This sequence forms a continuous cycle that can be revisited for curriculum review and improvement.

The four stages of the Tyler rationale

Following the four fundamental questions, the Tyler rationale advances through four stages (Figure 2.1). These are often termed the *Tylerian Application*.

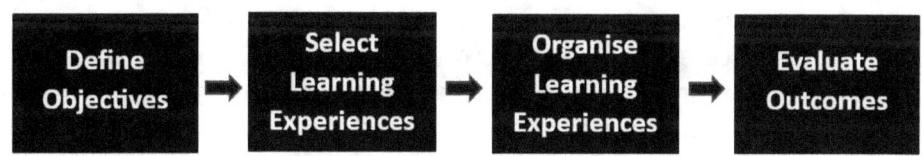

Figure 2.1 - Tyler's 4-Stage Rationale

Defining objectives: Curriculum development begins with publicly stated aims and objectives derived from wider educational values, learner needs, subject matter, and societal aspirations.

Selecting learning experiences: Educators identify content and activities suited to achieving the specified objectives, drawing upon insights from psychology, pedagogy, and discipline-specific knowledge.

Organising learning experiences: The curriculum is structured to sequence and integrate experiences efficiently, ensuring cumulative progression and alignment.

Evaluating outcomes: Assessment mechanisms are used to determine if the intended objectives have been met, providing data for ongoing curriculum refinement (Tyler, 2013).

Application in primary education

Tyler's rationale has significantly shaped the design of modern primary school curricula. National frameworks such as the English National Curriculum are anchored by clearly defined aims - such as promoting literacy, numeracy, and broader cognitive and personal development (DfE, 2014). Teachers and leaders are required to map these overall purposes onto subject- and age-specific learning objectives. In lesson and unit planning, primary educators routinely select and sequence experiences - e.g., phonics activities, science investigations, etc. - that build towards these objectives, applying Tyler's structure in practice (Burnett & Cremin, 2018).

Organisation is equally central: the progression of skills from Reception through Key Stage 2 often follows a spiral curriculum, resourcing knowledge in a carefully managed trajectory. Evaluation, both formative and summative, is intended to check that objectives are met, with assessment data feeding into curriculum adjustments for future cohorts (Black & Wiliam, 2009). Tyler's influence can be seen in the alignment of intended outcomes, classroom activity, and assessment that is now widely regarded as best practice in primary education.

Information

A **spiral curriculum** is an approach to curriculum design where key concepts and skills are revisited repeatedly over time, each time at a deeper and more advanced level. Instead of covering a topic just once, the spiral model spaces exposure to ideas and skills across different years or grades, ensuring that learners' understanding is gradually deepened as their cognitive abilities and prior knowledge expand.

Application in secondary education

Secondary schools also strongly reflect the logic of the Tyler rationale, especially in subject departments where specification-led planning and high-stakes assessment dominate (Priestley & Biesta, 2013). Here, educational purposes are often dictated by national standards and examination boards: each syllabus sets out what students must know and be able to do at various stages. Teachers are tasked with selecting and organising educational experiences - from experiments and group debates in science, to source analysis in history - carefully sequenced to scaffold students towards examination readiness and conceptual mastery.

Regular assessment and tracking, including mock exams and modular tests, make explicit the evaluative stage of Tyler's cycle. However, this focus can sometimes lead to overemphasis on measurable outputs ('teaching to the test'), a recognised limitation of strict Tylerian application (Biesta, 2015). Nonetheless, the clarity and structure provided by the rationale ensure subject progression and curricular coherence are prioritised.

Application in further education (FE)

In FE, where diversity of learner pathways and vocational orientation are prevailing features, the Tyler rationale helps provide structure and consistency. Qualifications such as BTECs, T Levels, and apprenticeships begin with explicit aims - e.g., competence in a trade, development of employability, or readiness for progression - which are mapped onto detail-rich learning objectives.

Curriculum designers select learning experiences through a combination of classroom delivery and practical, workplace-based activities, chosen specifically to meet required outcomes (Simmons, 2009). These experiences are typically structured into units or modules, with clear prerequisites and sequencing. The evaluation phase is heavily regulated: assignment briefs, competency portfolios, and observed assessments provide evidence that objectives have been met. Thus, the Tylerian model safeguards standards across institutions and supports transferability of qualifications.

Application in higher education (HE)

Higher education settings likewise utilise principles from the Tyler rationale, albeit with greater professional autonomy and flexibility. University programme specifications state intended learning outcomes - often developed to align with Quality Assurance Agency subject benchmarks or professional standards (QAA, 2024). Academic teams then design coherent sequences of modules and assessments to ensure that, on completion, graduates meet the intended aims.

HE curriculum development processes often involve 'constructive alignment' (Biggs, 2022), a concept entirely compatible with Tyler's logic, where learning activities and assessments are carefully and intentionally matched to articulated learning outcomes at both module and programme levels. In practice, evaluation in higher education is diverse and multifaceted, incorporating a wide range of methods including written examinations, coursework assignments, practical portfolios, and dissertations - each designed to provide evidence of student learning and achievement. The rationale behind constructive alignment also underpins regular curriculum review cycles, enabling outcomes and feedback from students, external examiners, and stakeholders to inform periodic redesign and continuous curriculum improvement. This responsive process ensures that HE programmes remain relevant, rigorous, and closely aligned with both evolving academic standards and professional expectations, supporting student progression and employability in a rapidly changing global environment (Biggs, 2022).

Strengths and limitations of the Tyler rationale

Strengths:

- Offers clarity and transparency for curriculum planning and communication.
- Supports accountability and alignment between aims, delivery, and assessment.
- Facilitates standardisation, comparability, and transfer across contexts.
- Encourages cyclical review and adaptation (Tyler, 2013).

Limitations:

- Can lead to excessive instrumentalism - overemphasising outcomes at the expense of process, creativity, or student agency (Biesta, 2015).
- May neglect hidden, informal, or unintended aspects of learning not readily measured by objectives or tests.
- Risks narrowing the curriculum to what is easily specified or assessed, reducing breadth and depth (Priestley & Biesta, 2013).
- Less suited to curriculum contexts valuing emergent knowledge or co-construction, such as inquiry-based or child-centred education.

Ongoing influence and adaptations

Despite various critiques, the Tyler rationale continues to serve as a foundational reference point for curriculum designers and theorists worldwide. Its clear, sequential structure has significantly shaped the evolution of subsequent models, informing approaches such as Taba's inductive strategy, Bruner's Spiral Curriculum, Stenhouse's Process Model, and Wiggins & McTighe's Backward Design method. Many educational institutions now reinterpret Tyler's original four-stage logic, adopting more flexible and contextually sensitive strategies. These contemporary adaptations are characterised by the inclusion of student voice, the use of formative assessment and feedback, and non-linear or cyclical curriculum planning processes that mitigate earlier limitations and support diverse learner needs (Kelly, 2009; Alexander, 2020).

Other design rationales

Contemporary curriculum design draws on a wide spectrum of theories and rationales that have evolved in response to both practical and philosophical questions about how best to organise knowledge and foster learning. While the Tyler rationale has dominated much of curriculum thought, numerous alternative models - some complementary, others fundamentally distinct - continue to enrich curriculum design across primary, secondary, further education (FE), and higher education (HE) contexts (Kelly, 2009; Ornstein & Hunkins, 2016).

Taba Model

The Taba Model, developed by Hilda Taba in the 1960s, is renowned for its inductive, grassroots approach to curriculum development. Unlike top-down models, Taba's process starts with the identification of specific learner needs, inviting teachers to play a central role. The model follows a sequence of diagnosis of needs, formulation of objectives, selection and organisation of content, selection and organisation of learning experiences, and evaluation (Taba, 1962; Print, 2021).

 **Information** — Taba strongly advocated for teachers to act as curriculum developers, asserting that their direct engagement with students places them in the best position to assess, interpret, and respond to learners' individual needs. She believed that teachers, being closest to the learning process, possess valuable insights into the developmental, social, and cognitive contexts of their students, making them uniquely qualified to design curriculum content and relevant and effective learning experiences.

- In primary and secondary education, the Taba Model supports developing responsive and relevant units based on pupils' needs.
- In FE and HE, it can underpin co-created modules with learners, engaging them in curriculum planning (Print, 2021).

Wiggins & McTighe's Backward Design (UbD)

Wiggins and McTighe's Backward Design, put forth in "Understanding by Design (UbD)", proposes that curriculum should be planned by starting with the desired learning outcomes. The process involves three stages: identifying desired results, determining acceptable evidence, and planning learning experiences and instruction (Wiggins & McTighe, 2011). This ensures alignment between outcomes, assessment, and pedagogy.

- In primary classrooms, backward design helps align lessons with clear goals and criteria.

- In secondary, FE, and HE contexts, it structures programme and module planning for deeper learning (Biggs, 2022).

Spiral Curriculum (Bruner)

Jerome Bruner introduced the Spiral Curriculum in the 1960s, arguing that a subject's fundamental ideas can be presented early and revisited at increasing depth and complexity. Each subsequent encounter builds on prior knowledge, promoting cumulative mastery (Bruner, 2009).

- In primary schools, core subjects are revisited each year at greater depth.

- In secondary, FE, and HE, spiral approaches revisit threshold concepts to deepen analysis and critical engagement (Burnett & Cremin, 2018; Biggs, 2022).

Stenhouse's Process Model

Lawrence Stenhouse's Process Model moves away from prescribed objectives, emphasising the experiences, processes, and interactions that occur during teaching and learning. Teachers and learners co-construct curriculum, with formative assessment embedded throughout (Stenhouse, 1975).

- In schools, this model supports project-based, inquiry-led and dialogic teaching, where the route to outcomes is flexible.

- In FE and HE, it underpins reflective portfolios, research projects, and collaborative learning (James & Biesta, 2007).

Wheeler Model

The Wheeler Model takes a cyclical approach to curriculum development, characterised by five interlinked stages: establishing aims and objectives, selecting learning experiences, choosing content, organising and integrating these elements, and then evaluating outcomes (Wheeler, 1967). Rather than a fixed sequence, the model highlights curriculum as an ongoing, iterative process that continuously re-examines and updates its stages to remain responsive and effective.

- In schools and colleges, it underpins regular curriculum review and adaptation for iterative improvement (Ornstein & Hunkins, 2016).

- In HE, the cycle can be used to evaluate and refresh programmes as contexts evolve.

Kerr Model

J.F. Kerr's model focuses on four elements: objectives, knowledge (content), school learning experiences, and evaluation (Kerr, 1968). These elements interact in a dynamic, non-linear fashion.

- In schools, the Kerr Model highlights the links between content, experience, goals, and assessment.
- In FE and HE, it supports holistic curriculum planning processes.

Eisner's Connoisseurship

Elliot Eisner's Connoisseurship Model emphasises qualitative judgement grounded in expert appreciation and artistic criticism, going beyond quantitative measures (Eisner, 1985). Connoisseurship enables nuanced curriculum evaluation.

- Significant in arts and creative subjects, this model is used to appraise portfolios and performances in both schools and universities.

Ornstein and Hunkins Framework

Ornstein and Hunkins offer a comprehensive framework, distinguishing technical-scientific and non-technical approaches and highlighting planning, implementation, and evaluation, all framed within value-laden, context-driven processes (Ornstein & Hunkins, 2016).

- The framework is used at all levels for comparing models and deciding on approaches suitable to local institutional aims.

Freire's Critical Pedagogy

Paulo Freire's Critical Pedagogy approaches curriculum as a tool for liberation and social justice, challenging the "banking model" of education and promoting dialogic, empowering and critically reflective learning (Freire, 1970). Learners are encouraged to question, critique, and transform their realities.

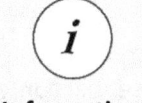

Information

The "banking model" of education is a term introduced by Paulo Freire in his influential work, *Pedagogy of the Oppressed* (Freire, 1970). It describes a traditional approach to teaching in which students are viewed as passive recipients of knowledge, and teachers are seen as all-knowing depositors of information.

- In schools, Freire's ideas inspire citizenship and anti-bias curricula.
- In FE and HE, they inform programmes on community education and adult learning.

Curriculum design example

Figure 2.2 briefly summarises an approach to curriculum design for a private sector company. It employs Tyler's Rationale and, for each of the 4 steps, outlines the work undertaken and who might undertake it.

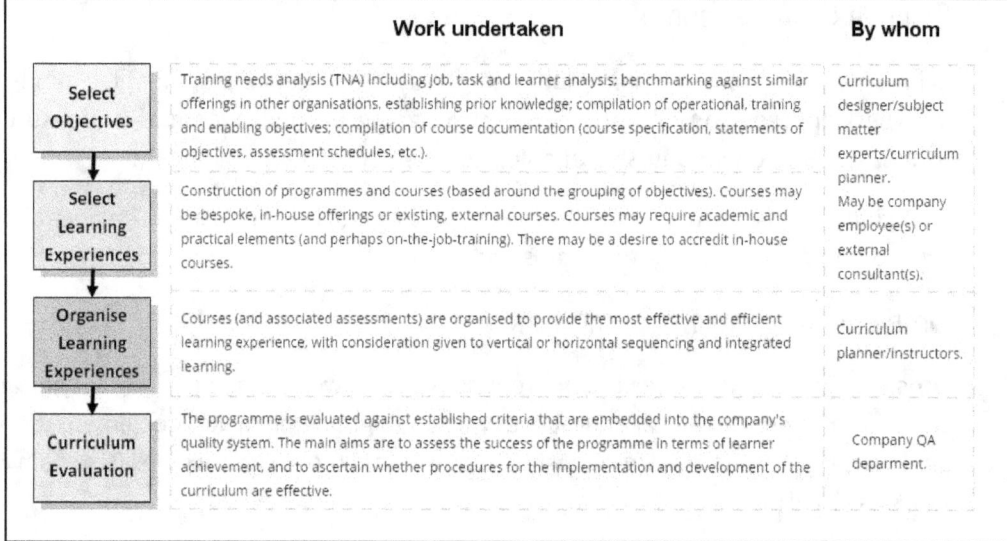

Figure 2.2 - Curriculum design example

This approach is not meant to be prescriptive - it is just one of many possibilities.

The example, though brief, does indicate that some organisations will have a greater degree of involvement in, and control over, their curriculum development. Some educational institutes may have little or no part to play in initial curriculum design and may feel restricted in their ability to review and evaluate it. This is perhaps a major disadvantage of curriculum frameworks such as a national curriculum.

Curriculum frameworks

A curriculum framework is an overarching guide that outlines the essential content, aims, and structure of an area of learning or qualification, providing the conceptual foundation for developing programmes, schemes of work, and assessment strategies. Unlike a prescriptive syllabus, a curriculum framework defines the scope and organisation of knowledge, skills, pedagogical principles, and learning progression, ensuring coherence and quality across educational contexts (Ornstein & Hunkins, 2016). Frameworks serve to standardise educational provision, offer guidance to practitioners, enable consistency, and support adaptability to local needs, while supplying benchmarks for review and improvement (DfE, 2014; ACARA, 2024).

While curriculum frameworks ensure standardisation and coherence, the best frameworks also enable local innovation and ongoing responsiveness to societal needs, preparing education for the demands of a changing world.

Framework content

- Rationale and guiding values.
- Key knowledge domains, skills, and capabilities.
- Staged learning progression.
- Content structure and learning outcomes.
- Principles for teaching, learning, and assessment.
- Accreditation and evaluation criteria.
- Guidelines for future review and adaptation.

Features of effective frameworks

- **Clarity:** Defines expectations and progression in accessible language (DfE, 2014).
- **Cohesion:** Structures learning logically across and within phases (Ornstein & Hunkins, 2016).
- **Inclusivity:** Guarantees all learners access to essential content and experiences (QAA, 2024).
- **Relevance:** Reflects current and future policy priorities (e.g. digital skills, sustainability) (OECD, 2020).
- **Adaptability:** Supports local and institutional customisation for context-specific needs (ACARA, 2024).
- **Evaluative basis:** Enables systematic monitoring and evidence-led improvement (Pearson, 2025).

Examples of frameworks

United Kingdom

Early Years Foundation Stage (EYFS) Statutory Framework

Sets standards for care and education for children from birth to five, detailing prime and specific learning areas, development goals, and assessment (DfE, 2024).

National Curriculum for England

A statutory document introduced in 1988 (revised in 2014), prescribing core and foundation subjects, key stages, attainment targets, and assessment guidelines for primary and secondary schools. It guarantees national entitlement while enabling some local adaptation in delivery and enrichment (DfE, 2014).

BTEC and Vocational Frameworks

Off-the-shelf frameworks such as the Pearson BTEC Level 3 National in Health and Social Care are widely used in FE. Each specification details units, guided learning hours, content, learning aims, and assessment criteria. Such frameworks ensure comparability and consistency across providers (Pearson, 2025).

T Levels

Introduced in England from 2020, T Levels represent a significant recent development in technical education for students aged 16-19. T Levels are two-year courses that are equivalent to three A Levels and are developed in collaboration with employers, sector bodies, and the Institute for Apprenticeships and Technical Education. Each T Level covers a specific industry and includes:

- A comprehensive technical qualification made up of core content and specialist options.

- 80% classroom-based learning, grounded in occupational standards.

- A substantial industry placement (minimum 315 hours or around 45 days), designed to provide real-world experience alongside classroom study.

- Detailed specifications covering core knowledge, key skills, synoptic assessments, grading, and progression routes.

T Level frameworks are published and maintained nationally to ensure high standards, comparability, and recognition by employers and higher education providers. Like BTEC frameworks, T Levels provide clarity about content, assessment, and expected outcomes - ensuring consistency and transferability across providers. However, T Levels place additional emphasis on direct employer involvement and extended work placement, aiming to bridge the gap between classroom learning and workplace practice (Institute for Apprenticeships and Technical Education, 2025; DfE, 2024).

Apprenticeship Standards

Developed by employer groups (trailblazers) and coordinated by bodies like CITB (2025), these frameworks set out occupational standards, knowledge, skills, behaviours, and high-stakes end-point assessment required for successful completion.

QAA Subject Benchmark Statements (HE)

The Quality Assurance Agency provides subject benchmarks for UK higher education, which articulate the knowledge, skills, and achievements expected of graduates in major subject areas - guiding programme design, monitoring, and external review (QAA, 2024).

Australia

The Australian Curriculum

Developed by ACARA, this provides a unified framework specifying content, achievement standards, general capabilities, and cross-curriculum priorities from Foundation to Year 12, with room for state-level adaptation (ACARA, 2024).

United States

Pennsylvania Standards Aligned System (SAS)

A state-level, standards-driven curriculum framework featuring clear content standards, "big ideas", skills, and assessment anchors for each discipline and grade (PDE, 2025).

International

International Primary Curriculum (IPC)

A thematic, cross-curricular framework used in schools worldwide, focusing on subject learning, personal skills, and global awareness. It offers learning goals, content, planning guidance, and adaptability to local contexts (Fieldwork Education, 2024).

OECD Education 2030

OECD promotes frameworks on global competencies, digital skills, and sustainability, supporting countries to develop future-oriented curricular frameworks with common reference points (Taguma & Frid, 2024).

Composition and use across contexts

Table 2.1 provides a composition of UK curriculum frameworks across the primary, secondary, FE and HE contexts.

Sector	Example framework	Key features
Primary	National Curriculum (England), EYFS	Core/foundation subjects, staged learning, entitlement
Secondary	National Curriculum, GCSE, IB, SAS (USA)	Subject progression, attainment targets, exam guidelines
FE	BTEC, T Level, Apprenticeship Standards	Unitised structure, skills lists, assessment benchmarks
HE	QAA Subject Benchmarks, AQF (Australia)	Graduate attributes, outcome descriptors, academic levels

Table 2.1 - Composition and use of frameworks across contexts

- In primary education, frameworks ensure breadth, progression, and entitlement to foundational learning.
- In secondary education, they clarify subject knowledge and progression, support exam readiness, and allow for some elective study.
- In further education, frameworks enable portability, skills training, and industry alignment.
- In higher education, subject benchmarks assure standards and comparability while supporting innovation.

Global comparison

Table 2.2 provides a global comparison of curriculum frameworks across primary, secondary, FE and HE contexts.

Country/ Organisation	Primary & Secondary	Further Education	Higher Education	Notable Features
England (UK)	National Curriculum	BTEC, T Level, Apprenticeship	QAA Subject Benchmarks	Entitlement, high standardisation, some adaptation
Australia	Australian Curriculum	VET Package Frameworks	AQF, HE Standards	National structure, state flexibility
USA (Pennsylvania)	SAS	State/Workforce frameworks	State university standards	Emphasis on "Big Ideas", local and state balance
International	IPC, IB, OECD 2030	IB Career Programme	IB Diploma Programme	Global skills, cross-curricular progression

Table 2.2 - Global comparisons of curriculum frameworks

Common pitfalls and challenges of curriculum design

Designing an effective curriculum is fraught with challenges, regardless of sector. Whether in primary, secondary, further education (FE), or higher education (HE), educators must navigate complex demands, competing priorities, and contextual constraints.

Among the most persistent pitfalls are those captured by Wiggins & McTighe's (2011) notion of the "Twin Sins" of curriculum design: activity-oriented teaching not anchored in purpose, and superficial curriculum coverage that sacrifices depth. However, these are just two of several interconnected risks that occur throughout curriculum planning, implementation, and review.

The twin sins of curriculum design

1. Activity-oriented design: The lure of engagement without purpose

A common temptation is to centre curriculum around engaging tasks - what Wiggins & McTighe (2011) term "the activity trap". In such cases, teachers select activities that are enjoyable, creative, or memorable, but which may lack direct alignment with clear learning goals.

> **Example**
>
> **Dressing up as Romans**
>
> A primary school might devote a history lesson to dressing up as Romans or re-enacting the Battle of Watling Street. While these activities encourage participation, there is a risk that learners focus on superficial features - such as the design of a tunic, or the feel of a sword - while neglecting key historical concepts or sources (Almond, 2020).

In secondary classrooms, this may appear as project weeks, poster presentations, or debates that are motivating but fail to build cumulative disciplinary knowledge. In FE, tutors may prioritise practical projects or context-based assignments that lack rigorous assessment or careful scaffolding. In HE, seminars may default to unstructured discussion or creative assignments without robust links to learning outcomes.

Almond (2020) highlights the importance of questioning the educational value and intended purpose of each activity: Does it directly support the curriculum aims? Is it an effective use of curriculum time? What knowledge or skills are actually being demonstrated? If such questions are not asked, activity-driven curricula risk prioritising entertainment over learning.

2. Superficial curriculum coverage: Rushing at the expense of depth

The second "sin" arises from the drive to cover extensive prescribed content, often under pressure from statutory curricula or examination expectations. Teachers may feel compelled to race through topics to keep pace with the scheme of work, curriculum map, or assessment timetable, sacrificing opportunities for consolidation or deeper understanding (Willingham, 2021).

A typical result is a breadth-over-depth approach: students encounter many topics superficially, but few concepts are explored in sufficient detail to ensure secure mastery or transfer of learning. In primary settings, this might manifest as rapid movement through science units, leaving students with isolated facts but limited conceptual frameworks. In secondary and FE, subject specifications can become checklists, where teachers "tick off" content coverage rather than supporting deep learning, critical analysis, or skill development.

In HE, the proliferation of modular courses can produce fragmented learning experiences, diluting coherence and impeding cumulative intellectual progress. This is especially problematic when individual modules are not mapped to broader programme outcomes, resulting in isolated knowledge "chunks" that are quickly forgotten after assessment (Knight & Yorke, 2003).

Willingham (2021) warns that such curriculum coverage creates shallow knowledge easily lost over time and rarely retained for transfer into new domains or future learning. Learners can appear to progress, but struggle to connect ideas or apply what they know in unfamiliar contexts.

Other common challenges in curriculum design

Lack of curriculum coherence

When curriculum is not constructed with clear end-points and logical progression in mind, it can lead to confusion, redundancy, or gaps in learner experience. Coherent curricula are carefully sequenced so that foundational knowledge and skills support later, more advanced study. Without this, learners may find themselves revisiting the same ideas without extension, or meeting complex topics without sufficient preparation (Wiliam, 2011).

In primary and secondary phases, lack of vertical alignment between year groups can lead to repetition or, worse, cumulative gaps. In FE and HE, poorly articulated pathways between modules or stages can leave students with uncertain progression routes, undermining confidence and attainment. The principle of "backwards design" (Wiggins & McTighe, 2011), which begins with end goals and plans backwards, is key to avoiding such incoherence.

Failure to consider progression and prior knowledge

Effective curricula are built on a recognition of what learners already know and are able to do. Where curriculum does not take into account prior learning or developmental readiness - whether through diagnostic assessment or transition planning - students may be presented with material that is either too easy or too challenging, leading to disengagement or misunderstanding (Ausubel, 1968; Black & Wiliam, 2009).

Overemphasis on assessment-driven teaching

Curricula designed primarily around high-stakes tests or external benchmarks can stifle creativity, intrinsic motivation, and deeper learning. When the focus shifts from holistic educational aims to "teaching to the test", teachers and students may neglect important but less easily examined areas, such as critical thinking, creativity, or values education (Biesta, 2015). This can be especially pronounced in secondary and FE contexts, where external accountability frameworks (e.g. Progress 8, BTEC or T Level specifications) dictate content selection and sequence.

Inadequate stakeholder involvement

Curriculum design is most successful when it incorporates input from a wide range of stakeholders, including learners, teachers, parents, employers, community representatives, and policy makers (Ornstein & Hunkins, 2016). Design processes led exclusively by a small team or single authority may fail to account for learner diversity, community context, or employer needs, leading to curricula that are disconnected from the realities of those they intend to serve.

Insufficient adaptation for diversity and inclusion

Another pitfall is designing curricula that overlook the need for personalised learning, differentiation, and inclusive practices. In all sectors, but particularly in FE and HE, curricula must address the needs of learners from varied backgrounds, prior attainment, learning differences, and aspirations. Failing to anticipate and plan for this diversity results in persistent achievement gaps and unequal outcomes (Ladson-Billings, 2021).

Neglect of informal and hidden curricula

Curriculum design that focuses solely on officially prescribed or assessed content may undervalue the impact of informal and hidden curricula - the social, emotional, and cultural factors that shape learners' attitudes and sense of belonging (Kelly, 2009). Ignoring these dimensions risks undermining engagement, motivation, and personal development, especially in sector contexts where identity and agency are formative (Leask, 2009).

Strategies for overcoming common pitfalls

- **Prioritise learning goals**: Anchor decisions in clearly defined and publicly shared end points, whether derived from national standards, employer expectations, or disciplinary benchmarks.

- **Balance breadth and depth**: Make deliberate choices about which content is essential for deep understanding, building in adequate time for rehearsal, consolidation, and extension.

- **Align activities with learning outcomes**: Select tasks that explicitly link to curricular aims, using a backward design approach to ensure coherence and progression (Wiggins & McTighe, 2011).

- **Sequence for progression**: Build vertical and horizontal alignment within and across year groups, modules, and qualifications to support cumulative learning (DfE, 2014; ACARA, 2024).

- **Integrate formative assessment**: Use diagnostic and on-going assessment to check understanding, inform teaching, and adapt pacing or challenge where needed (Black & Wiliam, 2009).

- **Promote teacher autonomy and collaboration**: Use professional expertise in designing, reviewing, and refining curriculum, while encouraging team-based planning and shared ownership (Stenhouse, 1975).

- **Regularly review and adapt**: Evaluate the effectiveness of curriculum through stakeholder feedback, learning data, and contemporary research, adapting as societal or sector needs evolve (Ornstein & Hunkins, 2016).

Learning outcomes, objectives and standards

In curriculum design and evaluation, the clarity of goals is crucial. Educational frameworks from early years through to higher education typically organise intended outcomes in terms of learning outcomes, objectives and standards. These elements shape what and how learners are expected to achieve and serve to structure the documents and processes by which curriculum content is planned, delivered, and assessed. Although these terms are sometimes conflated, they each serve distinct functions in the design, implementation, and evaluation of educational programmes across all sectors.

Learning outcomes

Learning outcomes describe the specific knowledge, skills, behaviours, or attitudes learners should demonstrate by the end of a course, unit, or lesson. As Spady (1993, p.10) stated, outcomes are "the clearly defined outcomes we want all students to demonstrate when they leave school". Outcomes are learner-focused, expressing what learners will be able to *do*, often in real-world or transferable terms.

For example, a learning outcome in a secondary science course might be: *"Evaluate the environmental impact of human activity on ecosystems, drawing on relevant data and case studies."*

Outcomes are typically written using *action verbs* (Appendix 1) aligned with a *learning taxonomy*, such as Bloom's Taxonomy (Appendix 2), to indicate the level of cognitive demand - ranging from recalling to creating (Anderson & Krathwohl, 2001).

In primary education, learning outcomes are simplistically worded to align with developmental levels. For instance, in Key Stage 1, a maths outcome may state: *"Pupils will be able to recognise and name common 2D shapes"*. In secondary schools, outcomes become more disciplinary and assessment-aligned. Examination boards define outcomes in specifications for GCSEs and A-levels, ensuring consistency across providers.

In FE, outcomes are written into vocational unit handbooks and apprenticeship standards. For example, the learning outcome for a unit in health and social care may read: *"Demonstrate effective communication using a range of methods in health and social care settings"* (Pearson, 2025).

In HE, outcomes often appear in course and module specifications and are aligned to subject benchmarks set by the Quality Assurance Agency (QAA, 2024). They are central to constructive alignment - the principle that teaching activities and assessments should be explicitly mapped to these outcomes (Biggs, 2022).

Learning objectives

Objectives are more specific than outcomes and are used primarily by teachers and curriculum designers to detail what learning activities will enable the learning outcomes to be achieved. Objectives can be thought of as building blocks that underpin broader outcomes (Marsh & Willis, 2003).

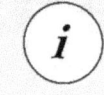

Information — While learning outcomes are valuable for clarifying expectations, judging success solely by them is unwise. This approach overlooks the richness of the learning process, risks superficial understanding, and ignores broader educational goals like critical thinking, creativity, and inclusion. A more balanced view considers both outcomes, achievement of objectives, and the quality of learning experiences.

In practice, objectives assist in medium- and short-term planning. For example, in a lesson plan focused on the outcome *"write in complete sentences"*, the supporting learning objectives might include:

- Identify subject and predicate in sample sentences.
- Differentiate between a phrase and a clause.
- Construct simple sentences with correct punctuation.

Objectives are useful in lesson plans, unit schemes, and medium-term documentation as they guide the sequencing, focus, and differentiation of instruction. In primary settings, especially within phonics or numeracy interventions, objectives help to align small, measurable steps with official progression maps. In secondary education, particularly in setting-specific or streamed classes, lesson objectives are differentiated to reflect learners' prior attainment and learning profile.

In FE and adult learning, objectives may be written as *enabling objectives*, phrased to describe behaviours or competences achieved under specific conditions. Many vocational courses make use of behaviourally based objectives, which specify:

- Evidence of achievement.

- Conditions of performance.

- Acceptable level of success.

"Correctly complete 3 out of 4 wiring tasks using appropriate tools, under supervision, following industry safety protocols".

Instructional objectives

Sometimes referred to as *micro-objectives*, instructional objectives are finely-grained, sequential steps within lessons or activities. These are particularly important in FE and HE settings where learners may need to demonstrate competency in work-based tasks. They are also vital in scaffolded learning, especially for students with additional learning needs.

Instructional objectives feed into formative assessment design - offering opportunities to test learning progression and to redirect teaching. Their use is common in adult basic skills, SEND contexts, and skills-based modules in HE.

Classifying objectives and outcomes

Objectives and outcomes can be classified into:

- **Cognitive domain**: Intellectual skills (e.g. analysis, application).

- **Affective domain**: Emotional and value-based responses (e.g. tolerance, motivation).

- **Psychomotor domain**: Manual or motor skills (e.g. construction, movement).

Bloom's Taxonomy (Appendix 2), and its later revisions, provide a hierarchy to structure content from lower-order ('remembering', 'understanding') to higher-order thinking processes ('evaluating', 'creating') (Anderson & Krathwohl, 2001).

Standards

Educational standards articulate the level of performance required, often mandated at a national or sector-wide level. They set benchmarks for what constitutes acceptable or exemplary achievement.

Standards differ slightly from outcomes: while outcomes are concerned with *what* students should do, standards express *how well* they should do it.

In England, standards appear in documents such as:

- The National Curriculum for key stages 1-4 (DfE, 2014).
- National Standards for Literacy and Numeracy (particularly in adult education).
- Apprenticeship Standards in technical and vocational education (IFATE, 2025).

In HE, standards are often codified through:

- Programme-level specifications.
- Subject benchmark statements (QAA, 2024).
- External examiner criteria.

Standards-based education broadly aligns with Outcome-Based Education (OBE), though critics argue that OBE focuses too heavily on measurable outputs, often neglecting the broader learning process and deeper educational aims (Spady, 1993; Biesta, 2015). Nevertheless, well-defined standards play an important role in clarifying expectations, promoting transparency, and ensuring comparability across institutions - particularly in systems where progression, transferability, or qualification equivalence are key features of educational accountability.

Associated curriculum documents

National curriculum documents

In primary and secondary schools, the National Curriculum and exam board specifications provide a concrete framework of outcomes, standards, and key content. Each subject has explicit attainment targets and progression goals by key stage (DfE, 2014).

Programme specifications

In FE and HE, a programme specification details the total structure of a course, including its aims, intended learning outcomes, curriculum map, entry requirements, and assessment strategy. These are formal QA tools used by awarding bodies and regulatory agencies.

Module specifications

Each module - within a programme, course or subject - has its own documented module specification, listing:

- Specific learning outcomes.
- Indicative content.
- Required readings or resources.
- Types of learning activity.
- Assessment methods.

In HE, module specs must show alignment with QAA benchmarks, institutional strategy, and often link to graduate attribute frameworks.

Appendices 3 and 4 provide sample programme and module specifications.

Schemes of work

Schemes of work are medium-term curriculum plans developed by teachers or departments. They translate curriculum frameworks into working units and lay out detailed weekly (or topic-based) goals, activities, resources, and assessment points. These are common in all sectors and are vital for ensuring consistency among parallel classes and long-term curriculum coherence.

Appendix 5 provides a sample scheme of work.

Lesson plans

Lesson plans break schemes of work into instructional episodes. At a minimum, they include:

- Learning objectives.
- Teaching steps and timings.
- Resources needed.

- Differentiation strategies.
- Plenary or assessment methods.

Lesson planning is mandatory in most primary and secondary contexts, less formalised (but still encouraged) in FE, and typically left to individual academic judgement in HE.

Appendix 6 provides a sample lesson plan.

The importance of alignment

Drawing on *constructive alignment* (Biggs, 2022), the robustness of a curriculum depends on systematically linking objectives and outcomes to teaching methods, resources, and assessment. This alignment ensures:

- Clear trajectory from initial aim to demonstrable impact.
- Consistency across teams and institutions.
- Transparency and accountability, especially in inspected or assessed organisations.

Misalignment can lead to confusion, inequity, or ineffectiveness - where what is taught does not match what is tested, or where assessments fail to measure intended outcomes.

Establishing the need for a curriculum

A critical foundation of curriculum design is determining what knowledge, skills, and values learners should acquire - and why. This reflective process, known as *needs analysis*, involves identifying the deeper educational aims a curriculum should fulfil, taking into account learners' prior knowledge, aspirations, cultural background, and broader societal conditions. It also considers institutional or professional imperatives, such as accreditation requirements, qualification frameworks, or labour market trends. While widely acknowledged in theory, needs analysis is often only partially addressed in practice. Traditional models like Tyler's (2013) include goal-setting as a key step, but do not always emphasise formal procedures for conducting detailed diagnostic work. Indeed, of all the sources used to establish 'need', the most common are texts written by subject matter specialists (Tyler, 2013).

Other models, such as Taba's inductive approach, afford greater attention to context-driven design. Nevertheless, across all sectors - primary, secondary, FE, and HE - establishing curricular need is vital for ensuring that content is relevant, inclusive, and flexible. It guides meaningful decisions about what to teach, how to teach it, and how learning is assessed and reviewed.

Model	Formal needs analysis?	How it is performed
Taba	Yes (explicit)	Diagnostic, teacher-driven
Tyler	Often implied	Stakeholder and learner review
Backward Design (UbD)	Implied/in practice	Reflection, goal setting, review
Spiral Curriculum (Bruner)	Informal/implicit	Teacher adapts via observation
Stenhouse Process	Ongoing/dynamic	Continual dialogue and reflection
Wheeler/Kerr	Yes (contextual/cyclical)	Initial and periodic reviews
Eisner's Connoisseurship	Limited/experiential	Professional qualitative judgement
Ornstein & Hunkins	Yes (explicit)	Formal diagnostic at outset
Freire's Critical Pedagogy	Dialogic/critical	Collective inquiry, context-driven

Table 2.3 - Needs analysis in major curriculum rationales

Information

While Taba's model includes an explicit needs analysis, she specifically advocates for this analysis to be led and conducted by teachers themselves (Taba, 1962). While this highlights professional agency, it has severe limitations including time constraints, lack of systemic coordination, variable expertise, and reduced access to broader data.

Why establish needs?

Deciding what students should learn is not a neutral process. It can serve varied aims - from promoting cultural transmission to enabling critical thinking or preparing for the workforce - and these aims will differ depending on sector, setting, and purpose. Needs analysis allows educators and curriculum designers to scrutinise the relevance and appropriateness of content for current and future learners. It also supports the alignment between learner needs, teaching methods, and expected outcomes, contributing to *curriculum coherence* and *educational equity* (Print, 2021; Kelly, 2009).

Needs analysis not only legitimises curricular choices but also functions as a safeguard against relying solely on top-down mandates or rigid subject traditions. In doing so, it opens space for innovation, responsiveness, and local variation.

Needs analysis in context

Primary education

In primary schools, curriculum needs are primarily framed around holistic child development, including not only cognitive but also physical, emotional, and social growth. Needs analysis in this phase often reflects developmental psychology (e.g. Piaget, Vygotsky) and focuses on what children are capable of understanding and doing at particular ages. Teachers play a central role in diagnosing needs based on formative assessment, observation, learner interests, and community context (Burnett & Cremin, 2018).

For example, identifying high levels of language delay in children entering Reception may lead schools to prioritise early literacy within a revised curriculum, including phonics interventions, structured storytelling, and oracy-based learning. At the same time, schools may integrate local cultural content or environmental learning if analysis suggests such inclusion will engage the community.

Needs analysis in primary contexts is therefore highly embedded in ongoing practice, often informal but crucial to adapting national curriculum aims to the lived realities of learners (Alexander, 2021).

Secondary education

By secondary education, needs analysis becomes more complex, as learners diverge in their developmental paths and curricula become more compartmentalised by subject. In this phase, needs analysis may include:

- Reviewing prior attainment and progression data (e.g. Key Stage 2 SATs, internal assessment).
- Considering post-16 aspirations (e.g. university, apprenticeships).
- Identifying gaps in knowledge or engagement across subject departments.
- Consulting student voice or parental input.

Curriculum needs in secondary settings are also shaped by performance metrics (e.g. Progress 8), which may pressure schools to prioritise "core" subjects. However, robust needs analysis can counteract narrow attainment focus by identifying the importance of broader wellbeing, citizenship education, or creative subjects (Whitty, 2010).

Secondary subject leaders frequently lead curriculum review cycles, drawing insights from results, lesson observations, and national research to realign schemes of work. Crucially, needs analysis at this level must balance statutory frameworks with responsive qualifications and engagement strategies.

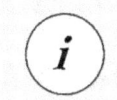

Information — Progress 8 is a key school performance measure in England that assesses the progress students make between the end of primary school (Key Stage 2) and the end of secondary school (Key Stage 4). It is a value-added measure, meaning it compares a school's results to those of other schools with students of similar prior attainment.

Further education (FE)

In FE, needs analysis is particularly formalised due to the diversity of student profiles and the vocational nature of many programmes. Students in FE may include:

- School leavers aiming for careers or university.
- Adult returners balancing education with work or caring responsibilities.
- Learners requiring additional support (e.g. SEND, ESOL).

For these groups, needs analysis includes both educational and societal diagnosis. Curriculum planners must determine what qualifications are needed for industry standards, what skills are deficient in the workforce, and what learners require in order to succeed personally and professionally.

Techniques used in FE for needs analysis include:

- Labour market analysis and engagement with Local Enterprise Partnerships (LEPs).
- Employer consultations and sector skills councils.
- Student entry profiles and prior qualification reviews.
- Targeted learner feedback on curriculum relevance.

For example, an FE provider may revise its construction curriculum to include sustainability skills such as heat pump installation, following emerging green job trends and industry demand.

Needs analysis in FE balances occupational readiness with wider goals such as citizenship, personal development, and flexibility - attributes that respond to the changing economy and learner diversity.

Higher education (HE)

In higher education, curriculum development is typically led by faculty, with attention to academic standards, research progression, and disciplinary coherence. However, needs analysis is increasingly formalised due to the expansion of HE access, internationalisation, and policy priorities around employability and graduate outcomes (Barnett & Coate, 2005). Universities undertake needs analysis by:

- Mapping subject benchmarks (QAA, 2024).
- Consulting industry advisory boards and accrediting bodies for vocational programmes.
- Reviewing student feedback (e.g. NSS), progression rates, and learner analytics.
- Engaging with alumni, employers, and university placement office data to understand market relevance.

Needs analysis might, for example, prompt the redesign of an engineering module to include digital engineering tools, or the inclusion of mental health literacy in teacher training programmes.

Unlike schools or FE colleges, HE must also consider needs related to higher-order thinking, research skills, interdisciplinarity, and global awareness - especially as curricula aim to prepare students for evolving knowledge economies (Knight & Yorke, 2003).

Education vs training: What differs?

Needs analysis also differs based on purpose. In education, the focus is broad and developmental, centred on fostering skills and dispositions for lifelong learning, active citizenship, creativity, and inquiry. In training, particularly for vocational or professional purposes, the emphasis is more on skill acquisition, competence assessment, and job-readiness.

- In education (e.g., secondary English or university history), needs analysis might identify the need for integrating critical thinking or decolonised content.

- In training (e.g., apprenticeship in hospitality), it focuses on operational standards, employer expectations, and qualification frameworks.

Nevertheless, the boundary is not clear-cut. Effective curriculum design in both settings is supported by a careful diagnosis of learner backgrounds, aspirations, challenges, and wider trends.

Methods of needs analysis

Curriculum designers and educators employ a diverse array of approaches to conduct needs analysis, ensuring that curriculum content aligns with learner requirements and broader educational goals. These approaches are typically grouped into two main categories: direct methods, which involve firsthand data collection from stakeholders, and indirect methods, which utilise existing records, research, or trend analysis to inform decisions. By combining both types of methods, educators gain a comprehensive perspective on learner needs, context, and priorities.

Direct methods:

- Student surveys and focus groups.
- Entry-level diagnostics or initial assessments.
- One-to-one interviews or personal learning plans.
- Stakeholder consultations (parents, employers, community leaders).

Indirect methods:

- Analysis of learner progression and attainment data.
- Review of national frameworks and policy documents.
- Labour market intelligence and employment forecasts.
- Literature reviews and curriculum benchmarking against peer organisations.

University criminology programme
In a UK university, a curriculum team are preparing a new criminology programme. The needs analysis combines:

- A literature review of similar UK qualifications.
- NSS data collection for student expectations in social sciences.

> - Consultation with criminal justice employers and probation services.
> - Assessment of research-active staff expertise to build specialist modules.
>
> The result is a curriculum that meets institutional rigour, market relevance, and learner interest - grounded in a thorough and triangulated needs analysis.

Limitations of needs analysis

The scope and richness of curriculum analysis at the school level are fundamentally constrained by the statutory requirements set out in the national curriculum framework. This centralised approach limits schools' ability to innovate or tailor content to local needs, in contrast to colleges and universities. Further and higher education institutions typically enjoy greater curricular autonomy, allowing for more diverse, flexible, and contextually responsive curriculum analysis and development.

1. Prescribed content and structure

- National curriculum frameworks prescribe in detail what is to be taught in schools, especially in the core and foundation subjects at primary and secondary levels (DfE, 2014).

- Schools must adhere to statutory programmes of study, attainment targets, and timetabled hours, drastically narrowing the scope for meaningful local adaptation.

- Because subject content, learning objectives, and even methods of assessment are centrally determined, schools have limited freedom to introduce new topics, pedagogies, or local priorities - reducing the potential for a nuanced analysis of curricular intent or innovation.

2. Reduced local flexibility

- Colleges and universities benefit from significant curriculum autonomy. They can design programmes to meet diverse community needs, regional employer demands, innovations in disciplinary knowledge, or developments in pedagogy (Barnett & Coate, 2005; QAA, 2024).

- In contrast, schools face legal and inspection requirements, which discourage deviation from the framework, leading to uniform practices across the country.

- As a result, analysis at school level often becomes a process of compliance-checking rather than of critically evaluating the curriculum's fitness for purpose in a specific context.

3. Limited stakeholder input

- In colleges and universities, curriculum design typically involves wider consultation with students, local employers, specialist staff, and professional bodies. This enables inclusion of current needs, feedback, and innovation.

- The school national curriculum, by contrast, is largely set at the policy level, with input mainly from government and national bodies, which constrains the ability to respond directly to student voice or local community priorities (Kelly, 2009).

4. Impact on needs analysis

- Effective needs analysis involves diagnosing learner requirements, local context, and broader social or economic trends. In colleges and universities, such analysis directly informs curricular changes and course content over time.

- In schools, the statutory framework limits the impact of any analysis; insights about learners' needs, local interests, or pedagogical innovation can rarely lead to meaningful changes in curriculum content, scope, or assessment structure - other than perhaps in optional extras or enrichment activities.

5. Implications for curriculum review

Table 2.4 outlines the implications of a number of aspects of curriculum review.

Aspect	School (National Curriculum)	College/University/Training
Content autonomy	Highly limited	Extensive
Pedagogical flexibility	Restricted	High
Responsiveness to local need	Minor (mainly in extra-curricular)	Significant (including course content)
Stakeholder influence	Minimal (mainly top-down)	Incorporated throughout the process
Scope for innovation	Low	High

Table 2.4 - Implications of curriculum review

Activity: Curriculum design, reflection and application

1. **Curriculum analysis:**
Choose a programme, module specification, scheme of work, or lesson plan from your own setting or experience (primary/secondary/FE/HE).

2. **Critical review:**
- Identify how the aims, objectives, learning outcomes, and standards are defined and communicated in the document.
- Evaluate how these guide the selection and sequencing of content, choice of teaching methods, and assessment strategies.
- Detect any evidence of the "twin sins" of curriculum design (activity-driven teaching without clear purpose, or superficial coverage rather than depth).

3. **Needs analysis:**
Reflect on whether and how learner needs were established in the curriculum design. Consider if the framework allows for inclusivity, progression, and local/contextual adaptation.

4. **Design improvement:**
Suggest two concrete changes you would make to improve curriculum coherence, depth, or relevance for learners - justifying your rationale with reference to chapter concepts or models.

5. **Discussion:**
Prepare to share your analysis and proposed changes in a peer discussion, drawing on insights from different sectors or approaches described in the chapter.

Summary

This chapter provided a comprehensive exploration of curriculum design, tracing key theories, rationales, and practical models used across primary, secondary, further, and higher education. It examined foundational frameworks such as Tyler's objectives-based approach, Taba's inductive model, and alternative designs including backward design, the spiral curriculum, and Stenhouse's process model.

The discussion highlighted how curriculum frameworks - whether national, vocational, or benchmark-based - structure content, progression, and assessment, while also balancing standardisation with the need for local adaptability and context.

Major curriculum design challenges were analysed, including the "twin sins" of activity-led planning and coverage at the expense of depth, the importance of curriculum coherence, and the risk of superficial or fragmented learning. The chapter also emphasised the centrality of needs analysis in establishing relevant content, and the crucial roles of objectives, learning outcomes, and standards in guiding curriculum intent and classroom practice.

Through an examination of supporting documents such as programme specifications, schemes of work, and lesson plans, the chapter reinforced that effective curriculum design is an iterative, evidence-informed process - requiring careful alignment between aims, pedagogy, and assessment to ensure meaningful, inclusive, and high-quality learning for all students.

3 ORGANISING THE CURRICULUM

Introduction

Effective curriculum organisation provides the structural backbone that ensures learning is purposeful, progressive, and accessible. This chapter introduces the core concepts and models that underpin how curricula are designed and implemented, from defining what curriculum organisation means to evaluating different approaches for grouping content, sequencing learning, and supporting varied educational pathways. Key frameworks, such as subject-based and integrated curricula, are explored alongside practical considerations like modularisation, credit transfer, and documentation. Special attention is given to how technological advancements and digital tools are reshaping curriculum structures, enabling greater flexibility and customisation for learners.

This chapter

- Examines the concept and significance of curriculum organisation across educational sectors.
- Discusses criteria and guiding principles for effective curriculum structuring.
- Explores the Gronlund Approach to taxonomic levels in organising learning objectives.
- Analyses the merits and challenges of subject-based versus integrated curricula.
- Illustrates practical methods and case studies of curriculum organisation in action.
- Reviews modularisation, credit transfer systems, and their impact on learner progression.
- Reflects on emerging models for using technology to organise and personalise learning experiences.

What is curriculum organisation?

Curriculum organisation refers to the structured arrangement of educational content, learning experiences, and pedagogical strategies to maximise the efficiency, coherence, and impact of teaching and learning over time. It encompasses how subject matter is selected, sequenced, connected, and delivered - both within individual subjects and across broader areas of learning. This process is a vital component of curriculum development and implementation, ensuring that learning builds cumulatively, reinforces key ideas, and fosters not only knowledge acquisition but also changes in skills, attitudes, and behaviour (Ornstein & Hunkins, 2016).

Effective organisation is not merely logistical. It plays a pedagogical role by shaping how learners encounter, engage with, and internalise content. As Hall & Burnett (2025) argue, learning should not be treated as a sequence of isolated objectives, but as the cumulative outcome of multiple, interrelated experiences. For this reason, the organisation of curriculum must ensure coherence both *vertically* - across time and developmental stages - and *horizontally* - across subjects and contexts at the same level.

Vertical and horizontal relationships

Vertical organisation refers to the sequencing of learning over time. It ensures continuity and progression from earlier to more advanced knowledge, skills, and concepts. For instance, in primary education, vertical curriculum alignment ensures that mathematical concepts introduced in Year 3 - such as place value - are deepened and extended in Year 4 and beyond. Similarly, vertical sequencing in secondary education is evident in how Key Stage 3 science introduces foundational biology knowledge that is then expanded upon in Key Stage 4 when pupils explore genetics or photosynthesis at a more complex level.

When vertical coherence is lacking - such as when learners are introduced to advanced topics without sufficient grounding - educational progress is hampered, and gaps in understanding emerge (Wiliam, 2011). In further education (FE), clear vertical organisation becomes especially important in competency-based frameworks, where vocational and technical skills must be built logically in preparation for workplace performance or higher-level study. In higher education (HE), vertical alignment often takes place through level descriptors and prerequisites, with learning outcomes mapped to national qualification frameworks such as the Framework for Higher Education Qualifications (QAA, 2024).

Horizontal organisation, by contrast, refers to the integration and alignment of learning across subjects or disciplines being taught concurrently. Its goal is to encourage meaningful connections between knowledge areas. In a primary curriculum, horizontal alignment might involve thematic units whereby learning in history, geography, and English are intentionally interlinked around a central concept, such as migration. This promotes reinforced learning, helping pupils develop a broader, more holistic understanding.

In secondary education, while subjects become more distinct, horizontal links between disciplines remain valuable. For example, the study of historical sources in history complements critical reading in English or the evaluation of evidence in science. When carefully planned, horizontal relationships can support learners in transferring skills - such as analysis, reasoning, or argument - from one domain to another (Bruner, 2009; Alexander, 2020).

In FE, cross-curricular connections might be made between employability and vocational units - where, for example, communication skills taught in a general education module are integrated with customer service in hospitality. In HE, horizontal alignment might occur across optional modules, when multiple courses contribute to a shared programme-level outcome such as ethical awareness, digital fluency, or research literacy.

Curriculum organisation and cumulative learning

Organisation is crucial for generating the *cumulative effect* of learning - where each new experience builds upon and reinforces prior knowledge. As Spady (1993) and others have noted, effective education is not merely about achieving discrete short-term goals, but about fostering deeper, lasting change over time. A well-organised curriculum enables learners to integrate new ideas with prior knowledge, reduce redundancy, and encounter key concepts multiple times in different forms.

Conversely, if learning experiences are poorly sequenced or disconnected, students may experience education as fragmented, leading to compartmentalised or superficial knowledge that fails to transfer into new situations (Willingham, 2021). For example, if ethical reasoning is taught in a citizenship module at Key Stage 3, but not reinforced in RE, history, or science, students may fail to see its wider application.

Curriculum organisation must also take account of developmental appropriateness, ensuring that learners encounter concepts when they are cognitively and emotionally ready. Vygotsky's (1978) *zone of proximal development* suggests that optimal learning occurs when new content is just beyond a student's current level, but within reach when supported. Thus, progression must be carefully mapped to avoid either repetition or overload.

Contextual variation in organising the curriculum

While the principles of vertical and horizontal organisation are universal, their expression varies significantly across educational contexts.

- In primary education, curriculum organisation is often guided by integrated or thematic models. Teachers, usually generalists, are responsible for multiple subjects, giving them greater scope to build horizontal links and tailor learning sequences day by day. However, this flexibility can also risk inconsistency without clear frameworks for progression (Alexander, 2021).

- In secondary education, timetabled subjects and specialist teaching make coordination more complex. Curriculum leaders often use tools such as curriculum maps, long-term plans, and assessment frameworks to promote coherence. Interdisciplinary initiatives - such as STEAM projects or cross-subject collaborations - are increasingly used to promote both horizontal and vertical alignment.

Information — A STEAM project is a multidisciplinary learning activity or unit that integrates elements from Science, Technology, Engineering, Arts, and Mathematics to solve real-world problems or address open-ended questions. The STEAM approach builds on the earlier STEM model by explicitly including the Arts, emphasising creativity, design, critical thinking, and communication alongside technical understanding.

- In FE, curriculum organisation must balance a wide range of learner journeys - academic, vocational, and personal. Modular units allow for flexibility, catering for full-time, part-time, and work-based learners. Effective planning helps ensure that learners can accumulate credits while progressing through clearly staged qualifications aligned with national standards and employer needs.

- In HE, curriculum organisation takes place at both the programme and module level. Credits, levels, and learning outcomes are organised according to qualification frameworks such as the QAA's Subject Benchmark Statements. Modular structures provide flexibility but require careful alignment to ensure progression. Responsiveness to research, student feedback, and industry developments also impacts how curricula are reviewed and restructured.

Criteria for effective organisation

The organisation of a curriculum is fundamental to ensuring that learning experiences promote sustained progress, coherence, and the transfer of knowledge and skills. Effective curriculum organisation ensures learners build meaningfully on prior learning, link concepts across disciplines, and experience education as a connected, cumulative process rather than a set of isolated encounters (Ornstein &

Hunkins, 2016). Across sectors - primary, secondary, further education (FE), and higher education (HE) - three interrelated criteria are widely recognised as foundational for organising learning: *continuity*, *sequence*, and *integration* (Tyler, 1949; Kelly, 2009).

1. Continuity

Continuity refers to the consistent reinforcement of core curriculum elements - concepts, skills, values - over time. It embodies the vertical dimension of curriculum organisation, ensuring that important ideas recur with increasing depth and complexity across key stages or academic levels (Tyler, 1949).

For example, in primary education, concepts such as number sense or sentence structure are revisited and developed in each successive year. In secondary science, the concept of energy may be introduced in Key Stage 3 through basic definitions and simple experiments, then revisited at Key Stage 4 in more complex contexts such as thermodynamics or chemical reactions.

Effective continuity strengthens memory and understanding, enables cumulative mastery, and prevents key elements from being forgotten or under-emphasised (Willingham, 2021). In FE settings, continuity can be seen as learners progress from foundational to advanced vocational skills, such as building basic customer service skills before advancing to managing complex client scenarios. In HE, disciplinary 'threshold concepts' - such as the scientific method in biology - are intentionally revisited at increasing levels of sophistication, supporting deep learning and the eventual development of expert thinking (Meyer & Land, 2005; QAA, 2024).

2. Sequence

While continuity ensures recurring emphasis, sequence focuses on progression - structuring learning so that each stage builds logically upon the last. Effective sequencing ensures each new learning experience arises naturally from previous encounters, increasing the sophistication or application of skills and knowledge (Bruner, 2009).

In primary mathematics, the move from adding two-digit numbers to manipulating three-digit numbers exemplifies sequence: initial skills are first consolidated, then extended to more complex and abstract scenarios. In secondary schools, teaching sequences in history progress from understanding sources and chronology, to conceptual themes such as causation or change over time, and, in upper years, to handling complex historiographical debates.

FE curricula are often explicitly modular, with units designed in a deliberate sequence so that foundational knowledge in, for example, food safety precedes more complex units such as managing hospitality operations. In HE, module pre-requisites ensure that students build the necessary background knowledge in 'level 4' courses before moving to specialisms at levels 5 or 6. Without deliberate sequencing, students may struggle with advanced content or experience topics as disconnected fragments (Knight & Yorke, 2003).

3. Integration

Integration refers to the horizontal relationships within the curriculum: how learning experiences in one area relate to, support, and reinforce others simultaneously being studied. The goal of integration is to foster a unified understanding and build connections across domains, promoting the transfer and synthesis of knowledge and skills (Beane, 1997).

In primary education, integration often takes the form of thematic or cross-curricular projects linking science, history, geography, and English. For instance, a theme such as 'water' might incorporate lessons on the water cycle in science, river studies in geography, and creative writing on these topics in English. Integration at this stage supports engagement, contextual understanding, and the application of skills across subjects (Alexander, 2021).

In secondary schools, although curricular structures tend to emphasise subject specialisation, there remain valuable opportunities for integration. These include joint, interdisciplinary projects such as sustainability challenges that connect geography, science, and citizenship, enabling students to address complex real-world issues from multiple perspectives. Additionally, aligned skills development - such as structuring an argument in both English and history - helps reinforce key competencies across disciplines. In further education (FE), functional skills in mathematics, English, and digital literacy are embedded within vocational pathways, ensuring students can contextualise their learning in work-related tasks. This applied integration strengthens practical outcomes and supports employability. In higher education (HE), integration is increasingly achieved through interdisciplinary modules, collaborative research opportunities, and co-curricular initiatives. HE institutions also map wider graduate attributes - such as critical thinking, ethical reasoning, and intercultural awareness - across disciplines, ensuring learners develop transferable, cross-sector competencies for an increasingly complex and globalised world (Barnett & Coate, 2005).

Organising threads (or strands)

A practical starting point for effective curriculum organisation is identifying "threads" or "strands", which are key elements that recur and evolve across year groups, subjects, or modules (Kelly, 2009).

- In mathematics, threads might include number, algebra, proportion, geometry, and statistics.
- In history, they could include historical enquiry, change and continuity, or significance.
- In music, threads might be performance, composing, listening, and notation.

Early and repeated exposure to these threads ensures learners not only encounter them in isolation but return to them at intervals, each time with enriched context and challenge. Threads also facilitate reinforcement across subjects - for example, understanding proportion in mathematics supports practical science investigations and recipes in food technology.

Reinforcement and the cumulative effect

Curriculum organisation must aim for *reinforcement*: deliberate revisiting of key concepts, skills, and values - not for repetition's sake, but to enable new layers of understanding (Willingham, 2021). Over time, this leads to the cumulative effect that is critical for deep learning: students not only retain information, but see connections, transfer understanding, and adapt to novel problems.

For instance, the importance of persuasive communication might start with show-and-tell in lower primary, build to formal presentations in secondary English, and culminate in debating and reflective arguments in FE or HE. Each stage draws on earlier experiences, yet adds complexity and sophistication (Knight & Yorke, 2003).

Applying the criteria across sectors

- In primary schools, continuity, sequence, and integration are essential for scaffolding new knowledge onto prior experiences and supporting holistic development. Organising threads help teachers plan across the year and connect learning for young children.

- In secondary settings, continuity and sequence support specialisation and exam-readiness, while deliberate integration (e.g., PSHE, cross-curricular themes) counters fragmentation.
- In FE, modularisation enables logical sequencing and flexibility for diverse cohorts; continuity and integration are increasingly built through spiralled functional skills and work-related learning.
- In HE, constructive alignment and modular frameworks ensure that students progress from foundational concepts to advanced, interdisciplinary application, while also catering for depth within specialisms and breadth through elective modules (Biggs, 2022; Barnett & Coate, 2005).

Challenges and considerations

Achieving all three criteria can be difficult. Overemphasis on sequence without periodic integration can lead to compartmentalised knowledge, while excessive integration without sequence may sacrifice depth for breadth. Curriculum leaders must therefore strike a balance, using documentation such as curriculum maps, schemes of work, and assessment plans to ensure clarity, consistency, and cumulative progression.

Institutional culture, teacher expertise, and available resources also play major roles in how successfully the criteria are enacted (Ornstein & Hunkins, 2016). Ongoing evaluation and curricula review are essential to monitor the cumulative effect and adapt organisation of the curriculum in response to student needs, policy changes, or emerging knowledge.

Taxonomic levels

Organising curriculum content effectively involves not only determining *what* should be taught but also in what *order* and to what *depth*. Taxonomies of learning provide educators with structured ways to classify educational objectives based on levels of knowledge, cognitive processing, and skills development. One influential framework is the *Gronlund Approach*, which builds on earlier taxonomies, such as those by *Bloom* and *Krathwohl*, but places particular emphasis on curriculum planning, assessment development, and learner progression across educational contexts.

This section examines the function and value of taxonomic approaches to curriculum organisation in primary, secondary, further education (FE), and higher education (HE) settings. Special attention is given to Gronlund's contribution in helping educators clarify learning outcomes, design assessments, and sequence learning to support progression from foundational to advanced capabilities.

Understanding taxonomies in curriculum design

Learning taxonomies - hierarchical frameworks for categorising educational objectives - serve several vital purposes in curriculum design. These include:

- Structuring learning outcomes from simple to complex.
- Supporting planning by sequencing content appropriately.
- Informing assessment through the alignment of objectives and evaluation tasks.
- Promoting transparency and shared understanding among educators and learners (Anderson & Krathwohl, 2001; Biggs, 2022).

The most widely known taxonomy is Bloom's (Appendix 2), later revised by Anderson & Krathwohl (2001), which classifies cognitive levels as:

- Remembering
- Understanding
- Applying
- Analysing
- Evaluating
- Creating

Gronlund, however, adapted this into a more simplified structure that particularly suits curriculum organisation and assessment development. He maintained clear links between instructional objectives and the levels of cognitive complexity, helping educators design teaching strategies and assessment tasks that match the intended outcome (Gronlund, 2000).

The Gronlund classification (adapted version)

In Gronlund's approach, objectives are commonly grouped into four broad levels within the *cognitive domain*:

- **Knowledge (Remembering):** Recalling facts, information, or procedures.
- **Comprehension (Understanding):** Demonstrating an understanding of meaning or interpretation.
- **Application (Applying):** Using knowledge in new and concrete situations.

- **Invention:** A holistic level combining analysis, synthesis, and evaluation - this relates to the development of new ideas, critical reflection, and problem-solving across disciplines.

Importantly, Gronlund acknowledged that these categories are not strictly hierarchical but often overlap. However, organising curriculum objectives in this way supports *vertical sequencing*, helping learners move incrementally from basic concepts to creative or evaluative tasks.

Applications across educational contexts

Primary education

In Key Stage 2, the Gronlund taxonomy can be particularly useful for organising progression in literacy and numeracy. For example, in English:

- At the knowledge level, pupils might recall key features of a fable.
- At the comprehension level, they explain the central message.
- At the application level, they write their own version using similar structure.
- At the invention level, they critique the moral implications or compare to modern issues.

Teachers can use this structure to build units of work that extend from basic understanding through to wider thinking and creativity. It also helps scaffold tasks for learners with varying levels of readiness and supports inclusive teaching (Burnett & Cremin, 2018).

In mathematics, the model allows learners to first recall key facts (e.g., times tables), understand how multiplication works, apply this to problems in real-life contexts, and eventually create their own investigations or explain different strategies to solve a problem - demonstrating both critical and creative thinking (DfE, 2014).

Secondary education

In secondary schools, curriculum organisation becomes more complex due to subject compartmentalisation. The taxonomy helps subject specialists map topics and skills against assessment frameworks. For GCSE history, for instance, outcomes can be framed as:

- Knowledge: Recall dates or key facts.
- Comprehension: Explain causes or consequences.

- Application: Use historical sources to support interpretations.
- Invention: Develop a sustained argument around interpretations or significance.

Integrating taxonomic thinking ensures learners are not exposed only to factual recall but to increasingly sophisticated intellectual challenges, aligned with both the National Curriculum and exam board specifications. Teachers designing schemes of work can use taxonomies to sequence lessons logically and vary the level of challenge (Sherrington, 2019).

Further education (FE)

In FE, particularly within vocational and applied qualifications like BTEC or T Levels, Gronlund's approach is valuable for linking theoretical content with practical application - a key requirement for workplace readiness.

Take, for example, a hospitality unit:

- Knowledge: Identify hygiene regulations.
- Comprehension: Explain the principles behind safe food storage.
- Application: Carry out a hygiene check or write a checklist for staff.
- Invention: Evaluate and revise a hygiene policy based on industry scenarios.

Many FE learners are assessed through portfolios or practical demonstrations. Clear taxonomic guidance ensures assessments capture a range of cognitive processes, from basic competence to problem-solving under new conditions, which can help both less confident learners and high achievers succeed through differentiated scaffolding.

Higher education (HE)

In HE, learning outcomes are formally documented in programme specifications and module descriptors, often referencing qualification frameworks such as the QAA's Framework for Higher Education Qualifications (QAA, 2024). Gronlund's model reinforces the idea that higher-level thinking (especially at levels 6 and above) involves an integration of critical evaluation, research application, and knowledge creation.

In a Level 6 electronic engineering module, for example:

- Knowledge: Explain fundamental concepts such as signal processing, circuit components, and semiconductor physics.

- Comprehension: Analyse circuit behaviour using simulation software and interpret measurement data.
- Application: Design, assemble, and test electronic circuits to meet specified functional requirements.
- Invention: Develop a novel electronic device or system, critically evaluate its performance, and propose improvements based on current research.

HE learning outcomes are expected to evidence deep engagement with abstract concepts. Gronlund's taxonomy, integrated with constructive alignment principles (Biggs, 2022), ensures that teaching, learning, and assessment strategies support progression from foundational knowledge to independent inquiry and innovation.

Sequencing and assessment

One core benefit of taxonomic classification is its role in *sequencing*. Educators use taxonomies to ensure that learning builds cumulatively, rather than exposing learners to complex demands too early. In planning, it allows curriculum designers to move from:

- Simple to complex.
- Concrete to abstract.
- Familiar to unfamiliar.

This sequencing is essential in project-based learning, scaffolding, and differentiated instruction across all levels of education.

In terms of assessment, taxonomic structures help ensure that assessment tasks accurately measure the level of understanding intended by the objective. For instance:

- Knowledge level: Multiple choice quiz.
- Application level: Problem-solving task or simulation.
- Invention level: Research paper or project presentation.

Without clear understanding and application of taxonomic levels in assessment design, there is a significant risk of misalignment between what is taught and what is evaluated. This misalignment can result in inaccurate measurement of learner achievement, overlooking critical aspects of deeper learning and cognitive development (Knight & Yorke, 2003).

Integrated or separate organisation

Taxonomic structuring also supports discussions around curriculum format. As noted in Gronlund's framework, the way objectives are classified can inform whether subjects are taught as distinct entities or via integrated models. In primary settings, integration is often achieved through cross-curricular themes (e.g., climate, conflict, identity), whereas in secondary, FE, and HE, a modular structure is more common. Regardless of structure, clear taxonomic classification ensures coherence, even within flexible or interdisciplinary formats.

An interdisciplinary project in HE focused on sustainability might involve:

- Geography module: Measuring environmental impact (application).
- Economics module: Analysing cost-benefit implications (evaluation).
- Politics module: Proposing new policy (creation).

This allows 'threads' to develop across domains while still tracking cognitive advancement.

Subject-based vs. integrated curricula

Curriculum organisation can follow multiple structural models, each reflecting different philosophies of education and pedagogical priorities. Two longstanding and often contrasting approaches are *subject-based* and *integrated* curricula. Each carries specific implications for the ways learners engage with knowledge, how teachers structure learning experiences, and how institutions meet national expectations or local needs. While subject-based curricula focus on maintaining disciplinary boundaries, integrated approaches promote interconnection across fields of knowledge - often aligning more closely with real-world problem-solving and multidisciplinary learning demands.

Subject-based curricula

Subject-based curricula are structured around discrete disciplines, such as mathematics, English, biology, or history, each with defined content, pedagogy, and assessment methods. These have traditionally been the dominant model in most formal education systems, particularly in secondary education (Figure 3.1) and higher education (Young et al., 2014). This approach ensures depth of knowledge, conceptual progression, and fidelity to subject-based 'ways of knowing', especially important in academic and technical education.

For example, in Key Stage 4 in England, learners study for General Certificates of Secondary Education (GCSEs) in clearly delineated subjects, with examination boards providing standardised content and assessments. In further education, many vocational programmes follow structured occupational areas (e.g., plumbing, health and social care) rooted in subject matter expertise and occupational standards. In higher education, departments often define curricula according to disciplinary traditions, with subject benchmarks ensuring that degrees reflect established canons of knowledge and skill (QAA, 2024).

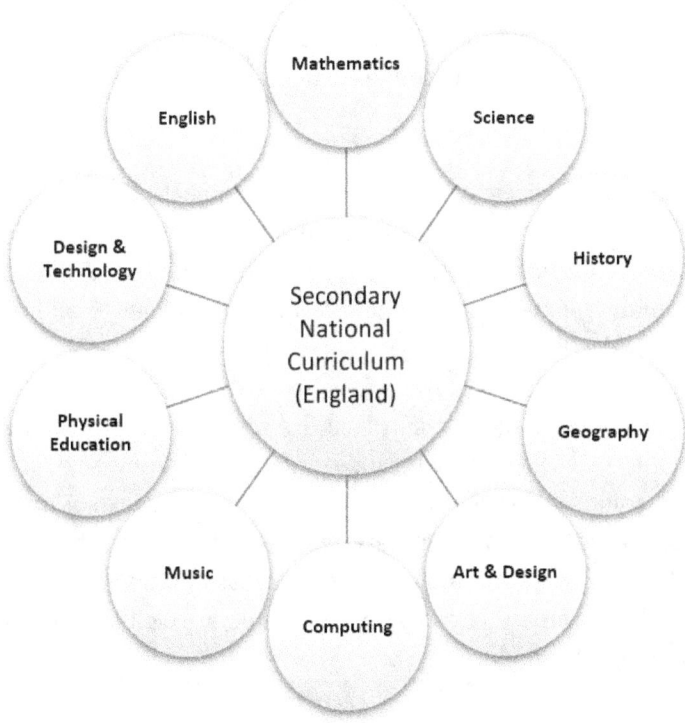

Figure 3.1 - Subject-based curricula

Supporters of subject-based curricula argue that they:

- Foster deep understanding and mastery within disciplines.
- Provide logical progression from basic concepts to advanced ideas.
- Align with teacher specialisms and standardised assessment (Kelly, 2009; Biesta, 2015).
- Prepare learners for discipline-specific knowledge required in further study or employment.

However, critics point to limitations. Subject-based approaches can promote *curricular fragmentation*, where learners struggle to make meaningful links between what they study in different classrooms. For instance, learners may not easily transfer mathematical reasoning into science or economics if they are not taught explicitly to do so (Learn, 2000). Content can also feel disconnected from real-world contexts, especially for students who thrive on practical or thematic learning (Apple & Apple, 2004).

Integrated curricula

In contrast, integrated curricula seek to connect or merge subjects to provide a more holistic, thematic, or problem-based learning experience. Integration can occur at various levels:

- **Intra-disciplinary**: Linking subfields within one subject.
- **Interdisciplinary**: Connecting two or more subjects under a shared theme.
- **Multidisciplinary**: Evoking multiple subjects while retaining distinct methods.
- **Transdisciplinary**: Extending beyond individual disciplines to address real-world issues holistically (Beane, 1997).

In primary education, integrated curricula are characteristic of thematic units. A topic like "Rainforests" (Figure 3.2) could combine geography, science, English, and art through reading persuasive texts about conservation, exploring habitats, and creating visual representations. Primary teachers often possess a broad range of expertise, allowing them to move flexibly across multiple subject areas. This versatility makes primary classrooms particularly well-suited to integrated curriculum models (Alexander, 2021).

In secondary education, where teachers are subject specialists, integration can be harder to coordinate but still achievable through cross-curricular projects or themed weeks. Some schools use approaches such as project-based learning (PBL), which centres learning around complex questions or real-world challenges. For example, a project on "Local Sustainability" might engage science, geography, design & technology, and citizenship, linking disciplinary knowledge to community-based solutions.

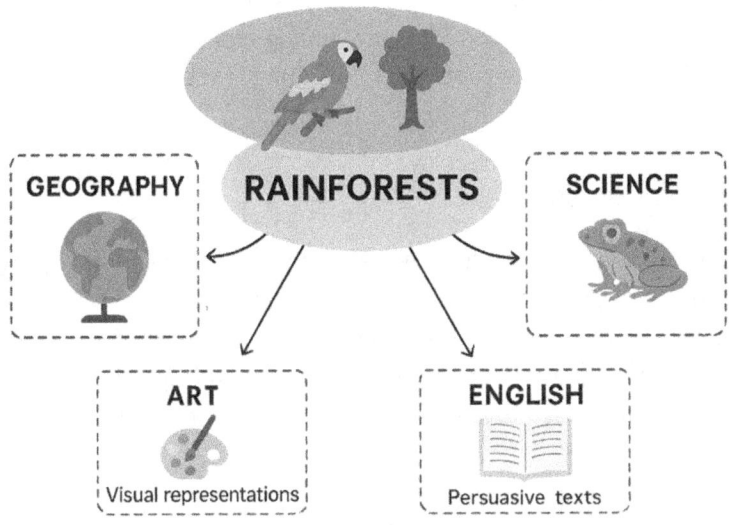

Figure 3.2 - Interdisciplinary integrated curricula

In FE, integrated approaches might align with employability skills or enterprise modules, using real-world briefs that naturally cross disciplinary lines. Learners on a hospitality and catering course, for instance, could explore nutrition (science), business planning (maths and economics), marketing (media), and client care (PSHE) in an integrated format tailored to their career path.

HE Institutions Increasingly adopt Interdisciplinary modules or liberal arts pathways to reflect the changing nature of knowledge and 21st-century skills. Integrated and team-taught modules in sustainability, digital futures, or global challenges invite learners to consider problems from multiple perspectives, building transferable skills like collaboration and critical enquiry (Barnett & Coate, 2005).

Proponents of integrated curricula cite the following advantages in that they:

- Reflect the interconnected nature of real-world problems.
- Promote deeper engagement, creativity, and learner autonomy.
- Encourage transfer of learning across contexts.
- Support inclusion by aligning with diverse learner strengths and interests.

However, there are trade-offs. Integrated curricula may risk diluting disciplinary rigor, especially if teachers are not well-supported in working beyond their specialisms. Assessing student progress becomes more complex, and national standards or subject inspection frameworks may be harder to align (Beane, 1997; Kelly, 2009). Furthermore, without clear planning and shared understanding among staff, integration can become superficial - resulting in thematic packaging of content rather than true interdisciplinary synthesis.

Balancing tradition and innovation

While subject-bound knowledge remains vital, especially for progression to examinations or employment standards, contemporary educational needs also demand flexibility, creativity, and responsiveness - qualities often better supported through integration. The challenge, therefore, is not to replace one model with the other, but to balance discrete knowledge-building with opportunities for connected learning.

One effective model is the *coordinated curriculum*, which seeks compromise. It links subjects through common themes or shared skills (e.g., digital literacy, oracy, wellbeing), while maintaining subject identities. This model is frequently seen in wider curriculum planning in secondary schools - such as combining history and English in joint units of study, or integrating enterprise skills across BTECs. Spiral curriculum designs also support integration by ensuring revisiting of key concepts through lenses of increasing complexity (Bruner, 2009).

Curriculum leaders need to consider how best to organise learning to support coherence, progression, and engagement. Effective curriculum organisation - whether subject-based, integrated, or hybrid - requires clear aims, communication among staff, appropriate assessment strategies, and responsiveness to both policy expectations and learner needs.

Case Study: Integrated curriculum in New Zealand

At a primary school in Wellington, New Zealand, Year 5 students explore the theme "Oceans and Us," integrating science, literacy, and social studies. Pupils research marine ecosystems, write persuasive letters on plastic pollution to local politicians, and learn about Māori environmental stewardship. This approach boosts engagement, especially for students previously struggling in science or writing.

In a rural South Island school, teachers use local heritage for integrated learning. Pupils visit historical sites, interview elders, create digital stories, and perform dramatisations about their community's past. This strengthens oral language, deepens historical understanding, and promotes inclusion. Teachers report enhanced collaboration and confidence among learners, notably improving Māori students' achievement.

Modularisation and credit transfer

The concepts of modularisation and credit transfer are central to contemporary curriculum organisation, particularly in further education (FE) and higher education (HE) but also with increasing influence in secondary settings. Modular structures provide flexibility, facilitate personalised learning pathways, and support lifelong learning, while credit systems underpin national and international recognition of learning, enabling student mobility and progression across institutions and borders (QAA, 2024; Barnett & Coate, 2005).

Understanding modularisation

Modularisation refers to the division of a curriculum into self-contained units or "modules", each with defined outcomes, content, assessment, and credit value. Students accumulate credits by successfully completing modules, which can be combined in different ways to achieve full qualifications. This system, widely adopted in FE and HE, is designed to break down programmes into manageable components, enabling students to tailor their studies to personal interests, career goals, or life circumstances (QAA, 2024).

A typical undergraduate degree in the UK is structured using a credit-based system known as the Credit Accumulation and Transfer Scheme (CATS). Under this framework, each module is assigned a specific number of CATS credits, commonly 20 or 30 per module, depending on its length and intensity. One CATS credit is equivalent to 10 hours of notional student effort, which includes lectures, seminars, independent study, assessment preparation, and revision. Over the course of a full-time academic year, a student will normally complete 120 CATS credits, building towards a total of 360 credits for a three-year honours degree (QAA, 2024).

In further education (FE), qualifications such as apprenticeships, BTECs, and T Levels, also use modular structures, with each unit contributing a defined credit value towards the overall qualification. Credits in these programmes are mapped to national qualification frameworks and enable flexibility, recognising different forms of learning and supporting progression across levels. In both HE and FE, accumulated credits serve not only to measure study volume, but also to provide a shared language for credit transfer between institutions, supporting student mobility and lifelong learning (Pearson, 2025; QAA, 2024).

Modularisation in context

- **Primary education:** Modularisation is less formalised but appears through thematic units or topic blocks - particularly in project-based learning or cross-curricular themes. While not linked to credit systems, this structure allows flexibility and differentiation in content delivery and assessment (Alexander, 2021).

- **Secondary education:** Modularisation is visible in GCSEs structured into components, and more so in post-16 education, where A-levels and vocational courses are typically divided into modules or units, each individually assessed and sometimes resitable. In international settings, the International Baccalaureate (IB) Middle Years Programme is modular in structure, facilitating cross-disciplinary options (IBO, 2024).

- **Further education (FE):** Modularisation underpins most FE programmes. Qualifications like BTECs, T Levels, and NVQs are built from units with specific learning objectives and credit values. This enables more flexible learning, transfer between pathways, and recognises prior learning, which is especially important for adult and part-time learners.

- **Higher education (HE):** Modular frameworks are the norm in UK universities and colleges, governed by schemes like CATS. Programmes are structured around compulsory and optional modules, allowing students to build degrees with some customisation. Modules may be shared across programmes, faculties and universities, supporting interdisciplinary study (Barnett & Coate, 2005).

Credit accumulation and transfer

Credit systems provide the "currency" for modularised learning and allows for:

- Completion of qualifications flexibly over time (full- or part-time).

- Recognition of learning from different providers (including work-based learning).

- Opportunities for students to "step-off and step-on" qualifications, supporting lifelong learning.

Credit transfer enables students to move academic credits earned at one educational institution to another, both within the same country and internationally. This system is instrumental in supporting student mobility, widening access to higher education, and fostering transnational collaboration. For example, students progressing from further education (FE) to higher education (HE) may use articulated agreements to transfer credits from foundation degrees towards honours degrees, streamlining academic trajectories and reducing duplication of study.

In addition, frameworks such as the European Credit Transfer and Accumulation System (ECTS) allow recognition of international study as part of UK qualifications, ensuring that learning achieved abroad is valued and facilitates global academic engagement (European Union, 2015). Credits acquired in one context are thus recognised across multiple learning environments, promoting flexibility, lifelong learning, and cross-border higher education participation.

Level	Typical credit size (UK)	System	Example
GCSE	Not credit-rated	—	—
A Level	180 CATS credits (full A level)	CATS	3 x full A-levels = 540 credits
BTEC Diploma	60-120 credits/unit	QCF (now RQF)	BTEC Level 3 National Diploma
Foundation degree	240 credits (2 years FT)	CATS	FdA/BSc/BA
UG Degree (BA/BSc)	360 credits (3 years FT)	CATS	BA (Hons)
ECTS (Europe)	60 ECTS/year (180 credits = 3 years)	ECTS	Erasmus+ exchange semester
Master's (UK)	180 credits (1-3 years FT)	CATS	MSc/MA

Table 3.1 - European credit transfer and accumulation system
(Adapted from: QAA, 2024; European Union, 2015; Pearson, 2025)

Advantages of modularisation and credit transfer

- **Flexibility & personalisation:** Students can tailor their programmes by selecting optional modules, enabling deeper engagement in chosen areas or interdisciplinary study (Barnett & Coate, 2005).

- **Mobility:** Credits can be transferred between institutions; students can change provider or pause/resume studies without penalty.

- **Recognition of prior learning:** Modular structures facilitate accreditation of prior experiential or work-based learning, supporting progression for non-traditional or mature learners.

- **Responsive curriculum:** Modularisation enables rapid updating or replacement of content in response to developments in knowledge, skills demand, or employer needs.

- **Support for key skills and competencies:** Modular systems support the embedding of key or transferable skills (sometimes called functional skills, core skills, or graduate attributes) across programmes, recognising achievement in problem-solving, digital literacy, teamwork, or communication alongside subject knowledge (Kelly, 2009).

Challenges and criticisms

- **Fragmentation:** Modularisation can risk compartmentalising knowledge, leading to poorly integrated learning and limited coherence across a programme. Without careful curriculum mapping, students may miss cumulative understanding (Knight & Yorke, 2003).

- **Assessment overload:** In heavily modular programmes, frequent assessment points can create high workloads and shallow learning, as students shift from one set of requirements to the next (Biggs, 2022).

- **Credit equivalence issues**: Credit transfer between institutions is not always seamless. Differences in module content, learning outcomes, or assessment standards may prevent full recognition, undermining student mobility (QAA, 2024).

- **Key skills integration**: Embedding core competencies across modules is often inconsistent. Programmes may claim to address problem-solving or digital literacy, but without explicit mapping or assessment, these skills risk being superficially covered or duplicated across modules (Young et al., 2014).

Key skills and competencies

Core or "key skills" are now frequently embedded in modularised curricula across sectors. These include:

- **Personal skills:** Self-management, teamwork, leadership, communication, social awareness.

- **Learning/academic skills:** Critical thinking, creativity, problem-solving, digital and data literacy, application of number.

For instance, in the English National Curriculum (Figure 3.3), functional skills are interwoven through subjects such as English (communication), maths (numeracy), and computing (ICT literacy) (DfE, 2014). In FE and HE, frameworks may include mandatory key skills units or require that modules evidence opportunities for learners to practise and develop wider competencies (QAA, 2024; Pearson, 2025).

	English	Maths	Science	History	Geography	Art	Music	ICT	DT
Problem-solving		X	X			X			X
Teamwork				X	X		X	X	
Critical thinking		X	X					X	X
Creativity	X				X	X	X		
Communication	X			X	X		X		

Figure 3.3 - Key skills competencies (English National Curriculum)

Modularisation beyond the UK

Credit and modular systems are used internationally, but structures vary. The European Credit Transfer and Accumulation System (ECTS) standardises credits, supporting student mobility across 40+ countries. These models underpin transnational education, helping recognise overseas qualifications, enable joint degrees, foster academic collaboration, and promote flexibility and global recognition of learning (European Union, 2015; OECD, 2020).

Sector	Modularisation	Credit transfer	Key skills integration
Primary	Thematic units, informal	Not formalised	Functional skills, cross-curricular themes
Secondary	GCSE/A-level, IB modules	A-level portability	Literacy, numeracy, oracy
Further Ed (FE)	BTEC, T Level, NVQ units	Unit transfer between providers	Communication, ICT, problem-solving
Higher Ed (HE)	Programme & module system	CATS, ECTS	Graduate attributes, employability

Table 3.2 - Modularisation and key skills integration
(Adapted from: DfE, 2014; IBO, 2024; Pearson, 2025; QAA, 2024)

Accreditation for prior learning and experience

Accreditation for Prior Learning and experience (APEL) - sometimes referred to as *Recognition of Prior Learning (RPL)* - is a method of formally acknowledging the knowledge, skills, and experiences that learners have gained outside of traditional academic contexts. It plays an increasingly important role in supporting flexible and lifelong learning pathways across primary, secondary, further education (FE), and higher education (HE). APEL enables learners to gain credit, exemption, or advanced standing for relevant prior learning, whether it is formal (achieved through recognised qualifications), non-formal (through work-based training), or informal (learned experientially or through self-directed learning) (QAA, 2024).

Principles of APEL

At the core of APEL is the principle that learning - rather than the duration of formal study - is the basis for recognition. This shifts the focus from where or how knowledge was acquired to what the learner knows and is able to do. It provides opportunities for diverse learners, particularly adults, career changers, refugees, and those with industry experience but no formal qualifications, to access or progress through education more quickly and equitably (ECDVT, 2009).

Generally, APEL is governed by three main criteria:

- **Validity:** The prior learning must match the intended learning outcomes.
- **Sufficiency:** There must be enough evidence to demonstrate competence.
- **Currency:** The learning must be recent enough to remain relevant.

The process often involves portfolio development, formative interviews, employer references, and performance assessments to ensure transparent, fair decision-making.

APEL in primary and secondary education

In primary and secondary education, formal APEL approaches are uncommon, owing to the statutory emphasis on age-based progression and standardised assessment frameworks. However, there are indirect examples of recognising prior learning. In initial assessments (e.g., baseline assessments in Reception or diagnostic assessments in Key Stages 2 and 3), prior knowledge informs teaching, differentiation, and intervention strategies (Alexander, 2021). Transitional planning - such as moving pupils between schools or countries - often depends on schools making informal judgements about prior experience to support placement and curriculum alignment.

In some cases, recognition of prior learning can shape accelerated pathways for high-performing students or provide tailored support for those with gaps in previous education, such as refugee and asylum-seeking children. Ofsted now encourages primary and secondary schools to start with what pupils already know and can do - a principle that underscores the pedagogical value of acknowledging prior learning, even if not formally accredited (Ofsted, 2019).

APEL in further education

In FE, APEL has a formal and well-established role. Many awarding bodies - including Pearson, City & Guilds, and the Open College Network - include APEL as part of their quality assurance frameworks. Learners can gain credit for previous qualifications, workplace experience, or unaccredited training, often aligned to National Occupational Standards or qualification specifications (Pearson, 2025).

APEL in FE supports:

- Work-based learning programmes, such as apprenticeships or vocational diplomas.

- Access to higher education programmes, where adult learners may lack traditional qualifications but have relevant professional or life experience.

- Flexible progression, allowing learners to advance into a qualification at a higher point, avoiding duplication.

A learner with 10 years' experience in retail but no formal qualification may be able to use APEL to access a Level 3 Business and Administration Diploma by providing documentation, employer testimonies, and a validated skills portfolio. APEL also supports re-skilling and up-skilling in a fast-changing labour market - an important function under the UK's Skills for Jobs agenda (DfE, 2021).

APEL in higher education

Higher education institutions (HEIs) have formal mechanisms for recognising prior learning, often expressed in policies that are aligned to frameworks such as the QAA's Recognition of Prior Learning guidance and the UK Quality Code for Higher Education (QAA, 2024).

APEL in HE supports:

- Entry to degree programmes without traditional A-level or Level 3 qualifications.
- Credit transfer for students progressing from FE via foundation degrees or HNDs.
- Advanced standing for individuals with relevant professional experience.

For example, learners who have completed a *foundation degree* in a related area may be able to use their prior learning to enter directly into the final year of a bachelor's degree. Similarly, an experienced project manager might be admitted onto an MBA without a first degree if they present a portfolio that evidences strategic decision-making, organisational leadership, and reflective practice - mapped against programme-level outcomes.

Institutional APEL policies typically restrict the proportion of credit that can be awarded for prior learning (e.g., up to 50% of total credits for an undergraduate degree) to maintain academic rigour and institutional benchmarking. Academic staff, recognition panels, and admissions tutors are usually involved in assessing APEL claims, ensuring evidence is robust, consistent, and transparent (HEA, 2013).

Challenges in implementing APEL

Despite its potential, APEL faces several challenges across sectors:

- **Administrative complexity:** Collecting, verifying, and evaluating prior learning evidence can be challenging and time-consuming.
- **Lack of consistency:** APEL policies and practices vary widely across institutions and sectors, leading to confusion or inequity.
- **Staff training needs:** Educators and assessors often require support to implement APEL processes fairly and reliably.
- **Equity concerns:** While APEL aims to widen participation, those with limited literacy, digital skills, or experience in self-assessment may struggle to present suitable evidence.
- **Cultural resistance:** Traditional models of education still value formal learning over informal or experiential learning, which may limit uptake.

These issues underline the importance of capacity building at institutional level and promoting a culture that values diverse learning trajectories.

APEL and lifelong learning

APEL is central to the broader goal of lifelong learning, which acknowledges that education does not end with initial qualifications but continues through life and work. The OECD (2023) and European Union (2022) identify recognition of informal and non-formal learning as key to economic adaptability, social inclusion, and personal fulfilment.

In response, several national initiatives have sought to expand APEL:

- Scotland's Recognition of Prior Learning Framework.
- Wales' Credit and Qualifications Framework.
- The European Guidelines for Validating Non-formal and Informal Learning (ECDVT, 2009).

Digital portfolios and open badges have also emerged as tools to support APEL, especially where formal documentation is lacking. These innovations align with HE efforts to make learning more modular, flexible, and responsive to learner needs (JISC, 2023).

APEL and inclusivity

APEL has strong relevance to inclusion and social justice. It provides non-traditional learners - such as migrants, carers, returners to education, or those who have experienced interrupted schooling - with a route into, or through, formal learning systems. It validates the knowledge gained through parenting, volunteering, activism, or frontline service practices - often undervalued in traditional curricula (Lumby & Coleman, 2007).

In this way, APEL challenges the deficit model that views certain learners - such as adult returners, migrants, or those with interrupted formal education - as lacking competence or qualifications. Instead, it reframes them as individuals possessing valid, though informally acquired, knowledge and skills gained through lived experience, employment, volunteering, or self-directed learning. Inclusive curriculum design must therefore integrate established APEL processes, enabling institutions to formally recognise this learning in ways that are flexible, accessible, and responsive to diverse educational and cultural contexts. This approach helps promote equity, widen participation, and validate diverse pathways into and through education.

>  **Activity: Organising the curriculum**
>
> 1. **Document analysis:**
> Select a curriculum document from your own or another relevant educational setting (e.g., a programme specification, scheme of work, or module outline).
> 2. **Structural audit:**
> Using the principles and models discussed in the chapter, analyse how the curriculum is organised. Consider:
> - Is the structure subject-based, integrated, modular, or a hybrid?
> - How are continuity, sequence, and integration addressed in its organisation?
> - Are taxonomic levels or key threads/strands (such as critical thinking, problem-solving, or digital skills) clearly mapped across the curriculum?
> 3. **Strengths and limitations:**
> Identify any aspects of the organisation that support deep, coherent learning and inclusivity. Note weaknesses, such as fragmentation, repetition, or lack of opportunity for credit transfer or progression.
> 4. **Practical scenario:**
> Imagine you are part of a curriculum review team. Based on your audit, suggest two specific changes to improve the organisation of this curriculum (e.g., integrating a cross-curricular project, improving the sequence of modules, embedding digital tools).
> 5. **Peer discussion:**
> Share your analysis and proposed improvements with a peer or in a study group. Reflect on how your context compares with those in other sectors (primary, secondary, FE, or HE), and discuss what you would adopt or adapt in your own practice.

Summary

Organising the curriculum ensures that learning is coherent, cumulative, and meaningful. Effective organisation involves structuring content through continuity (revisiting key concepts), sequence (progressing from simple to complex), and integration (connecting learning across subjects).

Subject-based models offer depth and disciplinary focus, while integrated models promote holistic understanding. Taxonomies, such as Gronlund's, support progression and assessment design. Modularisation and credit systems offer flexibility and transferability, especially in FE and HE. Key skills - like communication and problem-solving - are increasingly embedded across curricula to enhance employability and lifelong learning.

4 EXTERNAL INFLUENCES ON CURRICULUM

Introduction

Curriculum development is inextricably linked to broader societal forces and institutional frameworks. Although often perceived as a professional or academic endeavour, curriculum is fundamentally shaped by external influences that extend well beyond the classroom. In the UK, a network of national and international agencies, policy directives, and political dynamics define curriculum priorities, structures, and accountability measures. The idea of a national curriculum itself arises from the need to balance coherence, comparability, and local flexibility in response to societal changes, global benchmarking, and government agendas.

This chapter examines the principles underpinning national curricula, the practical and ideological challenges they pose, and the ways in which policy - whether local, national, or international - affects educational aims, content, and delivery. Through comparative perspectives and critical discussion, it also explores the ongoing negotiation between government involvement, global trends, and the professional autonomy of educators.

This chapter

- Examines the role of national and international agencies in shaping the UK curriculum.
- Discusses the foundational principles behind the creation of national curricula.
- Analyses persistent problems and tensions arising from national curriculum frameworks.
- Explores the challenge of balancing prescribed content with local autonomy and innovation.
- Assesses the political dimensions influencing curriculum direction and reform.
- Investigates how educational policy impacts curriculum at local, national, and international levels.
- Reviews the complex question of who is responsible for designing national curricula.
- Provides global perspectives and comparative analyses of national curriculum models.
- Explores the implications and controversies surrounding government interference in curriculum development.

Agencies for UK curriculum development

The development and ongoing evolution of the UK curriculum have been profoundly influenced by various national and international organisations. These agencies shape educational priorities, create statutory requirements, ensure quality and standards, and benchmark UK curriculum frameworks against global trends. Their influence spans all educational levels, including primary, secondary, further education (FE), and higher education (HE).

Historical context: Early agencies and developments

Until the mid-20th century, curriculum design in the UK was largely decentralised, with significant autonomy granted to individual schools and teachers. Primary education, in particular, embraced an experience-based approach, while secondary schools retained greater control over content and pedagogy. Concerns over the inconsistencies across schools led to the establishment of the *Schools Council for Curriculum and Examinations in England and Wales* in 1964. The Schools Council facilitated curriculum research, promoted teacher-led development, and advised government on examination and curriculum policy. Despite its initial success, its teacher-dominant structure and perceived limited impact led to its dissolution in 1984, marking a shift toward more centralised, politically-controlled curriculum bodies.

Statutory curriculum bodies: 1980s onwards

The *Education Reform Act 1988* was transformational, introducing the statutory National Curriculum in England and Wales. This curriculum aimed to standardise educational experiences, define attainment targets, and establish key stages. To administrate this, various quasi-independent bodies (quangos) were successively established:

- **National Curriculum Council (NCC):** Charged with developing and overseeing the National Curriculum.
- **School Examinations and Assessment Council (SEAC):** Responsible for assessments and qualifications. Their merger led to the School Curriculum and Assessment Authority (SCAA) in 1993, integrating curriculum and assessment governance.

In 1997, the Qualifications and Curriculum Authority (QCA) replaced SCAA, coordinating national curriculum reform and managing qualifications.

These bodies aimed to balance standardisation with some autonomy but increasingly came under direct government oversight, reflecting the political nature of curriculum governance.

Key current national agencies

Department for Education (DfE)

As the principal government department for education in England, the DfE holds ultimate responsibility for setting national policy and curriculum statutes. This includes determining the content and assessment arrangements for primary and secondary education, alongside reforms in FE and HE sectors.

Office of Qualifications and Examinations Regulation (Ofqual)

Established in 2010 as an independent regulator, Ofqual oversees qualifications and assessments, including GCSEs, A-levels, and vocational qualifications in England. It ensures standards, approves new qualifications, and balances educational rigor with fairness.

Ofsted

The Office for Standards in Education, Children's Services and Skills inspects educational institutions and influences curriculum direction indirectly through its inspection frameworks and reports. It evaluates curriculum *intent*, *implementation*, and *impact*, prompting schools and colleges to align with best practices.

Regional and devolved authorities

Scotland, Wales, and Northern Ireland operate distinct curriculum agencies reflecting local governance and contexts:

- **Education Scotland** manages the Curriculum for Excellence.
- **Curriculum and Assessment Authority for Wales** oversees the Curriculum for Wales.
- **Council for the Curriculum, Examinations and Assessment (CCEA)** fulfils this role in Northern Ireland.

These bodies adopt different curriculum philosophies and degrees of centralisation.

HE and post-16 education agencies

Higher education (HE) lacks a statutory national curriculum but is guided by:

- **Quality Assurance Agency (QAA),** which develops subject benchmark statements and qualification frameworks in the UK.
- **Office for Students (OfS),** the regulator ensuring quality, access, and standards.
- **Institute for Apprenticeships and Technical Education (IfATE),** responsible for apprenticeship and T Level development aligned with industry requirements.

These agencies ensure academic integrity, professional relevance, and responsiveness to changing educational landscapes.

Awarding bodies and sector-specific organisations

Several awarding organisations produce specifications and accredit qualifications used across education sectors. These include: Pearson (Edexcel); AQA; OCR; City & Guilds; and NCFE.

These bodies work within regulatory frameworks, collaborate with employers and professional bodies for vocational curricula, and influence pedagogy and content in schools, FE, and HE.

Professional and non-statutory organisations

Beyond statutory agencies, various professional associations (e.g., Association for Science Education, National Association for the Teaching of English), trade unions, and think tanks contribute to shaping curriculum discourse, advocating reform, providing research, and supporting teacher professional development.

International agencies with UK influence

- **OECD:** Its global assessments such as PISA influence UK curriculum priorities by emphasising core competencies and 21st-century skills.
- **UNESCO:** Promotes Education for Sustainable Development and Global Citizenship, encouraging value-based learning systems.
- **European Union (EU):** Prior to Brexit, the EU's frameworks, such as the European Qualifications Framework (EQF) and European Credit Transfer and Accumulation System (ECTS), underpinned cross-national comparability and credit transfer.
- Comparative curriculum models from countries like Australia, Finland, and Singapore inform UK educational reforms, particularly in curriculum breadth, progression, and skills orientation.

Agency influence across educational sectors

- **Primary education:** DfE and Ofsted dominate, with subject advisory bodies providing additional resources and guidance.

- **Secondary education:** A blend of DfE policy, regulatory bodies, awarding organisations, and international benchmarking shape content and assessment.

- **Further education:** Ofqual, IfATE, awarding bodies, and employer groups govern qualifications and curricula.

- **Higher education:** QAA and OfS coordinate quality assurance and regulatory frameworks, with evolving international standards influencing programme design.

Principles underpinning a national curriculum

A national curriculum is more than a list of subjects or prescribed content: it reflects fundamental values, societal expectations, and political intentions. It is underpinned by a set of guiding principles that aim to ensure equity, coherence, and relevance for all learners across a jurisdiction. In the UK context, the national curriculum has been framed to provide a structured, legally enforceable entitlement to education for children in maintained schools. This chapter examines the core principles that underpin a national curriculum and explores how they manifest across primary, secondary, further education (FE), and higher education (HE) contexts.

Equality of educational opportunity

At the heart of any national curriculum lies the ideal of equal access to high-quality education. In theory, this principle ensures that all pupils, regardless of background or geography, are entitled to a similar standard and breadth of learning. Equality of access is not determined solely by offering 'the same' to all, but by ensuring that no child misses out simply because their school does not offer certain subjects or resources (Whitty, 2010).

In primary education, the National Curriculum for England sets out core and foundation subjects - such as English, mathematics, science, and the arts - with clearly specified content across key stages. This establishes a minimum entitlement for all children, reducing disparities in provision that might arise from differing local policies or school leadership decisions.

In secondary schools, the principle of equality is operationalised through compulsory subjects leading to national qualifications, typically GCSEs. Metrics such as the Ebacc were introduced to encourage uptake of academic subjects by all students, particularly from disadvantaged backgrounds (DfE, 2014). Critics have argued, however, that strict adherence to specific qualification routes can inadvertently disadvantage learners with different needs or interests.

Information

The English Baccalaureate (Ebacc) is a performance measure used in England for secondary schools. It recognises students who achieve a good pass (usually grade 5 or above) in a specified set of academic GCSE subjects. The government introduced the Ebacc in 2010 to encourage a broader, academically rigorous curriculum, aiming to keep more pupils studying subjects that are considered essential for many higher education courses and careers.

In FE, equality of opportunity is embedded in frameworks like the Post-16 Study Programmes, which aim to ensure that all learners, including those on vocational courses, receive a balanced diet of learning: one that includes English and maths, work experience, and personal development.

While HE operates without a national curriculum per se, equality is promoted through widening participation strategies and the development of graduate attribute frameworks, ensuring that all students, regardless of prior advantage, gain access to broad, transferable skills (QAA, 2024).

A balanced educational experience

A core principle of a national curriculum is the promotion of balance - both across disciplines and in terms of knowledge, skills, and values. A national framework can help guard against overly narrow curriculum design, particularly where local priorities or institutional pressures might lead to imbalances.

In primary settings, a national curriculum requires schools to offer not just literacy and numeracy, but also art, music, physical education, and personal development. In doing so, it resists the marginalisation of non-core subjects, which are at risk when emphasis is placed primarily on tested outcomes (Alexander, 2021).

In secondary schools, curriculum balance ensures a mix of academic and creative subjects, though in practice this is often constrained by league table pressures and timetabling decisions (Whitty, 2010). National policy, such as guidance around 'broad and balanced' curricula in key stage 3, attempts to mitigate the risks of early specialism or curriculum narrowing.

In FE, balance is promoted through frameworks that encourage employability and vocational preparedness while retaining foundations in English, mathematics, and broader personal development (Simmons, 2009). In HE, balance is sometimes achieved through general education components or interdisciplinary modules that draw connections between disciplines and offer breadth alongside specialisation.

Maintenance of standards

Another key principle underpinning a national curriculum is the establishment and maintenance of national standards. By articulating clear learning outcomes, attainment targets, and assessment criteria, national curricula ensure that consistent expectations are placed upon learners across regions and institutions (Kelly, 2009).

At primary and secondary levels, this is most visible in subjects like English and mathematics, which are accompanied by assessment frameworks permitting comparability across schools. The use of standardised testing and national benchmarks allows policymakers to monitor system performance and intervene in cases of underachievement (Ofsted, 2019).

In FE, awarding bodies like Pearson and NCFE use unit-based outcomes to specify what counts as achievement. Ofqual's oversight ensures that vocational and academic qualifications meet agreed standards of difficulty and rigour, whether delivered in large colleges or by smaller training providers.

Though HE does not share the same national curriculum structure, standards are upheld through mechanisms such as subject benchmark statements and the Framework for Higher Education Qualifications (FHEQ). The emphasis on transparent learning outcomes, assessment criteria, and external examination provides quality assurance across the sector (QAA, 2024).

Relevance to national needs

A national curriculum is also designed to reflect the economic, social, and cultural needs of the country, developing graduates who are equipped to contribute to both community and national life (Young & Muller, 2016). Policymakers often position curriculum reform as a means of national investment - preparing learners not just for personal fulfilment, but for skilled employment, civic engagement, and cultural cohesion.

In primary and secondary education, this principle translates into compulsory citizenship education, digital literacy, and more recently, sustainability and climate education - areas deemed crucial for national development and global responsibility (OECD, 2020).

In FE, sector-specific standards and employer-led curriculum development highlight the importance of labour market alignment. T Level and apprenticeship standards are shaped through extensive stakeholder consultation, ensuring that knowledge and skills taught in vocational courses match employer expectations and occupational requirements (IFATE, 2023).

In HE, curricular responsiveness to national needs is mediated through funding incentives, graduate employability metrics, and the broader 'skills agenda'. Increasingly, institutions are expected to demonstrate how their programmes address national challenges such as digital transformation, public health, and social inequality.

A shared cultural and civic foundation

National curricula not only transmit knowledge and skills, but also play a crucial role in cultural reproduction and the formation of civic identity. This principle reflects the idea that shared learning experiences contribute to societal cohesion and mutual understanding.

In practice, this is reflected in subjects such as history, English literature, and RE, where national curriculum guidance outlines the importance of understanding Britain's heritage and global influences. While curricula are now more inclusive than in the past, tensions persist around *whose* knowledge and cultural narratives are prioritised - a critical concern within curriculum theory (Apple & Apple, 2004).

HE institutions have responded to criticism of narrow, Eurocentric curricula by embedding diversity and decolonisation goals within programme and module review processes, ensuring that a broader range of voices and perspectives are represented (Ladson-Billings, 2021).

Philosophical and epistemological foundations

The design of a national curriculum is inevitably shaped by theories of knowledge, pedagogy, and learning. Tensions exist between competing curriculum models: essentialist views that prioritise canonised knowledge versus progressivist approaches that emphasise learner-centred exploration and discovery (Young et al., 2014; Kelly, 2009).

The English National Curriculum for schools, for instance, has increasingly drawn on powerful knowledge theory, which advocates teaching disciplinary knowledge that enables learners to go beyond their everyday experiences (Young & Muller, 2016). However, critics argue such approaches risk prioritising abstract knowledge at the expense of relevance and equality.

In FE and HE, the construction of curricula often balances disciplinary traditions with experiential, applied, and constructivist models of learning - especially in vocational, professional, and interdisciplinary fields (Barnett & Coate, 2005). Thus, curriculum design is not purely a technical process but reflects broader epistemological questions about what is worth knowing and how that knowledge should be acquired.

Problems with a national curriculum

A national curriculum seeks to guarantee entitlement, standardisation, and coherence within a nation's education system. However, such ambitions are accompanied by persistent and significant problems across all sectors - primary, secondary, further education (FE), and higher education (HE). These challenges relate not only to the practicalities of policy design and implementation, but also to deep philosophical questions about the purposes and values of education in a diverse, changing society.

Commonality versus variety

One foundational problem with a national curriculum is its inherent tension between the pursuit of commonality and the need for variety. Kelly (2009) warns that "there is no logical connection between the idea of education for all and that of a common curriculum, nor do demands for educational equality imply that all must have the same educational diet" (p. 95). The Plowden Report (1967) similarly argues that equality of opportunity does not require curricular sameness.

A standardised curriculum risks homogenising experiences, ignoring the reality that learners enter education with diverse backgrounds, aspirations, and needs. In seeking to raise standards, national curricula may inadvertently stifle individual talents or fail to meet the particular needs of local communities and minority groups (Whitty, 2010; Apple & Apple, 2004). The diversity of the student body in the UK - whether economic, cultural, social, or linguistic - demands flexibility that many national frameworks struggle to provide.

Primary and secondary contexts

In primary schools, the problem is often most visible when broad statutory content pushes aside the need for local adaptation, cultural relevance, or child-centred approaches (Alexander, 2021). Teachers may find their professional judgement limited by prescriptive aims, with little scope to tailor learning to local heritage, languages, or the lived realities of children.

In secondary education, standardisation can drive a narrow focus on core academic subjects, with arts, vocational studies, and enrichment at risk of marginalisation due to accountability measures - particularly in disadvantaged or rural settings (Whitty, 2010).

FE and HE contexts

In FE, national specification led by central government or exam boards can result in programmes struggling to respond quickly to emerging industry trends or local employment needs, particularly where curriculum review processes are slow or inflexible.

While HE in the UK does not follow a national curriculum in the strictest sense, moves towards standards, learning outcomes, and subject benchmarks (e.g., via the QAA) raise similar concerns about over-homogenisation and constraints on institutional autonomy (Barnett & Coate, 2005).

Deciding on content: Whose knowledge counts?

A practical, persistent challenge for any national curriculum is the contentious process of deciding what content and values should be included.

Disputes often revolve around:

- Which subjects or topics are "core" (e.g. ICT, religious education, climate literacy)?
- How certain topics (e.g., history, literature, science) should be framed for diverse or multicultural populations?
- Which pedagogical approaches should be mandated (e.g. systematic synthetic vs. analytical phonics)?

These debates are rarely neutral. As Bernstein (2004) argued, all curriculum is a form of *cultural selection*, privileging particular types of knowledge, values, and dispositions over others. Decisions about curriculum content invariably reflect the interests, ideologies, and experiences of those with social or political power (Apple & Apple, 2004).

Primary examples abound: should the curriculum prioritise British history over world history, or place greater value on coding than on the arts? Such decisions may feel arbitrary or politically motivated, heightening controversy and undermining the legitimacy of a common curriculum. Even within seemingly objective domains such as science, selection of knowledge often lags behind advancements or fails to integrate contemporary ethical and cultural debates (Young et al., 2014).

State intervention and issues of control

The role of the state in imposing a national curriculum is among the most profound sources of controversy. In seeking to reflect and promote "national" values, state-imposed curricula risk rendering invisible the experiences of minority communities. This inadequacy is particularly acute in multicultural societies such as the UK, where a single national narrative or fixed cultural canon cannot suffice for all learners (Apple & Apple, 2004).

In practice:

- A statutory curriculum set at the national level may ignore the lived experiences or values of marginalised or migrant groups.
- Syllabuses for subjects such as history or citizenship may alienate students who fail to recognise their cultures or viewpoints reflected in lessons, contributing to disengagement and feelings of exclusion (Ladson-Billings, 2021).

Imposed state curricula can act as subtle forms of social control, reproducing dominant social norms and marginalising alternative perspectives or epistemologies (Apple & Apple, 2004; Kelly, 2009). One emblematic example is the enduring debate over whose histories are told in schools - a challenge not unique to the UK, but one that remains unresolved despite ongoing curriculum reform (Alexander, 2021).

Irrelevance and alienation

Mandating a uniform curriculum can also risk irrelevance for many students. If the curriculum is not meaningful or connected to learners' interests, backgrounds or aspirations, it loses its motivational power and reduces engagement (Biesta, 2010). Students may perceive much of the 'official knowledge' as too abstract, distant from their everyday lives, or inflexible in its presentation (James & Biesta, 2007).

For some groups:

- Content may seem alienating if it does not include positive or accurate representations of their cultures, identities, or histories.

- The structure and teaching methods favoured in a national curriculum may not reflect effective approaches for all learners, particularly those with SEND, EAL, or in alternative provision.

Many educators and researchers caution that the drive for universal standards must not come at the cost of personal connection, local relevance, or the ability to foster meaningful and affective learning (Barnett & Coate, 2005; Biesta, 2010).

Bureaucratisation and loss of professional autonomy

A further problem is the bureaucratic complexity that arises as governments attempt to regulate and monitor adherence to national curricula. Requirements to document, justify, assess, and report on prescribed learning outcomes have grown, alongside increasingly high-stakes accountability mechanisms (Ball, 2003).

For teachers and lecturers, this can result in:

- A culture of compliance, reduced innovation, and a narrowing of pedagogical repertoire.

- Less space to exercise professional judgement or adapt to class dynamics and emerging needs (Alexander, 2021; Kelly, 2009).

- Teaching to the test, with distorted curriculum priorities and the neglect of broader developmental aims (Biesta, 2015).

In FE and HE, the growing influence of central "quality assurance" often brings similar constraints, where innovation in programme design and delivery must be reconciled with relentless administrative and reporting burdens (Barnett & Coate, 2005).

Equity: Paradox and contradiction

Ironically, the pursuit of equity through commonality can generate new inequalities. While national curricula aim to level the playing field, they may overlook structural barriers such as resourcing disparities, local context, and personal circumstance (Whitty, 2010; Apple & Apple, 2004).

A curriculum that is equal in form may be unequal in effect if it does not account for:

- Different starting points and learning needs (Alexander, 2021).

- The additional support required in contexts of poverty, special educational need, or language acquisition.

- Institutional differences in capacity to deliver the prescribed curriculum (Barnett & Coate, 2005).

This can result in new forms of stratification - with rigid, test-based standards demotivating or penalising those less able to access the dominant culture and language, or whose family and community context offers little extra-curricular support.

Inflexibility and slow adaptation

National curricula often struggle to keep pace with rapid societal and technological change. Central review cycles are typically slow, and processes for curriculum update can lag behind developments in science, industry, culture, or digital technology (Young & Muller, 2016).

For sectors grappling with innovation - such as FE (in response to employer skill needs) or HE (as research disciplines advance) - a static curriculum model is especially problematic. Local and institutional autonomy is essential to meet new and evolving demands, yet may be frustrated by central prescription.

Balancing the curriculum

Achieving a balanced curriculum is a perennial challenge for educators, policy-makers, and curriculum designers across all educational sectors. "Balance" is neither a precise formula nor a universally agreed ideal, but rather an ongoing negotiation between competing aims - personal development, subject mastery, vocational readiness, social justice, and societal needs (Kelly, 2009). Fundamentally, a balanced curriculum is one in which learners experience a breadth and depth of knowledge, skills, and values, without disproportionate emphasis on any one domain to the exclusion of others.

Defining curriculum balance

Curriculum balance is more than allocating equal time to subjects; it involves thoughtfully structuring learning experiences to support the full development of each learner. This includes fostering intellectual, social, moral, emotional, and vocational growth, ensuring that no key aspect of human potential is overlooked (Alexander, 2021). A balanced curriculum provides all students - regardless of background - with meaningful opportunities to thrive while equipping them with the knowledge, skills, and values required to contribute effectively to society, the workforce, and wider global challenges.

Balance operates at different levels:

- **Between subjects:** For instance, ensuring the arts, humanities, sciences, and vocational areas are all valued.

- **Between forms of knowledge:** Propositional (knowing that), procedural (knowing how), and dispositional (attitudes and values).

- **Between aims:** Individual fulfilment, civic engagement, employment readiness, and global responsibility (Whitty, 2010).

- **Across the life course:** Achieving an age-appropriate mix of foundational knowledge, skills, and advanced specialism.

Critiques abound regarding what counts as an appropriate or sufficient balance. Educational traditions, political agendas, and changing societal circumstances frequently influence what is prioritised or marginalised in the curriculum.

Balance in primary education

Primary education frequently embodies calls for balance. Statutory frameworks such as the English National Curriculum mandate a mix of core subjects (English, maths, science) alongside foundation subjects (history, geography, art, music, PE, computing, etc.) (DfE, 2014). Official policy emphasises the "broad and balanced curriculum", requiring schools to provide for the spiritual, moral, cultural, mental, and physical development of pupils.

However, achieving this balance in practice is challenging. Pressure for accountability in literacy and numeracy often leads to curriculum narrowing, especially in schools facing challenging contexts or performance scrutiny (Alexander, 2021). The arts and humanities can become squeezed, and enrichment activities may be deprioritised. The Plowden Report (CACE, 1967) emphasised the holistic development of the child - a principle in tension with current performativity regimes and test-based priorities.

Schools that embrace thematic or integrated approaches, project-based learning, or regular enrichment are often better able to achieve a healthy balance, though this depends on school leadership, culture, and resourcing. Teachers' professional autonomy and skills in curriculum design are crucial factors (Lumby & Coleman, 2007).

Balance in secondary education

Secondary education sees a natural drift toward specialisation, but the need for balance remains paramount. The National Curriculum prescribes core and foundation subjects to age 14 or 16, and the "broad and balanced" requirement continues to apply (Whitty, 2010). However, constraints emerge as students select options for GCSE or equivalent qualifications.

Several factors disrupt balance at this stage:

- The Ebacc performance measure incentivises entry to academic subjects (languages, science, history/geography), sometimes to the detriment of practical, artistic, or technical subjects (Whitty, 2010).

- Time allocation and timetabling may express "hidden priorities", with some subjects allotted far less teaching time.

- High-stakes testing encourages "teaching to the test", narrowing what is experienced in classrooms (Biesta, 2010).

- Marginalised groups may be further disadvantaged if curriculum balance does not consciously address issues of equity, representation, and access (Apple & Apple, 2004).

Some schools counter these pressures by carving out dedicated curriculum time for personal development, PSHE, creative arts, and enrichment experiences, or by fostering cross-curricular projects that mix academic, practical, and civic learning.

Balance in further education (FE)

In FE, balance is influenced by sector diversity, funding, and the tension between meeting labour market needs and developing rounded citizens. Many FE programmes are highly vocational, focusing on occupational competence and employability, but national policy has increasingly recognised the need to embed English, maths, and broader "life skills".

Balance in FE also relates to:

- The inclusion of academic and vocational options for 16 to 19-year-olds.

- The integration of key or functional skills (communication, teamwork, digital literacy) across all programmes (DfE, 2014).

- Providing learner support, personal development, and enrichment to diverse adult and young populations.

Yet, challenges persist: emphasis on qualification outcomes can lead to "teaching to the specification" while holistic education may be sidelined due to funding or accountability constraints. Responsive curriculum planning, strong employer partnerships, and a commitment to social capital development can help maintain or restore balance.

Balance in higher education (HE)

HE curricula, typically constructed through modular frameworks, face their own balancing acts between depth and breadth, discipline and interdisciplinarity, academic and professional outcomes (Barnett & Coate, 2005). The QAA's requirement for graduate attributes (critical thinking, ethical reasoning, communication) has spurred broader curricular ambitions beyond narrow specialism (QAA, 2024).

Achieving balance in HE involves:

- Allowing students to combine major and minor subjects, or to select elective modules from diverse fields.

- Fostering interdisciplinary approaches through liberal arts pathways, joint honours degrees, or integrated projects.

- Balancing research, teaching, and applied learning, so that students develop both cognitive depth and transferable skills.

However, increased focus on employability and league table position can lead to vocational drift, at times detracting from academic breadth or critical, reflective learning (Barnett & Coate, 2005). Equity and student voice, as well as attention to the "hidden curriculum", play roles in ensuring the educational experience is genuinely balanced, inclusive, and forward-looking.

Subject choice and the curriculum as a whole

Efforts to achieve curriculum balance should move beyond piecemeal thinking and adopt a whole-curriculum perspective (Brundrett & Silcock, 2002). In primary and secondary settings, curriculum reviews, mapping, and cross-phase planning can help ensure continuity and intentional breadth. In FE and HE, modular design and credit accumulation systems, if not well-planned, risk fragmentation rather than balance (Knight & Yorke, 2003).

The predominance of the product model - lists of specific objectives, coverage requirements, detailed attainment targets - can tilt the balance toward compliance, uniformity, and a loss of teacher creativity. In contrast, developmental or process models, as advocated by reports such as Hadow (Board of Education, 1931) and

Plowden (CACE, 1967), emphasise a balance between structure and flexibility, professional agency, and learner engagement.

Achieving and sustaining curriculum balance

Both system-level and local initiatives play roles in balancing curricula:

- National policy can set minimum entitlements but should allow space for local and teacher innovation.

- Curriculum leaders can use audits, mapping, and assessment of pupil outcomes and engagement to identify imbalances needing attention.

- Student voice, parental input, and community partnerships can bring new perspectives to bear and highlight neglected areas.

- Reflective approaches, such as regular review cycles and collaborative professional development, are key to sustaining balance over time (Brundrett & Silcock, 2002; Alexander, 2021).

- Inclusion and diversity must be embraced, ensuring all learners experience challenge, creativity, and belonging (Ladson-Billings, 2021).

Ultimately, curriculum balance is context-specific and dynamic, constantly renegotiated in response to changing learner needs, social change, and fresh insights from practice and research.

The political influence on the national curriculum

The UK National Curriculum has always been more than a technical framework for what is taught in schools, colleges, and universities. It is a living document shaped by complex and sometimes competing influences - nowhere more powerfully than through political intervention at local, national, and international levels. Policy and politics have profoundly directed the evolution of curriculum content, scope, and priorities in primary, secondary, further education (FE), and higher education (HE), with significant consequences for educators and learners alike.

Political shaping of the national curriculum

Historical development and centralised control

The creation of the National Curriculum in 1988 under a Conservative government marked a decisive shift towards greater state control of education in England and Wales. Sparked by concerns over inconsistent standards and performance, the Education Reform Act established a legal requirement for all pupils to follow a clearly specified, centrally determined body of knowledge - initially featuring ten subjects with a strong emphasis on traditional academic disciplines and core skills. This move, championed by figures such as Kenneth Baker and Margaret Thatcher, sought to ensure every child received the same entitlement, regardless of location or background.

Yet, the political nature of curriculum design rapidly became apparent. Policymakers mandated not just what subjects to study, but also how they should be sequenced, delivered and assessed. As Ball (2008) observes, these political interventions reflected a growing culture of managerialism, performativity, and accountability in education, as governments sought to drive up standards, close perceived gaps, and benchmark the UK against international peers.

Curriculum reforms and alternation of priorities

The pattern of reform has reflected changes in political party, ideology, and priorities. Successive governments have used the curriculum as a mechanism to signal their educational philosophy and broader social values:

- *Conservative Governments (1988-1997; post-2010):* Emphasised traditional academic subjects, a strong knowledge base, and central direction. Michael Gove's reforms (2010-2014), for instance, promoted a "back to basics" agenda, reduced coursework, and gave greater weight to end-of-course examinations, echoing Hirsch's (2019) "core knowledge" philosophy.

- *New Labour (1997-2010):* Prioritised skills for the knowledge economy, broader social inclusion, and a balance between academic and practical learning. Initiatives like the National Literacy and Numeracy Strategies set national benchmarks at primary level, while the 2007 review increased emphasis on citizenship, diversity, and wellbeing. Curriculum reforms aimed to foster social cohesion and broader personal development beyond exam results.

- *Recent and current Labour Government (post-2024):* Early announcements point towards an even broader, more inclusive curriculum, with increased focus on digital literacy, arts, vocational education, environmental education, and the integration of diverse histories and perspectives. Weighted against this is an intention to make the statutory curriculum binding on all state schools and academies, signifying a reassertion of national direction.

Instability and the adjustment burden

One outcome of this politically mediated process has been *curriculum instability*. Frequent, ideologically motivated changes have resulted in phases of expansion and contraction, oscillating between detailed prescription and calls for professional autonomy. For example, the Dearing Review (1994) prompted a slimming-down of the curriculum after concerns of overload, but subsequent governments reintroduced or revised elements in line with political imperatives. For teachers and school leaders, this often means periods of major adjustment, retraining, and realignment, creating pressure and confusion in implementation.

Policymaking, ideology, and educational practice

Political priorities and ideological bias

Political intervention in curriculum rarely emerges solely from educational evidence. Instead, each iteration inevitably reflects current government ideology. This can be seen in the continued contest over the content of history or citizenship education - debates which illuminate whose knowledge and perspectives are at the forefront. Topics such as British imperial history or diversity in literature have at different times been included or downplayed depending on prevailing values. Scholars have criticised this as creating the risk of *ideological bias*, narrowing the scope of what young people learn and potentially undermining critical thinking and the development of balanced, independent views.

Policy and accountability culture

Policy decisions inform not only what is to be learned but also how it is measured. Periods of increased accountability have led to the adoption of high-stakes assessments and "teaching to the test", with performance data ranking schools and teachers by outcomes in core subjects. While intended to drive standards, these measures have often led to marginalisation of non-core content (e.g., creative arts, citizenship, PSHE) and increased stress for staff and students. The pressure to meet targets has drawn criticisms that the curriculum becomes narrowed and less responsive to individual or local needs.

Neglect of local and regional diversity

A persistent tension is the extent to which national policy recognises local and regional diversity. Critics point to the "one-size-fits-all" nature of prescriptive curricula, which may fail to address the unique histories, cultures, and priorities of particular regions or communities. In devolved jurisdictions - such as Scotland, Wales, and Northern Ireland - distinct approaches have been adopted, each reflecting local policy debates and educational philosophies. For example, the Curriculum for Wales promotes cross-curricular skills and a strong strand of local cultural heritage, reflecting devolved decision-making.

Policy and curriculum across sectors

Primary education

At primary level, the strong influence of central policy has led to greater consistency of provision and clearer entitlement to broad learning. However, it has also exposed practitioners to rapid cycles of change and increased prescription. Political initiatives such as the National Literacy and Numeracy Strategies set explicit benchmarks and priorities, but sometimes restricted teachers' agency to adapt the curriculum for their learners. Current moves towards a more inclusive and holistic curriculum again reflect the direction set by the government of the day.

Secondary education

For secondary schools, the intersection of political decision-making, performance measures, and accountability frameworks is especially acute. The introduction of the Ebacc measure and reforms to GCSEs and A-levels demonstrate the direct link between political priorities and subject value, with subjects outside the Ebacc suite often experiencing falling uptake and diminishing resources. Schools navigate a curriculum landscape shaped not only by DfE and Ofqual, but also by ideologically driven changes, media scrutiny, and local priorities.

Further education (FE)

In FE, government intervention has often sought to align curriculum provision with perceived national economic needs. Successive policy drives - from New Labour's focus on lifelong learning, to modern T Level and apprenticeship reforms - aim to ensure colleges produce a workforce equipped with relevant knowledge and technical skills. However, abrupt or centrally mandated changes to curriculum content and funding have sometimes disrupted longstanding provision or failed to address specific regional economic demands, highlighting the limits of central policy control alone.

Higher education (HE)

Although HE is not governed by a statutory national curriculum, its content and priorities are increasingly influenced by national and international policy. Mechanisms such as the Teaching Excellence Framework (TEF), QAA subject benchmarks, and employability metrics all reflect the need to respond to government-defined priorities and prove value. More recently, policy interventions regarding access, diversity, skills for the digital age, and global competitiveness have informed HE curriculum reform, often through funding incentives or league tables.

International and local policy influences

International comparisons and benchmarking

Successive governments have also been influenced by international policy trends and global benchmarking, notably through the OECD's PISA programme, UNESCO agendas, and the European Union's frameworks (prior to Brexit). Educational leaders and policymakers look to high-performance systems - such as those in Singapore or Finland - to justify reforms focused on knowledge acquisition, "21st-century skills", or inclusivity. The influence is two-way: the UK both shapes and is shaped by international policy discourses, especially in areas such as digital literacy, STEM education, and environmental sustainability.

Local policy and innovation

Despite centralisation, local authorities, multi-academy trusts, schools, colleges, and universities continue to exercise some influence over curriculum interpretation and innovation. Examples include the development of locally focused enrichment programmes, integration of regional history or languages, and the design of HE courses with local employers. These efforts are often in tension with - yet also sometimes supported by - national policy priorities, illustrating the ongoing negotiation between standardisation and local responsiveness.

The future: Towards a refreshed national curriculum

The recent shift in government (2024/25) signals another moment of curriculum review, with early indications suggesting a strong focus on broadening, modernising, and diversifying the National Curriculum. Priorities include the arts, digital skills, environmental education, resilience, and inclusion - each heavily influenced, once again, by the political values and societal imperatives of the moment. Whether this results in enhanced relevance and reduced instability will depend on how these reforms are enacted and the extent to which local, practitioner, and learner voice are meaningfully included.

Who designs the national curriculum?

The question of who designs the national curriculum is intricately bound to issues of authority, expertise, professional autonomy, and political power. The answer varies significantly across countries, sectors (primary, secondary, further education [FE], higher education [HE]) and points in history, but consistently reveals tensions between specialist and stakeholder input, government intervention, and the negotiation of local versus national priorities.

The English context

In England, the National Curriculum has historically been shaped through top-down processes initiated by central government, specifically the Department for Education (DfE). The 2014 National Curriculum framework was formulated by the DfE's National Curriculum Review Team, drawing heavily upon proposals and guidance from an 'Expert Panel' - a group consisting mainly of academic educationalists and policy advisors. While the Expert Panel consulted with various stakeholders (for example, teachers, employers, and subject associations), their recommendations remained advisory. The DfE ultimately retained decision-making power, enabling government ministers and departmental leaders to frame priorities and approve content in line with their wider political agenda (DfE, 2014; Alexander, 2021).

The 2011 review, which led to the most recent framework, articulated principles centred on freedom, responsibility, fairness, and a focus on 'essential knowledge', while advocating for school-level flexibility in delivery and enrichment. Despite this, the composition and remit of the curriculum design team are set by ministers, and government influence over content and structure remains considerable (Expert Panel, 2011).

The process of curriculum re-contextualisation

Curriculum development requires the re-contextualisation (Figure 4.1) of a vast body of disciplinary knowledge into teachable school and college subjects (Bernstein, 2004). This means not just selecting factual content, but choosing the most meaningful, transformative knowledge - or 'Powerful Knowledge' - which will equip learners to make sense of the world, challenge assumptions, and continue learning beyond formal education (Young, 2008).

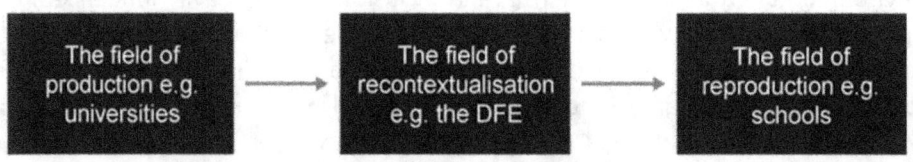

Figure 4.1 - Curriculum re-contextualisation

This process entails professional and epistemological judgement: curriculum designers (whether civil servants, academics, or expert teachers) must determine:

- What knowledge is most valuable for future citizenship?
- What content is essential for progression to further study or employment?
- How should knowledge be sequenced to produce deep, lasting understanding?

While official processes may claim to be evidence-based and consensus-seeking, the scope for actual debate and contestation remains shaped by broader socio-political forces and by the framing set by those with ultimate authority.

Political interference and calls for independence

The persistent possibility of government interference in curriculum development is a point of contention. Schools Minister David Laws (2014) famously warned against 'the corrosive impact of self-interested political meddling', advocating for an independent body to oversee curriculum design and standards (Coughlan, 2014). Critics argue that allowing elected officials disproportionate influence can lead to:

- Politically motivated swings in curriculum content (e.g., emphasis on 'British values', or changes to history syllabuses).

- Instability, as successive governments enact reforms reflecting ideological preference rather than educational evidence (Ball, 2008).
- A narrowing of curricular perspectives, particularly in controversial or value-laden subjects (Apple & Apple, 2004).

The alternative - an independent body - raises its own questions: Who should constitute such a body? Should it comprise senior academics, practising teachers, employer representatives, civic leaders, or members of the public? How can accountability be assured while insulating curriculum from transient political fashion? Different international models offer varying answers.

Question Reflect on your own educational context and consider the composition of an independent body, responsible for designing the curriculum in your own context. Who do you believe would best represent your interests? How would you justify their inclusion?

Comparative models of national curricula

Finland

Finland's curriculum process is often lauded for balancing central prescription with local autonomy. Core national objectives and values are set by the Finnish National Agency for Education, but municipalities and schools exercise significant freedom in interpreting and implementing them. Teachers are trusted professionals with a major voice in both design and adaptation (Sahlberg, 2021).

Singapore

Singapore's national curriculum is highly centralised, designed by the Ministry of Education in collaboration with subject specialist committees. Policy priorities such as national identity and competitiveness drive regular, systematic reviews, but a robust consultation process ensures input from educators and industry (Tan & Deneen, 2015).

Australia

Australia's curriculum is overseen by the Australian Curriculum, Assessment and Reporting Authority (ACARA), which draws on panels including teachers, academics, and community representatives from each state and territory. The result is a negotiated framework that sets national expectations while leaving implementation details to states and schools (ACARA, 2024).

United States

The US operates without a single national curriculum. Instead, state education departments set curricular standards, often drawing on frameworks proposed by national organisations (such as the Common Core State Standards). The fragmented structure enables strong local autonomy, but also leaves room for inequalities and widespread variance (Cuban, 2010).

Country	Who designs?	Role of government	Academic / professional input	Local adaptation
England	Central gov't; DfE, Expert Panel	Very strong	Consultative, subject to politics	Limited
Finland	National Agency + teachers	Moderate	High (teachers / academics)	Extensive
Singapore	Central gov't + specialist panels	Very strong	Considerable (committees, industry)	Some
Australia	Federal authority (ACARA), panels	Strong	High (all sectors involved)	Moderate
USA	State/local government	Weak (no national stds)	Variable by state, some national orgs	Extensive

Table 4.1 - Selected comparative models

Further education (FE) and higher education (HE) sectors

In FE, curriculum specification is frequently dictated by government policy (e.g., through T Levels or apprenticeships), with awarding organisations like Pearson and City & Guilds developing content under national oversight. However, many FE providers work closely with employer groups and regional agencies to ensure vocational relevance.

HE enjoys the greatest autonomy from direct political interference in both the UK and most comparative systems. Universities design programmes within broad regulatory parameters set by agencies like the Quality Assurance Agency (QAA), professional bodies, or funding councils (Barnett & Coate, 2005). External input may come from industry, academic consortia, and feedback from students, but institutional leaders and subject specialists retain final responsibility for curriculum content, subject to periodic validation, review, and external examination.

Even so, governments and non-governmental agencies can shape priorities through funding mechanisms, accountability frameworks, subject benchmarks, or national strategies relating to skills, diversity, or global competitiveness (QAA, 2024; Young & Muller, 2016).

Tensions and the path forward

There is no perfect answer to the question of 'who should design the curriculum.' Every model involves competing demands:

- Expertise vs. democratic voice.
- Stability vs. adaptability.
- National coherence vs. local relevance.
- Protection from political interference vs. the legitimacy of elected government.

Recent English experience, mirrored in international contexts, highlights an urgent need for more professionalised, transparent, and inclusive curriculum development processes (Whitty, 2010; Alexander, 2021). There is growing consensus that curriculum design should be driven by educational expertise and research evidence, rather than fluctuating political agendas or ministerial preferences. This has renewed calls for an independent, expert-led national curriculum authority, one that safeguards the rigour, balance, and inclusivity of curriculum design while maintaining accountability to the public and democratic oversight. Such a body could ensure greater continuity and coherence between successive curriculum reforms and respond more effectively to learner diversity, sector needs, and evolving societal challenges. Internationally, systems such as Finland and Australia have pointed to the value of hybrid models - where expert panels, teachers, and community stakeholders work in partnership to design, review, and adapt curricula in ways that are grounded in professionalism yet responsive to local and national needs.

Activity: Curriculum influence analysis

1. Select a current or recent policy initiative or official curriculum update (e.g., introduction of a new subject, change in assessment, or policy directive in primary/secondary/FE/HE settings).
2. Identify and map the external influences that led to this change, including the impact of agencies such as:
   - National agencies (e.g., Department for Education, Ofsted, Ofqual).
   - International agencies (e.g., OECD, UNESCO, European Union).
   - Political drivers (e.g., party manifestos, parliamentary debates).
   - Social/cultural influences (e.g., public campaigns, media coverage).

3. Critically evaluate:
   - Which influences were most significant in shaping the change?
   - What are the potential benefits and drawbacks for learners and educators?
   - How might different stakeholders (teachers, students, parents, employers) view the change?
4. Share your findings with peers or in a professional forum, and reflect on how such external influences might be navigated, challenged, or harnessed to achieve a more equitable and effective curriculum in your own context.

Summary

Curriculum development is fundamentally shaped by a web of external influences that extend from government agencies and political actors to international organisations and global trends. This chapter has explored how a national curriculum is shaped by both principled aims and political imperatives, and how agencies at multiple levels contribute to its direction, regulation, and reform.

Key debates include the tensions between standardisation and local flexibility, the effects of policy on curriculum content and pedagogy, and the rise of comparative, global models that challenge national priorities. By interrogating who controls the curriculum and to what end, the chapter highlights the ongoing negotiation required to balance accountability, inclusivity, and responsiveness in educational provision.

5 ARTICULATING CURRICULUM INTENT

Introduction

Intent goes beyond simply identifying the component objectives that make up a curriculum. It articulates the fundamental rationale behind what the curriculum is designed to achieve, answering core questions about educational purpose. This aligns closely with Ralph Tyler's (1949) foundational query: *What educational purposes should the institute seek to attain?*

Curriculum intent is formed 'before the fact' - it is the blueprint and guiding vision established prior to teaching and learning activities. As such, it provides a critical opportunity to evaluate and judge the quality and appropriateness of a curriculum in advance of its implementation, ensuring that curriculum design is purposeful, coherent, and aligned with both learner needs and long-term societal goals.

This chapter

- Examines the concept of curriculum intent and its significance in educational planning across sectors.
- Explores Ofsted's interpretation of intent in inspection frameworks and how this informs school self-evaluation.
- Analyses the historical shift from content-based to purpose-led curriculum development.
- Discusses how curriculum intent is applied differently in primary, secondary, further, and higher education.
- Evaluates the relationship between curriculum intent, sequencing, progression, and inclusion.
- Reflects on theoretical foundations underpinning purpose and intent in curriculum studies.

What is curriculum intent

Curriculum intent has emerged as an important component of contemporary curriculum evaluation and development, particularly in England following changes to Ofsted's Inspection Framework in 2019. Moving beyond a narrow focus on content or attainment alone, curriculum intent refers to the clarity and coherence of a school or institution's curriculum vision - what educators aim to teach, why they teach it, and what it is designed to achieve. This focus has profound implications across all sectors, including primary, secondary, further education (FE), and higher education (HE).

Defining curriculum intent

In its broadest sense, curriculum intent can be defined as the educational purpose and planned direction of a curriculum. It encompasses the rationale behind curriculum content choices, the sequencing of knowledge and skills, and the overarching aims regarding learner development (DfE, 2014).

Curriculum intent is not simply a list of subjects or topics, but rather an expression of underlying educational principles. It answers questions such as:

- What are we trying to achieve through our curriculum?
- What knowledge, skills, and values are most important for our learners?
- How will learners be prepared for the next stages of education, employment, and life?

According to Ofsted (2019), curriculum intent refers to "what pupils will learn over time and why." It involves planning that moves beyond compliance with national curriculum content to include ambition, inclusivity, and contextual responsiveness. Effective intent is grounded in a well-considered understanding of learner needs, educational research, and long-term enrichment, not just exam readiness.

Question — Have your students ever asked you "Why are we learning this?". Perhaps it's a question you sometimes ask yourself? Curriculum intent should provide the answer. At the beginning of a course, curriculum intent helps explain the overall purpose, aims, and relevance of the learning ahead. It outlines how each subject, topic, or skill connects to students' future education, life, and wider opportunities. It sets out not only what they will study, but also how it will help them develop essential knowledge, useful skills, and ways of thinking that prepare them for real-world challenges.

Intent acts as a vital bridge between the product and process models of curriculum theory. While it necessitates a clear specification of end points and desired outcomes - hallmarks of the product model - it also acknowledges the importance of educator agency, collaborative dialogue, and flexibility in curriculum enactment. This dual emphasis ensures that intent is not limited to predetermined objectives, but also embraces the adaptability, reflection, and responsive practice championed by process-oriented approaches to curriculum design and implementation (Kelly, 2009).

Is Curriculum Intent something new?

In the most recent version of its inspection handbook, Ofsted outlines the processes by which judgements on the quality of education are reached, placing particular emphasis on the role of curriculum 'intent'. Despite this clarity, a number of misconceptions about what 'intent' means have arisen across schools and settings. To address this, Ofsted has released a statement explaining the term in further detail. The summary below provides an overview of that explanation and serves to dispel commonly held misunderstandings about curriculum intent and its role in inspection.

> **Curriculum Intent**
>
> The term *intent*, as used in the revised framework, is based on extensive curriculum research and piloting. It refers simply to what leaders want pupils to learn. It includes all curriculum planning and decisions that occur **before** teaching begins. According to the Ofsted handbook, a strong curriculum intent exhibits the following characteristics:
>
> - It is *ambitious* for every pupil.
> - It is *coherently structured* and logically sequenced.
> - It is *adapted where necessary* to meet the needs of pupils with SEND.
> - It remains *broad and balanced*, offering opportunities across subjects.
>
> This concept is **not new**. There is no requirement for schools to rewrite websites or create new documents in response to this terminology. Intent is already embedded in curriculum planning - the phase that precedes instruction and prepares for the delivery of knowledge and skills in a systematic way.
>
> In practice, when inspectors assess 'intent', they focus on curriculum leadership - particularly the work of senior, subject, or curriculum leaders. They examine whether the curriculum is as broad and balanced as the national curriculum and whether it allows pupils, including those with additional needs or from disadvantaged backgrounds, to progress through a strong academic and/or technical offer.
>
> At the secondary level, inspectors consider whether curriculum breadth is maintained for as long as possible and whether pupils access a rich suite of academic subjects, such as those within the Ebacc. They also assess whether there is high ambition for all learners and whether any pupils or groups are missing out.
>
> Ofsted remains neutral on curriculum models. Schools are free to shape their curriculum around particular values, frameworks, or learning dispositions. Inspectors will examine how those curricular choices express educational substance - specifically, what leaders want pupils to understand and retain.
>
> If certain subjects - say, reading, mathematics, geography, or religious education - are underperforming, inspectors will look at the quality of subject planning. Are pupils acquiring essential knowledge in a logical progression? Are they being given the necessary building blocks to succeed and make progress?

> In short, curriculum intent concerns the ambition, structure, inclusivity, and clarity of a school's curriculum - up to the moment it is taught. It is not about an intent statement, but the curriculum itself.
>
> GOV•UK (2019)

Overview of Ofsted's inspection framework

The significance of intent was formally articulated in Ofsted's 2019 Inspection Framework, which restructured school inspection criteria around three interlinked elements: *intent*, *implementation*, and *impact*. Under this model, curriculum intent is central to the evaluation of the quality of education. This shift recognises that educational excellence depends not just on final outcomes, but on coherent and purposeful curriculum design from the outset.

According to Ofsted (2019), inspectors evaluate intent by considering whether:

- The curriculum is rooted in a "solid consensus of leaders about the knowledge and skills pupils need" to prepare them for future life and to address social disadvantage.

- There are clear end points that build logically from prior learning.

- Curriculum sequencing enables pupils to build knowledge progressively and connect new learning to existing knowledge structures.

- The curriculum addresses typical gaps in pupils' prior knowledge, particularly in underprivileged contexts.

- Academic ambition is equally high for all learners, including those who are disadvantaged or have special educational needs and disabilities (SEND).

- Reading is an academic priority, particularly to support engagement across the curriculum.

Importantly, Ofsted does not expect a prescriptive format for documenting curriculum intent (Ofsted, 2019). Instead, it assesses how clearly school and subject leaders can articulate their curriculum vision, justify its structure, and explain how they are enabling all pupils to achieve the curriculum's aims.

In practice, this renewed emphasis has prompted institutions - particularly in primary and secondary education - to reassess their curriculum design to ensure it is coherent, purposeful, and inclusive. It has led to a shift away from narrow, outcome-driven models of evaluation, encouraging schools to prioritise long-term learning, equity, and relevance for all pupils. Leaders are increasingly valued not only for raising attainment but for critically identifying weaknesses, engaging staff in reflective dialogue, and planning structured, sustained improvements. This underscores the understanding that strong curriculum intent is not fixed but evolves over time through collaborative reflection, professional development, and adaptive planning.

Historical context: The shift from content to intent

The concept of curriculum intent has evolved over time and reflects a broader shift in curriculum theory and practice, from a focus on prescribed content towards a more educationally purposeful and holistic approach.

Historically, early curriculum reforms in England, particularly under the 1988 Education Reform Act, focused closely on the specification of content and attainment targets, with detailed national curriculum programmes of study and high levels of central control. During this period, the dominating model was largely outcome-based, with clear attention to measurable achievements, often aligned to behaviourist principles and the Tylerian product model (Tyler, 1949; Kelly, 2009).

Tyler's model emphasises:

- Pre-specified objectives.
- Structured content delivery.
- Summative assessment to measure impact.

While this brought a degree of uniformity and comparability, critics argued that it reduced curriculum to little more than a "checklist" (Young, 2008), discouraged local innovation, and encouraged teaching to the test (Biesta, 2015). Content coverage often became equated with curriculum success, overlooking why particular topics were taught or how they were integrated into learners' broader educational journeys.

By the early 21st century, a new discourse began to emerge based on curriculum coherence, meaning-making, and equity. Studies of high-performing international systems (e.g., Finland and Singapore) suggested that clarity of educational purpose - rather than just prescribed content - was essential to learner success (Sahlberg, 2021).

Within the UK, the emphasis on curriculum intent gained momentum in response to:

- Growing educational inequality and attainment gaps.
- Recognition that learners were leaving school with shallow or disconnected knowledge.
- The need for greater alignment between curriculum, pedagogy, and assessment (Oates, 2011).

This culminated in Ofsted's 2019 reformulation, where curriculum intent became a formal category for evaluation.

Curriculum intent across educational contexts

Primary and secondary education

Curriculum intent in primary and secondary schools is now widely discussed among educators and leaders, particularly in relation to Ofsted's framework. Schools are encouraged to frame curricula around real learner needs - ensuring both ambitious academic standards and responsive local relevance.

Primary schools often interpret intent through values-led education, thematic learning, and cross-curricular planning that reflects the developmental stage of learners. For instance, early foundation subjects may be designed to instil curiosity, resilience, and core knowledge in literacy and numeracy, but also to provide cultural capital (Ofsted, 2019).

In secondary schools, curriculum intent must also address subject progression, leading towards terminal assessments such as GCSEs. Yet, the challenge here is to avoid over-prioritising outcomes, and instead develop subjects in ways that foster disciplinary thinking, critical literacy, and transferable skills (Whitty, 2010). Intent should articulate how each subject builds towards significant intellectual and civic goals - not just qualifications.

Further education (FE)

In the FE sector, curriculum intent is shaped by a diverse array of learners and outcomes - ranging from 16-19 study programmes to adult education, and from vocational qualifications to access courses. Here, intent often addresses both employability and personal development, focusing on real-world preparation and lifelong learning.

Providers are expected to articulate how their intent reflects:

- Local labour market need.

- Skills priorities nationally (e.g. digital or green skills).
- Learner diversity, especially for adult returners and those with interrupted formal education.

Evidence of intent often appears in programme specifications, employer partnership documentation, and course rationale statements - highlighting how content is selected and sequenced to support learner transitions into work or higher education.

Higher education (HE)

While HE institutions are not formally inspected by Ofsted, curriculum intent is evident in programme design and validation processes. Universities are increasingly required to demonstrate intent in terms of:

- Graduate attributes.
- Alignment with sector expectations (e.g. QAA benchmark statements).
- Inclusivity and global citizenship preparation (Barnett & Coate, 2005).

In many institutions, curriculum approval documents require a 'statement of intent' - detailing the intellectual, ethical, or professional foundations of a given programme. For example, a criminology degree may be designed to enhance critical thinking about justice systems, integrate real-world placements, and challenge structural inequalities. Such intent is justified through stakeholder consultation, market intelligence, and educational research.

While HE enjoys more autonomy in content selection, increasing accountability pressures have made curriculum intent a visible standard in quality assurance processes - particularly regarding employability, access, and civic responsibility.

Theoretical foundation of curriculum intent

Curriculum intent is more than a straightforward declaration of educational aims; it is grounded in complex, frequently debated theories regarding how people learn, what is worth knowing, and the ultimate goals of education. Across all sectors - primary, secondary, further education (FE), and higher education (HE) - curriculum intent embodies the ways educators engage with fundamental questions: what content should be prioritised, why it matters, and who it is designed to benefit. These theoretical underpinnings shape the values, principles, and priorities embedded in curriculum design. By appreciating the philosophical and pedagogical foundations that inform curriculum intent, educational leaders and teachers make better-informed decisions about planning, structuring, and justifying their curriculum, ensuring it aligns with broader purposes and meets learners' diverse needs.

Key educational theories

Behaviourism and the objectives model

One of the earliest theoretical influences on curriculum intent was behaviourism, which advocated for observable, measurable objectives as the starting point of the curriculum process. Ralph Tyler's influential rationale set out a model that begins with the identification of clear, specific educational purposes, which then drive the selection and organisation of learning experiences and the evaluation of outcomes (Tyler, 1949).

Tyler's model established the principle that curriculum design should begin with intent: what do we want learners to be able to do? This "objectives model" has been especially influential in primary and secondary education, driving the development of national curriculum aims, attainment targets, and lesson planning grounded in "learning objectives" (Kelly, 2009).

However, this logical-positivist approach has been critiqued for over-simplifying complex learning and neglecting broader aims such as criticality, creativity, and personal development (Stenhouse, 1975; Biesta, 2015).

Essentialism, perennialism, and the concept of 'powerful knowledge'

Essentialist and perennialist theories prioritise the transmission of core knowledge and disciplinary structures that represent society's intellectual heritage (Hirsch, 2019; Young & Muller, 2016). Michael Young's concept of "powerful knowledge" has been especially influential in contemporary English curriculum intent debates.

Young argues that intent should focus on giving all learners access to knowledge that is conceptually coherent, transformative, and allows them to understand and engage with the world beyond their everyday experiences (Young, 2008). This is a key justification for subject-based curricula with sequenced progression and high ambition - seen, for instance, in Ofsted's requirements that curriculum intent should make clear the core knowledge and skills needed for future success (Ofsted, 2019).

Perennialist intent is most visible in traditional academic curricula - secondary and HE especially - where curriculum is designed around established canons of knowledge with a view to cultivating intellectual independence and rigor.

Progressivism, constructivism, and the process model

Progressivist and constructivist theories, by contrast, centre on the idea that learners actively construct their own knowledge. John Dewey argued that intent should be grounded in the needs, experiences, and interests of learners (Dewey, 1938).

Laurence Stenhouse proposed the "process model", in which curriculum intent is framed less by fixed outcomes and more by principles of enquiry, democratic participation, and teacher autonomy (Stenhouse, 1975).

In this tradition, curriculum intent is inherently flexible. The focus is on transformative experiences that foster agency, critical thinking, and adaptability - a perspective influential in certain primary approaches (such as project or enquiry-based learning), alternative provision, liberal arts programmes in HE, and some FE settings (Alexander, 2021).

Bruner's spiral curriculum (Bruner, 2009) is another variant, in which intent revolves around key concepts revisited at increasing levels of complexity, supporting both breadth and depth.

Critical theory and social justice

Intent is also shaped by critical and emancipatory perspectives, which argue that curriculum should not only transmit powerful knowledge but empower learners to challenge inequality and promote social justice. Paulo Freire's critical pedagogy (Freire, 1970) characterises intent as the development of consciousness, dialogue, and criticality, enabling learners to interpret and change their world.

Such aims are increasingly represented in contemporary policy through requirements for curricula to address cultural diversity, global citizenship, and social disadvantage - explicit in the Ofsted framework's expectation that intent should address "social disadvantage" and promote high ambition for all (Ofsted, 2019).

Humanism and holistic education

A final theoretical thread is humanistic education, where the intent of curriculum is to foster self-actualisation, well-being, and personal growth (Rogers, 1969). Particularly visible in primary and alternative settings, this approach informs the inclusion of personal, social, health, and emotional education (PSHE), and underpins contemporary moves towards well-being-focused or inclusive curriculum intent statements.

The role of intent in curriculum design

From aims to implementation

Regardless of the underlying theoretical tradition, intent provides the guiding vision around which all subsequent curriculum decisions are made. In contemporary curriculum design models (e.g., Backward Design by Wiggins & McTighe, 2011), clarity of intent serves as the starting point: educators begin by specifying the desired knowledge, skills, and dispositions, then plan backwards through learning activities, resources, and assessment.

- In primary education, clear intent enables the integration of subjects, attention to developmental needs, and a focus on foundational learning, literacy, and numeracy.
- In secondary education, intent shapes subject sequencing, option choices, and alignment with key assessments, providing rationale for curriculum breadth and depth.
- In FE, intent guides vocational or academic pathways, employer and labour market engagement, and critical skills development for life and work.
- In HE, curriculum intent determines programme outcomes, graduate attributes, research skills, and disciplinary progression (Barnett & Coate, 2005).

Sequencing, progression, and adaptation

Intent also underpins decisions about sequencing and progression. In the Ofsted framework, a key indicator of strong intent is careful sequencing: curriculum content must build logically from prior learning and clearly signpost end-points (Ofsted, 2019). This echoes Bruner's spiral curriculum and Vygotsky's emphasis on the "zone of proximal development", where intent is to scaffold new learning just beyond what the learner already knows (Vygotsky, 1978).

- In primary, intent informs planning for age-appropriate progression and spaced reinforcement.
- In secondary and FE, subject and programme leaders align curriculum maps with assessment specifications and ensure cumulative skill-building (Knight & Yorke, 2003).
- In HE, intent is made explicit in programme specifications and module outcomes, which must be mapped to external quality frameworks and benchmarks (QAA, 2024).

Inclusion and responsiveness

The theoretical foundation of curriculum intent also acknowledges the necessity of inclusion and context-responsiveness. Curriculum intent must be adapted to fit the backgrounds, aspirations, and needs of learners - including those with SEND, EAL, social disadvantage, or those returning to education (Biesta, 2015; Alexander, 2021).

Ofsted (2019) considers curriculum intent in terms of how well it identifies and addresses specific gaps in knowledge and skills that are unique to each local context, while also ensuring ambitious aims are upheld for every pupil, regardless of background or starting point. In further education (FE) and higher education (HE), intent is further shaped by how programmes and modules respond to employer expectations, industry trends, and global developments, ensuring graduates are well-prepared for evolving workforce and societal demands.

Coherence, depth, and curriculum review

A theoretically robust approach to curriculum intent also requires coherence: intentional connections between aims, content, pedagogy, and assessment. Regular curriculum review, stakeholder engagement, and evidence-informed practice are essential to maintain alignment between theory and practice (Priestley & Biesta, 2013; Barnett & Coate, 2005).

This process promotes reflective professionalism - teachers and leaders as active curriculum thinkers, not just implementers - a theme in the work of Stenhouse (1975) and echoed in current Ofsted guidance, which values schools' articulation, justification, and ongoing development of their curriculum intent.

Ofsted's inspection framework: Intent explained

The concept of curriculum intent occupies a central place in the current evaluation of educational provision in England, as articulated in the Office for Standards in Education, Children's Services and Skills (Ofsted) inspection framework introduced in 2019. This framework marks a significant shift from focusing predominantly on outcomes and attainment to considering the intentions behind curriculum design and how these intentions translate into coherent, equitable, and ambitious educational experiences. Understanding Ofsted's definition of intent, alongside the key expectations it sets for schools, colleges, and other educational providers, is crucial for curriculum leaders and educators navigating the demands of quality assurance, accountability, and pedagogical excellence across contexts—primary, secondary, further education (FE), and higher education (HE).

Ofsted's definition of intent

Ofsted defines curriculum intent as the *what* and *why* of the curriculum - specifically, what knowledge, skills, and understanding pupils are expected to gain at each stage and the rationale for these choices (Ofsted, 2019). Intent embodies the educational ambition for learners and reflects the school's or institution's purpose and values. It frames curriculum as a structured, purposeful journey designed to prepare learners for future success, societal participation, and personal development.

Intent is not concerned merely with compliance or content coverage; rather, it focuses on how curriculum leadership interprets and applies educational research and evidence about effective learning. The Ofsted inspection handbook emphasises that:

- The curriculum should be underpinned by a solid consensus of school leaders about the essential knowledge and skills pupils need to face the opportunities, responsibilities, and experiences of later life.
- Clear end points or goals must be defined, enabling learners to know what they should know and be able to do at each stage.
- Content and skills should be planned and sequenced logically, progressively building on prior learning towards these agreed goals.
- The curriculum should respond to the school's local context, addressing known gaps in knowledge or disadvantage within the pupil population.
- The curriculum during the early years and as long as possible thereafter should remain broad, providing a comprehensive educational experience.
- Schools should maintain high academic and vocational ambitions for all pupils, including those who are disadvantaged or have special educational needs and disabilities (SEND), avoiding curriculum narrowing or reduction for these groups (Ofsted, 2019, paras 171-177).

For Ofsted, curriculum intent is a matter of leadership quality. Inspectors principally evaluate the clarity, coherence, and ambition of intent via discussion with senior and subject leaders and through documentary evidence such as programme specifications and schemes of work. Evidence includes how the curriculum aligns with statutory requirements or equivalent broad frameworks (in academies or independent schools), how gaps for disadvantaged pupils are addressed, and how curriculum content prioritises purposeful, useful, and progressive knowledge and skills (Ofsted, 2019, paras 179-181).

Because developing a fully embedded, effective curriculum takes time, the framework recognises that schools may be in various stages of implementing or refining intent. Inspectors will take a "best fit" approach, considering plans for improvement and the leadership team's accurate understanding of current practice when judging intent (Ofsted, 2019). This allows schools to demonstrate intent even when full implementation is ongoing.

Key expectations for schools and other settings

Primary education

In primary schools, Ofsted expects curriculum intent to support foundational knowledge and the development of literacy and numeracy, alongside a rich range of experiences across subjects. Leaders should articulate how early learning frameworks and the national curriculum translate into coherent progression across classes and year groups. Intent must explicitly consider the diverse needs of pupils, for example addressing language gaps or socio-economic disadvantage, and prioritise reading development as fundamental to accessibility across all subjects. Schools are encouraged to retain a broad and balanced curriculum as long as possible - combining core subjects with creative, physical, and personal development to promote well-rounded foundations (Ofsted, 2019).

Secondary education

Intent in secondary schools involves clear curriculum maps aligned with key stage milestones and terminal qualifications (such as GCSEs and vocational equivalents). There is particular emphasis on progression within core academic disciplines and subject-specific sequencing designed to build deeper knowledge and skills. Leaders must demonstrate how the curriculum supports a strong academic core, often linked to the Ebacc, while also providing vocational and creative options without compromise. Attention to inclusion and ambition for SEND and disadvantaged learners is crucial, ensuring no pupil is offered a narrowed or less challenging curriculum. Schools should explain how curriculum choices empower pupils for post-16 options and wider life opportunities (Ofsted, 2019).

Further education (FE)

Ofsted's approach to curriculum intent in FE reflects the sector's diversity and vocational focus. Providers must articulate curriculum purpose in terms of employability, skills progression, and personal development. Intent documents (such as programme specifications and learning plans) should show clarity about how curricula meet local labour market needs and enable progression within and beyond qualifications. FE curricula are expected to integrate wider key skills - English, maths, digital literacy - and to embed inclusivity and support for diverse learners. Providers should demonstrate ambitious intent that applies equally to vocational and academic provision, avoiding lower expectations or reduced curriculum for any student group (Ofsted, 2019).

Higher education (HE)

Though outside Ofsted's direct remit, the concept of curriculum intent in HE aligns with QAA quality codes and institutional programme approval processes. Universities and colleges craft curriculum intent by defining programme learning outcomes, ensuring coherence between curriculum aims, curriculum content, learning activities, and assessment (QAA, 2024). Clear articulation of intent supports both academic rigour and the multiple purposes of HE, including research integration and lifelong learning readiness (Barnett & Coate, 2005).

Summary of expectations

Across all sectors, Ofsted expects curriculum intent to be:

- **Clear and ambitious:** providing all learners with challenging, coherent, and purposeful learning.

- **Well sequenced:** ensuring knowledge and skills build progressively across phases and stages.
- **Inclusive and equitable:** responding to learner diversity and working to close gaps.
- **Contextually relevant:** addressing local needs and national priorities without reducing breadth.
- **Reflective and developmental:** recognised as an evolving framework requiring ongoing review and leadership insight.

The impact of these expectations is broad and significant, encouraging educational institutions to move well beyond mere compliance with curriculum mandates. They foster curriculum design that is deeply imbued with clear educational intention - intent that is firmly anchored in robust research evidence, responsive to the diverse needs of learners across all contexts, and framed by a coherent, transparent sense of purpose. This evolving emphasis on curriculum intent prompts leaders and educators to prioritise thoughtful sequencing, inclusivity, and ambition, rather than superficial content coverage. Consequently, institutions are encouraged to adopt a more strategic, reflective, and evidence-informed approach that contributes to equitable and meaningful learning experiences for all students.

Here is a sample excerpt from the "Intent" section of a typical Ofsted inspection report. It has been carefully written to reflect the tone, structure, and evaluative language used in official Ofsted documentation. This example illustrates how curriculum intent is typically described across primary, secondary, and further education (FE) settings.

Intent

Leaders have constructed a curriculum that is ambitious, broad, and designed to give all pupils, including those with SEND and those who are disadvantaged, the knowledge and cultural capital they need to succeed in life. The curriculum is coherently planned and sequenced, ensuring that pupils build on prior learning and make clear progress through each subject area. Leaders have identified the key knowledge and skills that pupils should acquire at each stage, with clear end points towards which teaching is directed.

The curriculum reflects the needs and context of the school community. Leaders demonstrate a clear understanding of local gaps in pupils' knowledge and have adapted the curriculum accordingly, ensuring that disadvantaged pupils and those who speak English as an additional language are well supported. The curriculum remains as broad as possible for as long as possible, including a wide range of subjects beyond English and mathematics.

Subject leaders have reviewed and mapped out the essential content of their areas to ensure progression and challenge for all. Leaders have high expectations for what all pupils can achieve and have established a curriculum that provides opportunities for pupils to gain

> a depth of understanding and to develop skills that prepare them well for the next stage of education or employment.
>
> The school's curriculum intent is communicated effectively by leaders, ensuring clarity of purpose across all levels of staff. Teachers and wider school personnel demonstrate a secure understanding of why particular content has been chosen and how it fits into the school's wider educational aims. This shared understanding enables coherent planning and consistent delivery across subjects and key stages, supporting pupils' long-term academic development, personal growth, and readiness for future education, employment, and participation in wider society.

Developing a school's curriculum intent

Developing a curriculum intent that is both principled and practical involves articulating a clear educational purpose, rooted in the values and vision of a school or educational institution. Across settings - including primary, secondary, further education (FE), and higher education (HE) - curriculum intent must respond meaningfully to learners' needs, local contexts, and broader societal aims. The process of developing this intent requires thoughtful reflection, stakeholder engagement, and evidence-informed planning. It involves more than just compliance with statutory requirements; it seeks to define what a school or provider believes education should accomplish and how curriculum design will support that vision.

Establishing core values and vision

At the foundation of any strong curriculum intent is a well-defined school vision - a guiding set of beliefs about what learners should become and how the curriculum should support their development. Establishing this vision is a collective, strategic process that involves leadership, staff, governors, learners, and often parents and community partners (Brundrett & Rhodes, 2010). The vision encapsulates what the organisation sees as the purpose of education and the kind of citizen, worker, or thinker it hopes its learners will grow to be.

Core values such as respect, inclusion, creativity, resilience, and aspiration are frequently expressed through school ethos statements. However, for these values to be meaningful, they must be intentionally woven into curriculum design, content, and pedagogy (Alexander, 2021). That is, the curriculum should not merely prepare pupils for assessments or qualifications; it must also cultivate personal growth, social responsibility, and intellectual curiosity.

In primary schools, values often take the form of 'whole child development', where literacy and numeracy goals are supported by emotional learning and broad cultural exposure. For example, a vision that prioritises empathy and global citizenship might lead to thematic units on environmental sustainability or social justice, enabling intent to encompass both academic rigour and moral education.

In secondary schools, values are frequently aligned with future-readiness and academic excellence. A school aiming to develop independent thinkers might design a history curriculum rooted not only in factual recall but in source evaluation, argument formation, and the exploration of contested narratives.

FE institutions, especially those serving diverse and often underrepresented learners, typically articulate intent around employability, inclusion, and social mobility. Establishing a core vision in these contexts often involves balancing vocational purpose with broader developmental aims such as confidence-building, citizenship, and re-engagement with learning.

In HE, vision statements are commonly tied to disciplinary excellence, critical inquiry, graduate employability, and increasingly, global citizenship and sustainability (Barnett & Coate, 2005). Curriculum intent in universities is often cascaded through programme specifications, module outlines and graduate attribute frameworks, and is developed with reference to national benchmarks and subject-specific expectations (QAA, 2024).

Aligning intent with school community needs

While a school's values and vision may provide the philosophical backbone, curriculum intent must also respond pragmatically to context. That means understanding and addressing the lived realities of the community it serves - its demographic composition, cultural history, socio-economic challenges, and learner aspirations (Ofsted, 2019).

In Ofsted's terms, one role of intent is to address typical gaps in knowledge and skills, especially for those at risk of underachievement, such as disadvantaged pupils or those with SEND. This is not merely about differentiating provision; it is about setting ambitious, inclusive goals that ensure equity of access to academic and cultural capital - both in content and opportunity (Ofsted, 2019, para. 172).

Curriculum leaders must begin by gathering and analysing a rich set of community data, including:

- Attainment outcomes by group or subject.
- Pupil premium reports.
- Community demographic profiles.
- Pupil voice and parental feedback.
- Local economic and career opportunities.

- Safeguarding and well-being indicators.

In primary education, this might mean explicitly planning aspects of the curriculum to fill vocabulary gaps, nurture reading fluency, or build the cultural knowledge learners need to access higher-order concepts later. For example, a thematic geography unit on "Our Local Area" might incorporate map skills, writing tasks, and community visits as part of a broader aim to build place identity and spoken language confidence.

In secondary contexts, intent may require tailoring curricula to redress prior disadvantage while keeping pathways broad and aspirational. For schools in areas of high deprivation, this could mean increasing exposure to canonical texts in English or deliberately sequencing science content to enable success at GCSE and transition to post-16 study, even when pupils arrive with low prior attainment. A key consideration is to avoid "curriculum narrowing", which is when learners - especially those seen as less able - are offered a reduced, less challenging curriculum that curtails their opportunities (Whitty, 2010).

In FE, alignment with community needs is even more prominent, given the diversity of learners and the institution's explicit role in local workforce planning and social inclusion. For example, an FE college in an area experiencing growth in digital industries might embed coding, project-based learning, and employer-led qualifications into its study programmes, aligning its curriculum intent with local economic strategy and national skills priorities. Colleges are also tasked with addressing the educational and pastoral needs of adult learners, many of whom bring life experiences that require a curriculum rooted in trust, respect, and flexibility.

In HE, responsiveness to community needs is evolving. Increasingly, institutions align their curriculum intent with global and local policy priorities - including sustainability (UNESCO, 2020), equality, and employability. A university located in an area with high minority ethnic populations, for example, may develop inclusive reading lists and community-based research opportunities to reflect and serve its context. Planning curriculum intent here involves horizon-scanning, policy awareness, employer partnerships, and participatory design with students, especially in courses that interweave community engagement and applied knowledge.

Shared ownership and participatory design

Developing curriculum intent is most powerful when it is a collaborative and participatory process. Leaders alone cannot shape a meaningful curriculum vision without the involvement of those who teach it and those who learn from it. Staff voice, student experience, and parental input all contribute to an intent that is contextual, relevant, and inclusive.

Teachers must be given time and structure to contribute to curriculum planning. Subject leaders should be supported to reflect on content choices and progression structures, especially through curriculum mapping exercises and peer dialogue that bring coherence to subject intent vertically (across key stages) and horizontally (across disciplines).

Similarly, students can provide critical insights into what works, what is meaningful, and what barriers they encounter. Involving students in curriculum conversations—especially in secondary and tertiary settings - fuels engagement and ownership while revealing gaps between declared intent and lived experience (Biesta, 2015).

An emerging practice, particularly in HE and some progressive schools, is co-construction, where learners and educators collectively shape aspects of the content and approach of the curriculum. Such methods build curriculum intent around principles of democracy, responsiveness, and critical inquiry, reflecting process models of curriculum theory (Stenhouse, 1975; Kelly, 2009).

Statements of intent

Schools in England are not formally required by Ofsted or the Department for Education (DfE) to produce a specific "statement of curriculum intent". However, Ofsted's Education Inspection Framework (EIF) does require schools to be able to clearly articulate and demonstrate the intent behind their curriculum. Inspectors look to see whether leaders and staff can explain: what their curriculum aims to achieve, including the knowledge and skills pupils should gain at each stage; how the school's values, ambitions, and local context shape curriculum decisions; and how intent informs curriculum sequencing, inclusion, and opportunities for all learners, including those with SEND and from disadvantaged backgrounds. This answers fundamental questions about what education should accomplish, which knowledge and skills are most important for learners, and how education prepares them for future stages in life, learning, and work.

How Is Intent Evaluated?

During inspection, inspectors primarily assess curriculum intent through discussions with senior and subject leaders. They focus on how well these leaders can articulate what pupils are expected to learn, the rationale behind the curriculum choices made, and how the curriculum is thoughtfully planned and sequenced to promote progressive learning. Inspectors may review curriculum planning documents as evidence, but schools are not required to produce a formal "intent statement" or submit documentation in any prescribed format solely for inspection purposes (Ofsted, 2019). The emphasis is on understanding the coherence and ambition embedded in curriculum intent rather than on specific paperwork.

"Intent is about what leaders intend pupils to learn. It's as simple as that. Intent is everything up to the point at which teaching happens... There's no need to write new statements, adapt websites or restructure staffing to cover intent. Intent is not the next big thing".

Ofsted (2019)

Common Practice in Schools

Despite it not being a statutory or Ofsted-mandated requirement, many schools choose to write and publish a statement of curriculum intent. This statement helps:

- Sharpen and unify the school's curriculum vision
- Communicate aims and principles to staff, parents, and inspectors
- Provide clarity for curriculum planning and professional development

Such statements are commonly found on school websites or within curriculum policies, but their content, length, and style are decided locally.

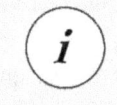

Some schools frame their curriculum intent primarily around broad visions and core values, such as respect, inclusion, and personal development, rather than focusing explicitly on detailed curriculum content or academic objectives. This approach risks diluting the clarity and specificity needed in a curriculum that effectively guides teaching and learning. Without a clear articulation of intended knowledge and skills, there is a danger that curriculum planning becomes vague, limiting teacher guidance and potentially reducing educational rigour and consistency across subjects (see Appendix 7 for sample statements).

Ongoing review and refinement

Curriculum intent is not static. It requires ongoing review and clear articulation in response to evolving learner needs, policy changes, and reflective practice by staff. Many institutions embed curriculum development within their annual self-evaluation cycles, using data analysis and professional dialogue to continually enhance the curriculum's effectiveness. Ofsted acknowledges this dynamic process, noting that leaders involved in evidence-based redesign who can clearly communicate their intent are viewed positively during inspection (Ofsted, 2019).

A strong curriculum intent framework also empowers teaching staff, governors, and wider stakeholders to engage consistently and meaningfully with the school's educational purpose. It supports ongoing dialogue about priorities, ensures decisions align with shared values, and facilitates the translation of intent into effective planning, teaching, and learning outcomes.

>  **Activity: Articulating and evaluating curriculum intent**
> 1. Select a curriculum from your own or a familiar educational setting (e.g., a subject in primary or secondary school, an FE programme, or a HE module).
> 2. Analyse the curriculum by responding to the following prompts:
> - What are the stated or implied *intentions* of this curriculum?
> - How clearly are end points defined? Are these academic, vocational, social, or a combination?
> - How is knowledge sequenced to support progression towards these goals?
> - How does the curriculum address inclusion and differentiation?
> - To what extent is intent informed by learners' local context or future aspirations?
> 3. Compare the curriculum intentions with actual practice (implementation) and outcomes (impact). Where do you observe alignment or misalignment?
> 4. Reflection and redesign: Draft a revised statement of curriculum intent for that context, ensuring clarity, ambition, inclusion, and relevance. Identify one structural or pedagogical adjustment that would better realise this intent in practice.
>
> Optional: Share your revised intent and rationale in a group setting or peer discussion to gather alternative perspectives.

Summary

Curriculum intent provides the philosophical and practical foundation upon which educational design is built. Whether describing what learners should know, the kinds of thinking and skills they should develop, or how they will be prepared for life beyond education, intent invites curriculum designers to clarify their values and assumptions about learning.

Over time, there has been a notable shift from delivering content for its own sake to prioritising coherent, ambitious, and contextualised curriculum planning. Articulating and evaluating intent is essential for curriculum coherence, learner engagement, and educational equity. Systems such as Ofsted's Inspection Framework have formalised this focus, but its impact reaches far deeper, challenging educators to align pedagogy, assessment, and institutional mission with a clear and meaningful educational purpose.

6 CURRICULUM IMPLEMENTATION

Introduction

Curriculum implementation refers to the process of translating planned curriculum design into authentic learning experiences and measurable outcomes. This stage bridges the gap between theory and practice, involving the adaptation of policies, content, and teaching methods to suit unique classrooms, learners, and institutional cultures. Effective implementation demands more than mere adherence to prescribed materials: it requires skilled teaching, thoughtful adaptation to local needs, robust evaluation, and responsiveness to feedback.

As educational environments become increasingly complex - fuelled by technological advancements and policy shifts - it is more important than ever to understand the practical realities, challenges, and support needed for curriculum to truly enrich learners' lives. This chapter provides a comprehensive exploration of the implementation process, spanning factors that influence successful delivery, the pivotal role of teachers, and the evolving impact of digital tools.

This chapter

- Defines what is meant by curriculum implementation and why it matters across all education sectors.
- Examines the factors influencing implementation, including organisational culture, leadership, and resistance to change.
- Explores the range of learning experiences that bring curriculum to life for learners.
- Discusses the critical role of teachers in adapting, mediating, and enacting curriculum in diverse settings.
- Evaluates models and tools for measuring implementation effectiveness and impact during delivery.
- Considers national approaches and challenges to implementing curriculum reforms at scale.
- Investigates the place of technology in supporting implementation, with a focus on digital tools for teaching and assessment.
- Reflects on current and emerging trends in curriculum implementation, with practical strategies for continuous improvement.

What is curriculum implementation?

Curriculum implementation is the complex and ongoing process of transforming a designed curriculum into actual learning experiences that occur within educational settings. It involves moving beyond written plans and intentions to a practical enactment of curriculum ambitions through teaching, learning activities, assessment, and engagement with learners' needs. Instead of a simple transmission of content, implementation is dynamic, shaped by interpretation, adaptation, context, and reflection that occurs daily within classrooms, workshops, lecture halls, and online.

Defining curriculum implementation

At its core, curriculum implementation refers to the practical enactment and delivery of the curriculum framework - whether a national syllabus, a school-based programme, or HE module learning outcomes. It is the bridge between policy or design and the lived reality of learners and educators (Figure 6.1).

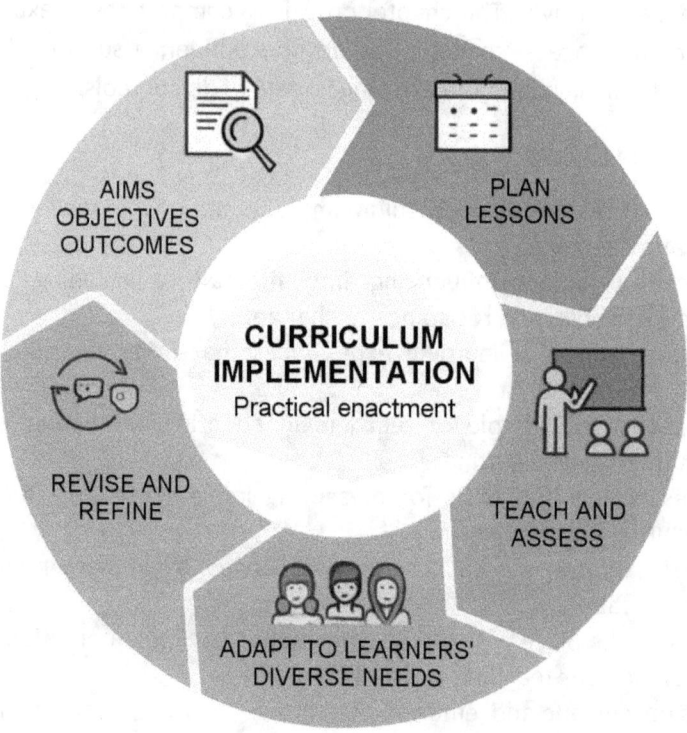

Figure 6.1 - Curriculum implementation

The process includes:

- Interpreting curriculum documents and frameworks, translating aims and objectives into tangible learning outcomes.
- Planning lessons, units, or modules in ways that organise knowledge, skills, and experiences coherently.
- Employing teaching methods, resources, and assessments that facilitate learning and measure progress according to curriculum goals.
- Adapting content and pedagogical approaches to fit the diverse needs, backgrounds, and interests of learners.
- Revising and refining curriculum delivery based on formative feedback, learner responses, assessment outcomes, and changing contexts.

This cyclical process (Figure 6.1) acknowledges that curriculum implementation is never a one-off event but a continual negotiation between prescribed intentions and classroom realities (Fullan, 2016; Kelly, 2009).

Curriculum implementation across educational contexts

Primary education

In primary education, teachers typically deliver a broad national curriculum that covers multiple subjects. Curriculum implementation here is integrated and developmental, focused on foundational skills like literacy and numeracy, along with creative, physical, and social learning experiences. Teachers must:

- Sequence subject content according to learners' developmental stages.
- Adapt activities to accommodate varied abilities, including pupils with special educational needs and disabilities (SEND) or English as an Additional Language (EAL).
- Provide rich, engaging experiences that balance statutory requirements with local context.
- Scaffold learning to enable acquisition of fundamental skills that underpin success across subjects.

Effective implementation demands flexibility, ongoing formative assessment, and responsive teaching strategies to maximise engagement and progress (Alexander, 2021).

Secondary education

Secondary curriculum implementation is still aligned with national curriculum but shifts towards greater subject specialisation and complexity. Teachers deliver discipline-specific content aligned to external qualifications like GCSEs and A-levels. Key considerations include:

- Ensuring curriculum coherence within and between subjects through sequencing concepts and skills.
- Balancing the breadth of subjects with depth and rigour, mindful of national benchmarks and accountability measures.
- Differentiating instruction to address diverse learning preferences and achievement levels.
- Managing practical constraints such as timetabling and departmental resource allocation.

Subject leaders play a pivotal role in aligning school-level curriculum delivery with national standards and examination requirements, while encouraging adaptation to school-specific learner profiles (Whitty, 2010).

Further education (FE)

In FE, implementation addresses the diversity of learners, including school leavers, adult returners, and apprentices, across highly varied vocational and academic programmes. The delivery of curriculum is influenced by:

- The necessity to meet nationally regulated qualification frameworks (e.g., BTECs, T Levels).
- Direct links with employer needs and workplace learning opportunities.
- Integration of functional skills such as English, maths, and digital literacy within vocational curricula.
- Flexible pedagogies to suit a wide range of learner ages, experiences, and motivation.

FE teachers skilfully adapt national or awarding body specifications to create meaningful, contextualised learning experiences that balance theoretical knowledge with practical application. They often tailor content to reflect local economic demands and social priorities, ensuring that learners gain relevant skills for employment and community engagement.

Higher education (HE)

HE curriculum implementation is characterised by a high degree of autonomy, with academics designing modules and programmes aligned with institutional mission, discipline standards, and external accrediting frameworks (e.g., QAA subject benchmarks). Implementation involves:

- Designing teaching and learning experiences that foster critical thinking, disciplinary depth, and research engagement.
- Aligning assessments with intended graduate attributes and learning outcomes.
- Emphasising student-centred, active learning strategies.
- Incorporating diverse assessment modes and increasing use of blended and digital learning pedagogies.

HE implementation is sensitive to the needs of an increasingly diverse and international student body and is closely monitored through quality assurance and enhancement processes (Barnett & Coate, 2005).

Implementation as an ongoing, evaluative process

Curriculum implementation is not a fixed act but an evolving, cyclical process. Effective implementation involves monitoring actual classroom practice and learner outcomes, reflecting on successes and challenges, and making timely adjustments in response to data and feedback. This iterative process supports continuous improvement in teaching quality and student achievement across all sectors (Priestley & Biesta, 2013).

Influences on curriculum implementation

Curriculum implementation is a complex and multifaceted process shaped by a dynamic interplay of technical, political, cultural, and contextual factors. These influences can vary substantially between educational settings, affecting how well curriculum intentions are realised in practice. Success depends not only on meticulous planning and resource allocation, but also on the commitment of educators, effective leadership, and ongoing professional development. It is essential to engage stakeholders at all levels, address diverse learner needs, and ensure clear communication throughout the process. Also, managing resistance to change and fostering a collaborative culture are critical for translating curricular goals into genuine, sustained educational improvement.

Factors affecting implementation

Technical factors

Technical factors relate to the practical and logistical considerations assumed to be addressable through systematic planning and provision of resources (House, 1979). They often form the foundation upon which other factors operate and include:

- *Curriculum clarity and complexity*: Well-structured and clearly articulated curricula promote consistent and faithful implementation. Overly complex or vague curriculum documents can confuse practitioners and dilute focus. Primary teachers, who typically deliver multiple subjects, may find densely packed curricula overwhelming, which can compromise the scaffolding of key knowledge and skills (Kelly, 2009).

- *Resources and infrastructure*: Adequate teaching materials, technology, laboratories, and appropriate learning environments are essential for effective delivery. This is especially critical in FE, where industry-standard equipment and workplace simulation facilities enable authentic vocational learning.

- *Professional development and training*: Continuous, well-targeted training ensures teachers and lecturers possess up-to-date content knowledge and pedagogical skills necessary to enact curriculum innovations confidently. In HE, where curriculum reforms often involve new assessments or interdisciplinary approaches, professional development supports alignment and quality assurance (Barnett & Coate, 2005).

- *Time and workload*: Teachers require sufficient time to plan, adapt, and reflect on curriculum delivery. Secondary contexts often face pressures from large class sizes and tight timetables, which can restrict flexibility and experimentation (Fullan, 2016).

- *Communication and guidance*: Clear articulation of curriculum aims, rationale, and expectations enhances understanding among educators and reduces implementation ambiguities. Effective leadership communication fosters coherence and shared commitment (Priestley & Biesta, 2013).

Political factors

Political factors encompass the power dynamics, policy environments, and stakeholder interests shaping curriculum implementation:

- *Government and policy alignment*: Curriculum implementation is heavily influenced by national and regional policy directives. For example, the mandatory

National Curriculum in England requires compliance, but frequent policy changes or ideological shifts can destabilise teacher confidence and continuity (Ball, 2008).

- *Leadership and institutional support*: School and departmental leaders act as catalysts or barriers. Effective leaders provide vision, allocate resources, and cultivate a collaborative culture supportive of curriculum change. Conversely, weak or sceptical leadership can erode motivation and stifle innovation (Leithwood et al., 2008).

- *Teacher agency and involvement*: Teachers' participation in curriculum development fosters ownership and commitment. Where curricula are imposed top-down without consultation - common in national reforms - resistance or perfunctory compliance often follows, notably in professionalised settings like HE (Alexander, 2021).

- *Stakeholder engagement*: Collaboration with parents, governors, employers, and the wider community increases the legitimacy and relevance of curriculum initiatives. Especially in FE and HE, employer involvement ensures alignment with labour market needs and enhances learner motivation.

- *Accountability regimes*: High-stakes testing, external inspections, and league tables can restrict curriculum breadth as teachers may "teach to the test" rather than fully realise curriculum intent, narrowing learning experiences (Biesta, 2015).

Cultural factors

Cultural aspects reflect the deeply ingrained beliefs, values, and traditions within educational institutions and stakeholder groups:

- *Institutional culture*: Established pedagogic norms, subject traditions, and school histories profoundly influence openness to curriculum change. Departments with strong identities may resist alterations that threaten longstanding practices (Whitty, 2010).

- *Teacher beliefs and professional identity*: Educators' philosophies about teaching, learning, and their professional roles condition how curriculum is enacted. Resistance can stem from anxieties about autonomy, perceived threats to expertise, or disagreement with reform purposes (Barnett & Coate, 2005).

- *Learner culture and community values*: Curriculum relevance is mediated by alignment with learners' socio-cultural backgrounds and local community expectations. Mismatches between curriculum content and learner identities can lead to disengagement, highlighting the importance of culturally responsive adaptations (Gay, 2018).

- *Peer collaboration and support*: Collegial networks and professional learning communities foster mutual reinforcement of curriculum change efforts. Isolation often correlates with lower implementation fidelity and teacher dissatisfaction.

Learner diversity and differentiation

Effective implementation recognises that learners arrive with diverse prior knowledge, abilities, languages, motivational levels, and cultural backgrounds, necessitating adaptation and differentiation. In primary education, this may mean scaffolding language development for EAL pupils or personalising interventions for SEND learners. Secondary and FE contexts grapple with diverse learner trajectories and aspirations, requiring flexible pedagogies. In HE, widening participation policies and internationalisation introduce further diversity that shapes curriculum delivery (Fullan, 2016).

Teacher expertise and beliefs

The subject knowledge, pedagogical skills, confidence, and personal attitudes of teachers significantly influence curriculum enactment. Teachers adept in curriculum content and flexible in pedagogy tend to implement curricula more faithfully and innovatively. Conversely, teachers questioning the value or feasibility of curriculum reforms may unintentionally dilute or skew delivery (Priestley & Biesta, 2013).

Leadership and culture

Supportive, visionary leadership nurtures an environment conducive to curriculum innovation. Leaders who communicate clear aims, provide resources, encourage collaboration, and value professional development embolden teachers to embrace change. Conversely, leadership deficits or ambiguous priorities often undercut implementation efforts (Leithwood et al., 2008).

Resource availability

Adequate access to teaching materials, technological resources, suitable physical spaces, and specialist support staff is fundamental to delivering a high-quality curriculum. However, resource limitations frequently pose significant challenges across all education sectors, particularly when curricula require advanced technologies or specialised practical facilities to meet learning objectives effectively.

External pressures

Curriculum implementation also faces external pressures from policy mandates, assessment frameworks, inspection regimes, and accountability measures. These may either support or hinder curriculum breadth and pedagogical innovation depending on how they are structured and enacted (Ball, 2008; Biesta, 2015).

Environmental and contextual factors

Socio-economic contexts, community expectations, demographic shifts, and historic institutional practices all shape the curriculum's perceived relevance and the engagement of learners and teachers. Responsive curriculum design and implementation that acknowledge these realities are more likely to succeed (Fullan, 2016).

Resistance to change

Resistance is an expected response to curriculum innovation and can be classified as:

- *Passive resistance*: Compliance without genuine engagement or adaptation, leading to superficial implementation.
- *Active resistance*: Open opposition, refusal to change teaching practices, or promoting alternative approaches.
- *Cultural resistance*: Rooted in conflicting educational values or identity, particularly where reforms challenge traditional roles or pedagogies (House, 1979).

Resistance tends to arise when changes are rapid, imposed without consultation, or unsupported by sufficient training and resources. In sectors valuing academic autonomy - such as HE - resistance to mandated curriculum changes is particularly prevalent (Alexander, 2021).

Managing factors and promoting successful implementation

Research demonstrates that curriculum implementation is most successful when change strategies address technical, political, and cultural dimensions simultaneously (Corbett & Rossman, 1989). Key strategies include:

- Involving teachers early and meaningfully in design and planning to build ownership.
- Providing timely, relevant professional development and resources.

- Establishing clear communication channels and coherent leadership.
- Encouraging professional collaboration and reflective practice.
- Acknowledging and addressing cultural concerns and institutional history.
- Balancing pressure for change with adequate support and evaluation.

Contextual examples

In primary settings, successful curriculum implementation often hinges on supporting generalist teachers with rich professional learning and manageable curriculum demands that reflect local pupil needs (Alexander, 2021). In secondary schools, navigating departmental autonomy and examination requirements requires strong leadership and clear curriculum mapping (Whitty, 2010). In FE, diversity of learner profiles and close employer links necessitate flexible, context-responsive implementation practices. HE curricula depend on collaborative governance and academic freedom balanced with quality assurance and student-centred learning design (Barnett & Coate, 2005).

Creating learning experiences

Creating meaningful learning experiences is fundamental to curriculum implementation in all educational settings. The concept of a 'learning experience' centres on how learners engage with activities, content, peers, and environments, rather than solely on what has been planned or intended by the teacher. Because learning is an inherently personal and social process, students in the same class, module, or workshop may have different experiences, influenced by their prior knowledge, motivation, cultural background, and confidence (Kolb, 2014; Illeris, 2018). It is, therefore, the responsibility of educators to design and facilitate opportunities that maximise the likelihood of equitable, engaging, and worthwhile experiences for all learners, regardless of context or starting point.

The nature of learning experiences

Learning experiences go beyond the mere completion of predetermined tasks. They encompass the cognitive, emotional, and social processes of sense-making, practice, collaboration, and reflection. Crucially, a teacher's plan does not guarantee a uniform experience for every student. While one learner may be fully absorbed in solving a problem or exploring a text, another may feel lost, disengaged, or unsupported. This diversity of experience underscores the need for teachers to design activities that are *multi-faceted* and flexible enough to accommodate the varied needs, abilities, and aspirations of all students (Alexander, 2021).

Aligning experiences with objectives

A core principle in designing learning experiences is *alignment*: activities should directly support progress towards clear learning objectives or outcomes (Tyler, 1949; Biggs, 2022). If an objective is to develop mathematical reasoning, for example, then activities must allow students to grapple meaningfully with challenging mathematical ideas, not simply follow rote procedures. In a science context, if the objective is to foster scientific inquiry, students should be given authentic opportunities to formulate hypotheses, conduct experiments, and critically interpret evidence. This alignment is crucial in ensuring experiences are not just engaging, but *purposeful*, driving progression and deep understanding.

The nature of the objective - cognitive, practical, or affective - will often determine the most suitable type of experience (Bloom, 1956; Anderson & Krathwohl, 2001). Problem-based learning, for instance, is well-suited to objectives centred on synthesis, application, or evaluation.

Principles for selecting and designing learning experiences

Regardless of objective, several general principles should guide the selection and structuring of learning experiences (Kelly, 2009):

- **Authenticity and relevance**: Learners are more likely to engage with activities that connect to real-life scenarios or personal interests. In FE, for example, hospitality students benefit from experiences that replicate industry settings, such as case studies, role plays, or workplace simulations. In HE, seminar discussions around current disciplinary debates foster motivation and critical engagement.

- **Opportunities for application**: Experiences should allow learners to *apply* newly acquired knowledge and skills. A primary science lesson might involve designing and carrying out experiments. In secondary English, students may write for real or simulated audiences. In HE, research projects and placements enable students to synthesise theoretical learning with practical demands.

- **Satisfaction and motivation**: Learners should derive satisfaction from the experiences themselves - solving problems, creating artefacts, or achieving personal milestones. Enjoyment and sense of accomplishment underpin motivation and, ultimately, deeper learning (Ryan & Deci, 2000).

- **Attainability and progression**: Learning experiences must be pitched at a level that challenges students but remains within their *zone of proximal development* (Vygotsky, 1978). This means teachers need secure understanding of learners' current attainment and capacity, supporting progression through scaffolding, differentiation, and formative assessment.

- **Variety and adaptability**: Multiple routes often lead to the same goal. Offering a range of experiences (e.g., group work, independent research, active investigation) increases the likelihood that most learners will find an accessible pathway. This flexibility is especially important for students with Special Educational Needs and Disabilities (SEND), English as an Additional Language (EAL), or other additional needs.

- **Reflection and feedback**: Opportunities for structured reflection and responsive feedback help learners consolidate experience and make sense of new information. In all sectors, strategies such as learning journals, peer discussions, or formative quizzes can serve this function.

Learning experiences across sectors

Primary education

Primary education places particular emphasis on *active, developmental, and multimodal* experiences. Here, teachers integrate play, storytelling, hands-on investigation, and collaborative tasks - ensuring the curriculum is accessible and stimulating for younger learners (Alexander, 2021). Structured routines offer security, but variety and autonomy are essential to nurture curiosity and foundational skill development. Problem-solving tasks, creative arts, and local community engagement are common approaches to making learning relevant and memorable.

Secondary education

In secondary settings, learning experiences become more subject-specific and often more abstract. Teachers design experiences to develop deeper subject knowledge and critical skills, employing techniques such as debates, experimental work, source analysis, simulations, or extended project work (Whitty, 2010). Differentiation within classes and across ability sets ensures learners of varying backgrounds and prior attainment can engage meaningfully. The capacity to provide multiple approaches remains vital; for example, a history lesson may combine timelines, primary source evaluation, and drama to reach a diverse range of students.

Further education (FE)

FE students, spanning diverse ages and ambitions, particularly benefit from learning experiences that integrate practical and theoretical knowledge. Industry placements, simulations, and task-based learning tie classroom content to workplace realities - enhancing engagement and employability. Creative use of assessment (such as portfolios, group projects, and performances) allows for individual strengths and learning needs to be recognised and developed. Attention to inclusivity and adult learning principles (andragogy) is essential, responding to learners' life stages and previous experiences (Knowles et al., 2014).

Higher education (HE)

HE increasingly emphasises *student-centred, inquiry-led* experiences. Seminars, research projects, and interdisciplinary learning require students to take more responsibility for their progress, developing skills of independence, collaboration, and metacognition (Barnett & Coate, 2005). Project-based learning, case analyses, placements, and international experiences promote graduate attributes such as critical thinking, problem solving, and global awareness. HE educators must continually adapt experiences to suit a growing diversity of learners - including international students and those entering via non-traditional routes.

The challenge of equity and Inclusion

Because the same planned activity can evoke different learning experiences for different students, equity in learning is a major challenge. Teachers must identify and address barriers - whether cognitive, linguistic, or affective - and design experiences that scaffold participation and success for all. Universal Design for Learning (Rose & Meyer, 2002) offers principles for creating flexible curricula that accommodate human variability. In practice, this might mean providing materials in multiple formats, supporting learners to use assistive technologies, or structuring peer collaboration to support social learning for less confident students.

Balancing structure and choice

While it is important to ensure all students meet curriculum objectives, overly rigid structuring of experiences can suppress autonomy and reduce motivation. Conversely, unstructured approaches may leave some learners directionless or unsupported. The most effective learning experiences balance clear structure with meaningful choice, challenge, and adaptability (Biggs, 2022; Biesta, 2015). Teachers act as facilitators - guiding, provoking, and responding to student ideas - while maintaining clarity about aims and progression.

Evaluating and enhancing learning experiences

Continuous evaluation is essential. Teachers use formative assessment, observation, and feedback from learners to monitor whether experiences are achieving intended outcomes and to make real-time adjustments. Sharing of practice, reflective dialogue, and professional development all contribute to improving the quality of learning experiences across sectors (Priestley & Biesta, 2013).

The importance of the teacher

The teacher's role in curriculum implementation is central and multi-layered, acting as the critical bridge between planned intentions and the lived experiences of learners. While curriculum frameworks may be expertly designed, their realisation depends on the skill, professional judgement, and agency of those delivering them. Teachers interpret, adapt, and breathe life into curricula, shaping not only what is taught, but also how, why, and to whom. The nature and quality of curriculum implementation hinge on teachers' expertise, beliefs, and interactions with their students and contexts.

Teachers as curriculum mediators

A curriculum, no matter how well constructed, only becomes effective when enacted thoughtfully by teachers (Marsh, 2009). Teachers do much more than follow prescribed plans; they are curriculum mediators who constantly interpret learning objectives, adapt teaching strategies to pupil realities, and select resources that fit local needs (Kelly, 2009). This mediation is not mechanical compliance but a matter of professional artistry - requiring deep knowledge of subject matter, understanding of pedagogy, and sensitivity to student diversity.

In primary settings, teachers exercise autonomy in integrating subjects, differentiating for a broad range of abilities, and fostering holistic development. In secondary, subject specialists translate curricular aims into classroom practice, often adapting content sequences, designing assessments, and promoting disciplinary skills. In FE and HE, where curricular structures can be highly prescribed or modular, teachers and lecturers must navigate complex specifications, qualification requirements, and increasingly diverse student populations while still enabling meaningful, individualised learning (James & Biesta, 2007; Barnett & Coate, 2005).

The primacy of pedagogical skill

The assertion that *'how you teach is more important than what you teach'* (Taba, 1962) is borne out in research and practice. Great teaching goes beyond mere coverage of content: it involves designing and facilitating learning experiences that motivate, challenge, and support students on their learning journeys. Pedagogical skill is evident in teachers' abilities to:

- Select and sequence activities to maximise engagement and progression.
- Employ differentiated and inclusive strategies that ensure accessibility for all learners, including those with SEND, EAL, or varying prior attainment.
- Use questioning, feedback, and dialogue to stimulate thinking, check understanding and address misconceptions effectively.
- Generate and use formative assessment to adapt teaching in real-time, closing gaps and reinforcing key concepts (Black & Wiliam, 2009).
- Build positive relationships and classroom climates that encourage confidence, resilience, and collaboration among students (Alexander, 2021).

This capacity is particularly vital in contexts facing rapid change, curriculum reform, or where statutory curricula reduce teacher agency. In such cases, it is teachers' pedagogical decision-making - what Hilda Taba terms "diagnostic artistry" - that ensures intended curriculum outcomes are genuinely realised for learners (Taba, 1962; Marsh, 2009).

Teacher agency and curriculum adaptation

Teachers are not passive implementers. They exercise *agency* in adapting official curriculum documents to suit their classes, schools, and communities (Priestley et al., 2015). Agency involves both autonomy (professional freedom) and accountability (responsibility to learners and curriculum aims). Research shows that where teachers are involved in curriculum design and have opportunities to exercise agency, implementation is not only more faithful but often more innovative and responsive (Oates, 2011; Stenhouse, 1975).

For example, a primary teacher may revise or supplement a scheme of work to address vocabulary gaps identified within their class, often arising from variations in socioeconomic background or language exposure in the local community. In a secondary setting, a science department might work collaboratively to adjust the sequence or emphasis of curriculum topics, ensuring that teaching is strategically aligned with the specific strengths and weaknesses revealed through cohort performance data, ultimately aiming to boost GCSE attainment. In FE, teachers are often required to interpret externally set qualification frameworks flexibly, embedding current employability skills or responding to feedback from local employers to ensure relevance. In HE, module leaders may frequently adapt reading lists, update case studies, and refine assessment methods in response to student evaluations and shifts in disciplinary thinking or industry standards, thereby keeping courses engaging and academically current (Barnett & Coate, 2005).

Relational expertise: Knowing the learner

High-quality curriculum implementation requires teachers to know their learners deeply. This encompasses understanding students' prior knowledge, interests, cultural backgrounds, and aspirations, as well as any barriers to learning. By forging strong, respectful relationships, teachers can tailor the curriculum to make it relevant, supportive, and challenging (Nieto, 2013; Biesta, 2015). In primary schools, the nurturing of curiosity and emotional wellbeing is as crucial as academic progress. In FE and HE, recognising the diverse pathways, motivations, and needs of adult learners underpins inclusive practice (James & Biesta, 2007).

Teachers as reflective practitioners

Curriculum implementation is not static: effective teachers are reflective practitioners who continually evaluate the impact of their practice, seek professional learning, and respond to feedback (Schön, 2017; Black & Wiliam, 2009). This cyclic process of *plan-deliver-reflect-adapt* is the hallmark of professional growth, enabling teachers to meet evolving curricular demands and emerging learner needs.

Structures such as professional learning communities, lesson study, and coaching cycles provide systemic support for teacher reflection and shared improvement, leading to greater consistency, innovation, and curricular depth (Priestley & Biesta, 2013; Alexander, 2021).

The teacher's role in shaping culture and expectations

Teachers are key agents in constructing classroom and institutional culture. Through daily routines, expectations, language, and attitudes, they transmit not just the explicit curriculum but also values, norms, and aspirations - the so-called 'hidden curriculum' (Jackson, 1968). In primary and secondary schools, teachers model respect, inclusion, and high ambition, guiding learners to see themselves as capable and valued. In FE and HE, the teacher's approach can signal whether classrooms are open to diversity, critical thought, and student agency.

Teacher leadership and collaboration

Implementation is rarely a solo endeavour. Effective curriculum enactment frequently relies on collaborative planning and shared professional dialogue, both within and across departments or subject areas. Teacher leadership - formally (e.g., heads of department, curriculum leads) or informally (as mentors or innovators) - drives forward curricular adaptation, quality assurance, and professional learning initiatives. In FE, where teaching teams are often multidisciplinary, collaboration supports coherence and relevance. In HE, team teaching, module co-ordination, and partnership with external stakeholders enhance both quality and alignment with programme aims (Barnett & Coate, 2005).

The critical role of ongoing professional development

Continuous professional development (CPD) is essential in empowering teachers to implement curricula effectively and confidently. It supports educators by updating their subject knowledge, enhancing pedagogical approaches, and strengthening their technical skills, enabling them to meet new or complex curricular demands with greater assurance (Cordingley et al., 2015). Particularly when reforms introduce novel content, technologies, or assessment methods, targeted and sustained CPD ensures these innovations are translated successfully into everyday classroom practice. Effective CPD is ongoing, collaborative, and closely connected to teaching realities, moving beyond isolated or one-off training events to foster meaningful, reflective professional growth across all educational sectors.

Sector-specific perspectives

- **Primary education:** Teachers' proximity to learners and their central pastoral role mean they are uniquely positioned to make the curriculum accessible and developmental. Their skill in integrating subjects and scaffolding foundational skills is key to early learning success.

- **Secondary education:** Subject expertise and pedagogical skill combine to enable deep, progressive learning. Teachers' abilities to differentiate, integrate skills across curricula (e.g., literacy in science), and foster disciplinary thinking are critical.

- **Further education:** Teachers must flexibly interpret qualification requirements, bridge theory and practical skill acquisition, and support learners from varied backgrounds, balancing compliance and innovation.

- **Higher education:** Lecturers and module leaders interpret subject benchmarks and graduate outcomes, often exercising significant autonomy. Their academic expertise, ability to create inquiry-based experiences, and responsiveness to feedback underpin high-quality curriculum implementation.

Teachers as the linchpin of successful implementation

As researchers and policy documents repeatedly affirm, no curriculum can be better than the quality of its implementation - and this relies fundamentally on teachers' knowledge, judgement, and relationships with learners (Ofsted, 2019; Alexander, 2021). High-quality teaching is not merely about delivering content but about enacting a curriculum in ways that foster long-term understanding, skills, and personal development.

Teachers are not simply vehicles for external prescriptions: they are co-constructors, translators, and, often, innovators, continually negotiating between curriculum aims, contextual realities, and the best interests of their learners. Their central role must be recognised and supported through meaningful involvement in curriculum design, robust professional development, and institutional cultures that value professional agency and learning.

Measuring implementation

Measuring curriculum implementation involves assessing how the intended curriculum - its materials, pedagogy, and aims - is translated into actual classroom practice and, ultimately, learner outcomes. Evaluation must consider what is delivered, how it is delivered, how learners engage, and what is achieved. Given the intricacies of teaching and learning across contexts from primary to higher education (HE), deciding what and when to measure - and how to interpret findings - requires nuanced approaches aligned with educational goals and practical constraints.

What to measure?

A key challenge in measuring implementation is identifying focus points. Implementation comprises three interrelated domains: curriculum materials, teacher actions, and student engagement. Observations or data collection that target only one domain risk an incomplete picture. For instance, curriculum materials may be rich and appropriate, but if teachers lack confidence or expertise to use them effectively, implementation suffers. Likewise, learners might engage only superficially despite strong materials and teaching.

Educators and researchers thus face questions such as:

- Should measurement focus on the fidelity and quality of curriculum materials?

- How can teacher practice and interactions be assessed effectively?

- What indicators of student engagement and learning best reflect implementation success?
- When in the implementation timeline - immediately, after six months, or later - should measurements be taken for meaningful insights?

These decisions determine data types collected (e.g., observations, interviews, document analysis, self-report questionnaires) and their analysis frameworks (Fullan, 2016; Kelly, 2009).

Measuring student activities and achievements

Student outcomes form a critical but partial measure of implementation quality. Summative assessments such as tests and examinations provide clear, quantifiable data on achievement and progress relative to curriculum goals. In primary and secondary settings, standardised testing data often serve this function, while FE and HE use specialised qualification results, assignments, and projects. However, such data alone cannot reveal *why* implementation succeeded or faltered.

More authentic measures include:

- Formative assessments along the way.
- Portfolios showcasing progression, depth, and breadth of student work.
- Observations of student engagement and interaction during lessons.
- Student self-assessments and reflections indicating understanding and metacognition.

These approaches align better with process models of curriculum that value learning experiences alongside outcomes (Priestley & Biesta, 2013). Additionally, they can capture differentiated progress for diverse learners, providing insight into inclusion and equity in implementation (Biesta, 2015).

Measuring curriculum materials

Curriculum materials such as schemes of work, textbooks, digital content, and assessment instruments, are foundational to implementation. Their design, accessibility, and relevance directly influence teaching and learning. Measuring how these materials are used and perceived is therefore essential.

UK institution often evaluate curriculum materials using purpose-developed checklists and quality assurance protocols. These frameworks typically consider criteria such as alignment with the National Curriculum, clarity, inclusivity, accessibility, and the extent to which materials promote progression and depth of knowledge. Quality assurance in UK institutes also involves systematic processes like self-evaluation, lesson observations, student work scrutiny, and feedback from staff and students to monitor the effectiveness of teaching materials and their impact on learning.

In the US, materials are often evaluated against criteria in a Curriculum Materials Analysis Scheme (CMAS), or using checklists in an Innovations Configuration (IC). ICs identify the major components of a new educational programme such as objectives, materials, learning activities and assessment (Fixsen, 2005). They promote a consistent approach to implementation, and act as a means of judging successful implementation within an acceptable tolerance (variation).

Systematic review of curriculum materials helps identify gaps, inconsistencies, and adaptations that occur in practice, informing future development or professional learning.

Measurement methods and data sources

Implementation measurement spans quantitative and qualitative methods, often involving mixed approaches to provide balanced evidence.

- **Observations:** Classroom or online observations offer direct evidence of curriculum delivery styles, student-teacher interactions, and use of materials. Structured observation protocols ensure consistency and focus but are time-intensive to conduct (Alexander, 2021).

- **Interviews and focus groups:** Engaging teachers, learners, and leaders in structured conversations can uncover deeper insights into perceptions, challenges, and contextual adaptations during implementation.

- **Self-assessment tools:** Teacher self-reports, using validated questionnaires or rating scales, are popular due to ease of administration. Instruments often map onto developmental models like the Stages of Concern (SoC) framework (Table 6.1), which captures emotional and cognitive responses to innovation (Hall et al, 1975).

- **Document analysis:** Reviewing lesson plans, schemes of work, assessment data, and learner portfolios provides tangible evidence but requires interpretative expertise.

- **Student feedback:** Surveys and reflections help gauge learner perceptions of curriculum coherence, engagement, and relevance.

Blending multiple data sources creates a more comprehensive implementation picture, helping to triangulate findings and validate conclusions (Fullan, 2016).

Stages of Concern (SoC) and measuring teacher attitudes

Among approaches to measuring implementation readiness and progress, the Stages of Concern model (Table 6.1) developed by Hall and colleagues is prominent (Hall et al., 1975).

IMPACT	6	Refocusing	The individual focuses on exploring ways to reap more universal benefits from the innovation, including the possibility of making major changes to it or replacing it with a more powerful alternative.
	5	Collaboration	The individual focuses on coordinating and cooperating with others regarding use of the innovation.
	4	Consequence	The individual focuses on the innovation's impact on students in his or her immediate sphere of influence. Considerations include the relevance of the innovation for students; the evaluation of student outcomes, including performance and competencies; and the changes needed to improve student outcomes.
TASK	3	Management	The individual focuses on the processes and tasks of using the innovation and the best use of information and resources. Issues related to efficiency, organising, managing, and scheduling dominate.
SELF	2	Personal	The individual is uncertain about the demands of the innovation, his or her adequacy to meet those demands, and/or his or her role with the innovation. The individual is analysing his or her relationship to the reward structure of the organization, determining his or her part in decision making, and considering potential conflicts with existing structures or personal commitment. Concerns also might involve the financial or status implications of the programme for the individual and his or her colleagues.
	1	Informational	The individual indicates a general awareness of the innovation and interest in learning more details about it. The individual does not seem to be worried about himself or herself in relation to the innovation. Any interest is in impersonal, substantive aspects of the innovation, such as its general characteristics, effects, and requirements for use.
	0	Unconcerned	The individual indicates little concern about or involvement with the innovation.

Table 6.1 - Stages of Concern (SoC)
Source: George et al., 2014

The model categorises teacher concerns about curriculum innovation into sequential stages, highlighting emotional, cognitive, and practical adjustments during implementation

Seven stages of concern (0-6) regarding an innovation have been identified. These are called stages because individuals typically move through them in a developmental sequence. This means a person using the innovation may feel one type of concern strongly at first, which then decreases as a new concern arises. Similar to Frances Fuller's study on teaching concerns (1969), these stages evolve from minimal or no worry, through personal or self-related concerns, then to concerns about managing the innovation's tasks, and finally to concerns about the innovation's effects.

The Stages of Concern Questionnaire (SoCQ) is the main tool used to determine an individual's current stage. This process appears developmental, as earlier concerns generally need to lessen before later ones increase. Research indicates this pattern applies to most innovations involving processes or products, although it is not guaranteed in every case.

Both the Stages of Concern (SoC) model and the concept of resistance to change are frameworks for understanding how individuals and groups respond - emotionally, cognitively, and behaviourally - to the introduction of new practices, innovations, or reforms, particularly in educational contexts. While each model is distinct, there are notable similarities and overlaps between them.

Using SoC surveys, professional development providers or school leaders can diagnose readiness, tailor support, and monitor progress during curriculum change. This approach highlights that successful implementation depends not only on technical competence but also on emotional and social processes (Fullan, 2016).

Timing and continuity in measurement

Determining optimal timing for measuring implementation is essential. Initial stages capture adoption challenges, teacher concerns, and early use of materials. Later stages reveal more about sustained practice, refinement, and ultimate impact on student learning. Longitudinal measurement provides insight into implementation evolution, helping to distinguish transient resistance from persistent barriers or enablers (Corbett & Rossman, 1989).

For example, evaluating after six months may diagnose initial adjustments and resource needs, while a year-on assessment can better gauge curriculum embedding and outcomes. In HE, where modules or programmes span semesters or years, continuous feedback loops ensure rapid responsiveness to emerging issues (Barnett & Coate, 2005).

Challenges in measuring implementation

Measuring curriculum implementation involves several inherent challenges:

- **Simultaneity of processes**: Curriculum materials, teaching practices, and learning activities occur simultaneously and influence each other, complicating efforts to isolate variables.

- **Contextual variability**: Different classrooms, schools, or institutions adapt curricula to diverse cultural, social, and learner needs, making standardised measurement problematic.

- **Attribution issues**: Linking student achievement or engagement exclusively to curriculum implementation, rather than other factors such as socioeconomic status or teacher quality, is difficult.

- **Data reliability**: Self-report measures may be biased by social desirability or misunderstanding. Observation can be intrusive and alter behaviour.

- **Resource intensiveness**: Comprehensive and repeated measures demand significant time, expertise, and funding.

Recognising these difficulties, evaluators increasingly favour mixed-method approaches, iterative measurement, and participatory evaluation involving teachers and learners as co-constructors of evidence (Priestley & Biesta, 2013).

Measuring implementation in different contexts

Primary education

In primary schools, measuring implementation often involves classroom observations focusing on teacher facilitation of active, developmental learning experiences in literacy, numeracy, and thematic areas. Assessment data from national tests and formative assessments provides objective measures of student progress. Portfolios, reading logs, and teacher journals supplement formal data with qualitative insights into learning processes (Alexander, 2021).

Teacher and parent feedback surveys offer valuable insights into how relevant and engaging the curriculum is for students, while also highlighting whether the specific needs of pupils with SEND and those learning English as an Additional Language (EAL) are being addressed effectively (DfE, 2014).

Secondary education

Secondary contexts integrate measurement of curriculum delivery across multiple subject areas and teacher teams. Observational protocols examine pedagogical strategies, differentiation, and use of resources. Assessment outcomes - GCSE, A-level results, or vocational qualifications - offer quantitative markers, while student voice exercises reveal engagement levels and perceived curriculum coherence (Whitty, 2010).

Teacher collaboration and leadership evaluations also gauge how subject teams manage curriculum alignment and adaptability (Leithwood et al., 2008).

Further education (FE)

FE measurement includes evaluation of practical skills acquisition alongside academic achievements. Observations and employer feedback on workplace learning components are critical. Learner portfolios, self-assessments, and attendance data help capture engagement and progression. Vocational relevance and employability outcomes are central performance indicators, with feedback loops between trainers, employers, and learners informing continuous improvement.

Higher education (HE)

HE prioritises measurement of curriculum delivery through student feedback surveys (e.g., NSS in the UK), qualitative peer review of teaching, and analysis of progression and employability statistics. Module evaluations assess the alignment of teaching methods with intended learning outcomes. Academic boards and external examiners monitor curriculum coherence and assessment integrity. Reflective teaching portfolios and scholarship of teaching and learning (SoTL) activities contribute to evidence of implementation quality (Barnett & Coate, 2005).

What do Ofsted say about implementation?

Ofsted shapes and defines expectations around curriculum implementation in England, exerting considerable influence from primary settings through to further education (FE) and, increasingly, higher education (HE) contexts. While its formal inspection remit focuses on schools and FE providers, Ofsted's frameworks and published commentary provide a widely-adopted lens for understanding and evaluating how curricula are put into practice.

Ofsted's framework and approach to implementation

Ofsted's Education Inspection Framework (EIF), first launched in 2019 and further developed in the years since, places curriculum implementation at the centre of quality judgments. Implementation is defined as "the curriculum in action" - not merely what is written, but how the intended curriculum is enacted in classrooms, workshops, and lecture spaces (Ofsted, 2019). Inspectors do not just focus on coverage of content, but closely examine depth, sequencing, teaching quality, and the extent to which implementation realises curricular intent in ways that support progression for all learners.

Crucially, Ofsted's focus is on whether the curriculum is "taught well through effective and consistent pedagogy", paying close attention to coherency, inclusivity, ambition, and practical adaptation for local needs (Ofsted, 2019).

Expectations in primary settings

In primary schools, Ofsted expects to see learning sequences that build foundational knowledge - particularly in reading, mathematics, and core subjects - delivered in a coherent and cumulative manner. Inspection priorities include:

- Strong, systematic teaching of phonics and early reading as a bedrock for future learning.
- Well-paced and differentiated instruction that addresses the needs of pupils with SEND, English as an Additional Language (EAL), and other vulnerabilities.
- Broad, concept-rich curricular experiences that develop curiosity and engage learners in meaningful contexts.
- Teachers making regular, formative assessments to adapt their practice responsively.

Inspectors look for clear evidence of curriculum coherence, purposeful sequencing, and staff confidence in delivering all required content areas (Ofsted, 2019).

Implementation in secondary and FE

For secondary schools, Ofsted's expectations shift towards:

- Subject specialists offering well-structured, progressively sequenced content that builds towards key assessment objectives (e.g. GCSE or A levels).

- Retaining subject breadth for as long as possible before qualification choices narrow the curriculum.

- Robust support for students who need additional help - through interventions or adapted teaching - while also offering challenge for the more able.

- Assessment practices that inform planning and support learners to progress, not just measure outcomes.

In FE, the focus is on the combination of academic and vocational content, delivered in ways aligned with qualification frameworks and labour market requirements. High-quality implementation demonstrates:

- Sequenced programmes that develop both technical and transferable skills.

- Teachers bringing together subject expertise with inclusive, adaptable teaching methods suitable for diverse and sometimes adult cohorts.

- Diagnostic assessment and timely support to address learning gaps or barriers.

- Responsiveness to employer and community needs, supporting progression to work or higher education.

Quality assurance and leadership

A notable Ofsted emphasis is on the role of leadership in securing effective implementation. Inspectors look for:

- Clear guidance and professional development enabling teachers to confidently enact the curriculum.

- Monitoring systems (such as lesson observations, work scrutiny, and pupil progress reviews) embedded within continuous quality assurance.

- Decision-making informed by data, professional expertise, and reflective practice - promoting ongoing curriculum adaptation where necessary.

Effective leadership is seen as setting the overall "tone" for successful curriculum implementation, ensuring that all staff clearly understand curriculum priorities and pedagogical expectations. Beyond communication, leaders actively foster a collaborative and positive school culture, build shared vision, and address challenges proactively. They provide timely, practical support, allocate the necessary resources, and model high expectations. By supporting professional growth and encouraging reflective practice, leaders ensure continuous improvement, effective adaptation to obstacles, and confidence among staff at all stages of implementation.

Measuring successful implementation

Ofsted bases judgments of implementation on multiple forms of evidence, including:

- Discussion with school and subject leaders about curriculum design, sequencing, and adaptation.
- Classroom observations evaluating how plans are enacted and how well teachers engage all pupils.
- Scrutiny of pupil work, assessment information, and tracking data to trace progression and identify impact.
- Documentation on how schools address statutory requirements and adapt provision for SEND, EAL, and disadvantaged students.

Crucially, Ofsted emphasises that effective implementation is not about mechanical consistency, but skilled adaptation - where practice matches intent, responds to feedback, and meets the evolving needs of learners.

Adaptation and context

Ofsted recognises that curriculum implementation must reflect local context, student cohorts, and particular community challenges. Schools are encouraged to customise their approaches - provided this does not undermine statutory breadth, progression, or ambition. For example, schools in areas of high linguistic diversity may focus greater early attention on vocabulary; FE colleges in areas of skill shortages may tailor curriculum pathways to employer demands. Inspectors seek evidence that such adaptations are strategic and lead to stronger outcomes for all groups of pupils.

Challenges and improvement priorities

Ofsted's inspection reports and research identify frequent implementation challenges, including:

- Narrowing the curriculum (reducing subject breadth too early in pursuit of performance data).
- Variable teaching quality, often linked to lack of training or poor curriculum leadership.
- Weak differentiation, risking some learners being left behind.

- Poor use of formative assessment, meaning teachers are less able to close gaps or extend learning.
- Gaps between intended and actual curriculum - where what is taught diverges from curriculum plans.

Schools and colleges are expected to address these through targeted professional development, leadership support, and robust monitoring systems (Ofsted, 2019).

Professional development and teaching quality

A strong message throughout Ofsted's publications is the primacy of high-quality teaching as the main vehicle for curriculum implementation. Regardless of how well the curriculum is designed, it only delivers pupil progression if teachers have the subject knowledge, pedagogical skill, and confidence to enact it effectively. Thus, the quality and regularity of staff training, peer support, and reflective practice are key inspection focuses. This is reiterated in Ofsted's own Annual Reports, which praise providers where "teachers adapt learning to the needs of their pupils and continually refine their practice according to evidence of what works" (Ofsted, 2021).

Ofsted and higher education

While Ofsted does not inspect universities, its frameworks do guide inspection of HE provision delivered in FE colleges. The underlying principles - coherence, progression, adaptation, inclusion, and responsiveness - are increasingly reflected in the Quality Assurance Agency (QAA) Quality Code and OfS (Office for Students) guidance for the sector. These frameworks expect providers to evidence how curriculum implementation supports progression and achievement for all student groups, including those with non-traditional backgrounds, SEND, or other additional needs (QAA, 2024).

Key messages and leadership implications

Ofsted's message is clear: curriculum implementation should embody ambition, high expectations, and inclusivity. To achieve this, leaders are expected to prioritise professional learning so that staff can implement curricula confidently and adaptively, while also monitoring and supporting implementation through both formal and informal review cycles. They are responsible for fostering a culture of reflection, collaboration, and continuous improvement, recognising that implementation is an ongoing, developmental process. Additionally, leaders should use research and evidence to guide the adoption of models, resources, and interventions best suited to their specific context.

Providers who can evidence that their curriculum is well-implemented, regularly reviewed, and improving in impact are more likely to be judged as offering high-quality education.

>  **Activity: Curriculum implementation audit and reflection**
> 1. Select a curriculum implementation scenario from your context or recent professional experience. This could be a new subject introduction, a shift to digital learning, or the rollout of a revised scheme of work.
> 2. Analyse the implementation process using the prompts below:
> - What factors supported or hindered successful implementation (e.g. leadership, resources, staff attitudes, external pressures)?
> - How did teachers adapt plans in response to learner feedback, challenges, or contextual changes?
> - What evidence was used to measure or evaluate implementation effectiveness?
> - How did digital tools or assessment practices shape experiences for teachers and learners?
> 3. Reflect on what was learned from the process and identify two changes that might improve future implementations.
> 4. Discussion: Share your findings with a colleague or peer group, comparing similarities and differences in implementation experiences across sectors or settings. Consider how your reflections could inform future planning or professional development.

Summary

Curriculum implementation is where vision meets classroom reality - a stage shaped by teacher expertise, institutional support, learner diversity, and technological innovation. Successful implementation depends on understanding the complexities of institutional cultures, engaging stakeholders, and responding flexibly to resistance or unforeseen challenges. Teachers play a pivotal role, designing learning experiences that are inclusive and vibrant, even as they adapt to evolving expectations and assessment practices.

Measuring and evaluating implementation in real time enables institutions to identify strengths, address obstacles, and ensure curriculum intentions are being fulfilled. With the expanding influence of digital tools and increased emphasis on evidence-based practice, effective curriculum implementation remains at the heart of educational success - demanding ongoing attention, support, and professional reflection.

7 CURRICULUM EVALUATION

Introduction

Evaluating curriculum is vital for understanding whether intended learning outcomes are being achieved, identifying strengths and areas for improvement, and ensuring the curriculum remains fit for purpose. Curriculum evaluation is not merely about accountability or external judgement - it permeates every level of educational practice, informing decision-making and supporting continuous development. Both summative and formative approaches have distinct roles: the former provides judgement on overall effectiveness and value, while the latter fuels ongoing refinement and professional learning.

Through the lens of *impact*, this chapter explores the theoretical underpinnings, tools, and models of curriculum evaluation, and considers how they operate in practice. It also examines Ofsted's expectations and practice regarding evaluation of curriculum impact.

This chapter

- Explores fundamental theories and purposes of curriculum evaluation.
- Examines the rationale for measuring curriculum impact at different levels of education.
- Distinguishes between summative and formative evaluation approaches, discussing their uses and limitations.
- Reviews key evaluation models and phases, including practical examples of their application.
- Considers the documentation and evidence generated during the evaluation process.
- Summarises current Ofsted expectations and practice regarding evaluation of curriculum impact.

Measuring impact

Evaluating the *impact* of the curriculum is a fundamental process in ensuring educational quality and improvement. Impact, in this context, refers to the degree to which intended learning outcomes are being achieved, and whether learners have acquired the expected knowledge, understanding, skills, and dispositions. Curriculum evaluation is both a theoretical field and a practical task, addressing questions not only of "did it work?" but also "how and for whom did it work?" and "how can we do better?" It provides crucial insights at all educational levels, and in all contexts, enabling leaders, teachers, and policymakers to make judicious decisions about ongoing curriculum development.

Theoretical foundations of curriculum evaluation

Curriculum evaluation has been shaped by a variety of philosophical and methodological approaches. The Tylerian tradition, arising from Ralph Tyler's influential work (1949), conceptualises evaluation as the process of measuring the extent to which educational objectives have been attained. This product-oriented approach, while foundational, has since been complemented by models that expand the scope of evaluation beyond test scores, encompassing the experiences of learners and the broader context in which learning takes place (Stufflebeam & Shinkfield, 2014).

Scriven's (1967) distinction between formative and summative evaluation was particularly influential, clarifying that evaluation is not simply about final judgments but has a vital role in supporting ongoing improvement. Stenhouse (1975) further advanced the case for a process-oriented evaluation, emphasising the significance of the learning journey, and arguing that teachers should act as curriculum evaluators - gathering and interpreting evidence from multiple sources.

Evaluation theory today recognises the need to balance quantitative evidence (such as attainment data) with qualitative insights (such as learner voice, classroom observation, and work scrutiny) to gain a holistic picture of impact (Kelly, 2009; Biesta, 2015).

The purpose of impact evaluation

The impact of the curriculum should be understood as more than just examination results or qualifications. As Ofsted's Education Inspection Framework (EIF, 2019) states, impact evaluation encompasses the whole learning journey, triangulating test data with first-hand evidence from observations, interviews, and documentation. Bromley (2021, p.74) usefully summarises the threefold purpose:

1. To evaluate the effectiveness of curriculum design.

2. To evaluate the effectiveness of curriculum implementation.

3. To evaluate the pace of pupil progress, outcomes, and learners' preparedness for their next steps.

This approach acknowledges that true impact includes not only how pupils perform at the point of final assessment, but also how well they are supported to thrive throughout and beyond the curriculum - socially, emotionally, and in terms of progression.

Impact evaluation in practice

Primary education:

In primary settings, evaluation of impact takes place at multiple stages. National tests (such as Key Stage 2 SATs in England) provide summative data, but schools also gather evidence from teacher assessments, learning journals, work samples, and formative standardised tests. Inspectors and leaders are increasingly interested in 'progression maps' that document how well pupils are accumulating critical knowledge and skills over time (Ofsted, 2019). Pupil voice - listening to children's perspectives on what and how they learn - offers important qualitative input about engagement and inclusivity.

Secondary education:

The secondary phase sees a shift to high-stakes public examinations (e.g., GCSEs, A-levels) as summative evaluative tools, but these are supplemented by internal tracking systems and monitoring of student work. Evaluation encompasses not only attainment and progress measures but also wider curriculum goals - such as developing personal agency, critical thinking, and readiness for post-16 study or employment. Departmental reviews, peer observations, and scrutiny of classwork or coursework portfolios all contribute to a rounded judgement of impact (Whitty, 2010; Ofsted, 2019).

Further education (FE):

Further Education (FE) impact evaluation places significant emphasis on both academic achievements and vocational outcomes, reflecting the sector's commitment to addressing diverse learner goals. While successful completion of qualifications remains a core indicator of effectiveness, evaluators also assess a broad range of evidence including portfolios of practical work, demonstrations of applied skills, and qualitative feedback from workplace mentors and employers. Crucially, progression rates into meaningful destinations - such as sustained employment, apprenticeships, or higher education - serve as vital metrics of success. These comprehensive measures underscore FE's close alignment with labour market needs and its essential role in equipping learners with the skills and competencies necessary for active participation in their communities and the wider economy.

Higher education (HE):

In HE, curriculum impact is evaluated through a combination of student attainment (degree classification, module marks), retention and progression data, employability and graduate destinations, and external review processes (such as QAA audits). Student surveys - including the National Student Survey (NSS) - offer additional, often critical, perspectives on the quality of the learning journey. Increasingly, institutions use portfolios, reflective accounts, and evidence of skill development across programmes to complement exam-based evaluation (Barnett & Coate, 2005; QAA, 2024).

The learning journey and staged impact evaluation

Impact evaluation is not merely an end-point activity. The learning journey can be conceptualised as a succession of stages - each of which should prepare learners for the next, and be assessed on its contribution to progression. For example, a well-sequenced primary mathematics curriculum tracks how foundational concepts build towards later mastery; a secondary science programme maps learning from core principles to advanced application in preparation for subject specialisms; a degree scheme ensures students develop baseline academic skills before progressing to research or industry placements.

At each transition point, evidence is gathered to confirm that learners are well equipped for subsequent challenges - whether that be moving between Key Stages, transitioning from school to college, or progressing from undergraduate to postgraduate study.

Triangulation of evidence: balancing data sources

High-quality impact evaluation draws on multiple forms of evidence, recognising the limitations of any single source. While standardised assessments are useful benchmarks, Ofsted and evaluative theorists highlight the importance of triangulating these with:

- **Work scrutiny:** Examining samples of pupil work to evaluate depth, progression, and consistency.

- **Observational data:** Analysing teaching and learning interactions, classroom climate, and student engagement.

- **Interviews and student voice:** Gathering qualitative evidence on how learners are experiencing the curriculum in practice.

- **Documentary review:** Reviewing schemes of work, assessment records, and other planning materials for coherence and intent.

Triangulation guards against over-reliance on test data, enabling evaluators to capture aspects such as creativity, collaboration, or resilience that formal metrics might miss (Ofsted, 2019; Priestley & Biesta, 2013).

Responsive and developmental evaluation

Curriculum evaluation must also support continuous development. Formative approaches - built into everyday teaching, departmental meetings, and programme reviews - enable rapid responses to emerging challenges and promote ongoing professional growth (Black & Wiliam, 2009). Summative evaluation provides accountability and strategic direction, but formative cycles drive quality improvement and innovation over time.

This distinction is vital across all educational tiers. For example, in FE and HE, module or course reviews allow for iterative refinement based on student feedback, assessment analysis, and employer or accreditor input. In primary and secondary schools, lesson study and collaborative planning sessions foster shared reflection and adaptive curriculum improvement.

Theory into practice: Challenges and future prospects

Despite the centrality of impact evaluation, significant challenges remain. These include:

- The risk of focusing too narrowly on quantifiable outcomes at the expense of broader educational aims (Biesta, 2015).
- Difficulty in attributing changes in pupil outcomes to curriculum modifications as opposed to other variables.
- Ensuring that evaluation tools are fit for diverse learner needs, especially in inclusive or multidisciplinary contexts.

Summative and formative evaluation

Evaluation includes both summative and formative approaches, each essential for assessing and enhancing educational quality across all levels. Summative evaluation typically measures outcomes at the end of a learning period, providing overall judgements, while formative evaluation occurs continuously to offer timely feedback. Together, they help educators monitor effectiveness, guide improvements, and support the ongoing development of curriculum and teaching practices.

Summative evaluation

Summative evaluation (Figure 7.1) is conducted after a curriculum, course, module, or programme has been implemented. Its primary function is to determine whether predetermined goals and learning outcomes have been achieved (Scriven, 1967; Stufflebeam & Shinkfield, 2007). This 'reactive' form of evaluation typically takes place at the end of an instructional period - such as the conclusion of a school year, a module in FE, or a trimester in HE. Summative evaluation may be carried out immediately or several months to years after implementation, depending on institutional review cycles.

Typical evidence used in summative evaluation includes national examination results such as Key Stage tests, GCSEs, and A-levels, as well as final grades earned in FE assignments and degree classifications awarded in higher education. However, summative evaluation extends beyond formal testing; it also incorporates data gathered from course-completion surveys, feedback collected during external inspections like Ofsted reports, and comprehensive programme reviews. These varied sources contribute to building a holistic judgement of curriculum effectiveness, providing insights into both learner achievement and the quality of educational provision (Barnett & Coate, 2005).

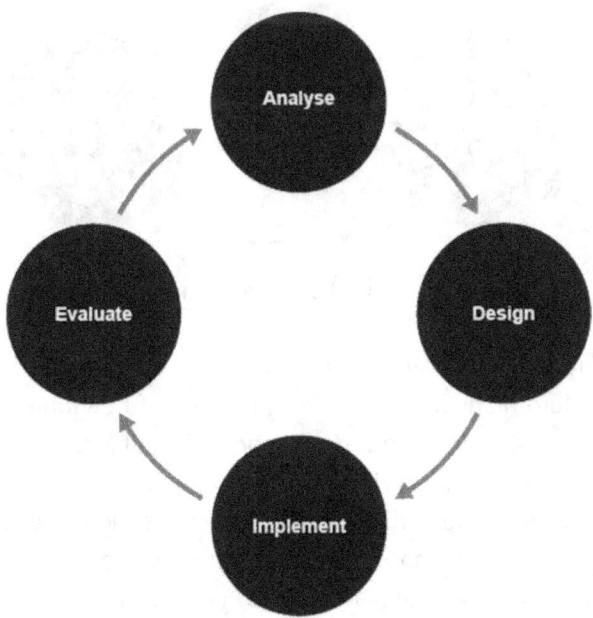

Figure 7.1 - Summative curriculum evaluation

The key limitation of summative evaluation is its timing - it evaluates after the event - providing useful evidence to inform future iterations of the curriculum but often too late to impact current learners directly (Scriven, 1967). It is most closely associated with improvement to overall teaching and learning, rather than immediate responsiveness within the delivery phase.

Formative evaluation

Formative evaluation (Figure 7.2), by contrast, is proactive and occurs throughout the development and delivery of curriculum, aiming to provide timely feedback for adjustment and enhancement (Black & Wiliam, 2009). It supports ongoing curriculum formation by identifying mismatches, gaps, or areas for development - such as learning outcomes that are not matched by appropriate activities or assessments.

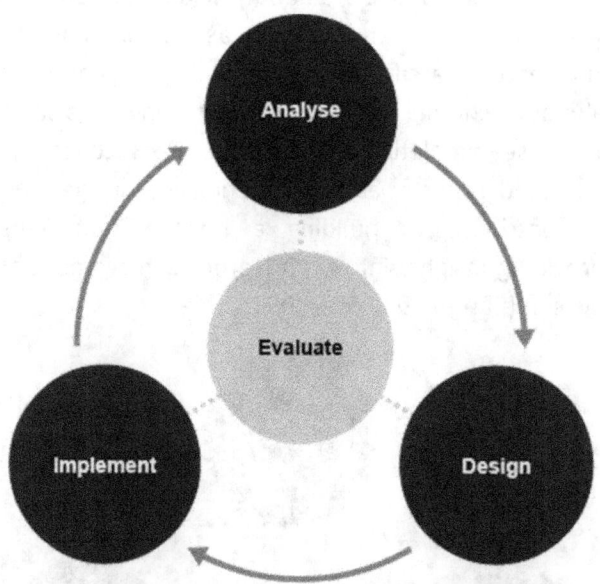

Figure 7.2 - Formative curriculum evaluation

Formative evaluation is highly iterative and collaborative. It can involve expert review of curriculum plans prior to rollout, piloting of new units or materials with representative groups, and structured collection of feedback from both learners and staff. For example, teachers in primary schools may adjust sequences of activities mid-term in response to pupils' difficulties or misconceptions, while in HE, formative module evaluation surveys enable real-time alteration of content or pedagogical approach (Barnett & Coate, 2005; Priestley & Biesta, 2013).

Critically, formative evaluation "connects" to all stages of curriculum development, from initial planning through to in-class adjustment: its evidence helps not only to refine teaching and learning as it happens, but also to inform future curriculum design and resource development.

Application across settings

In primary and secondary settings, formative evaluation is embedded in ongoing assessment for learning, lesson studies, and peer observation; summative evaluation underpins year-end reporting and statutory accountability. In FE, formative approaches include workplace feedback or continuous portfolio review, while summative evaluation might take the form of graded practical assessments. In HE, formative mechanisms (such as ongoing self- and peer-assessment and course feedback) complement summative evaluation via examinations, dissertations, and external review.

Complementary roles

Both forms of evaluation are vital: formative evaluation enables agile, student-focused improvement, while summative evaluation ensures accountability and broad curricular effectiveness (Stufflebeam & Shinkfield, 2014; Black & Wiliam, 2009). Effective educational institutions use both to promote excellence, responsiveness, and sustained impact.

Evaluation models

As curriculum evaluation has developed as both a field of theory and a practical necessity, numerous models have emerged to guide how educational impact, quality, and improvement are assessed across all phases of education. Each model provides a conceptual framework that helps evaluators navigate the complex process of judging curriculum effectiveness, whether the focus is on primary, secondary, further, or higher education. These models range from the outcome-oriented, objectives-based approach of Tyler, to process-focused frameworks that prioritise ongoing improvement and responsiveness, such as the CIPP model. Other widely used perspectives - like Stake's Countenance Model, Scriven's Goal-Free Evaluation, and qualitative models such as Eisner's Educational Connoisseurship - extend the possibilities for evaluating curriculum by incorporating stakeholder perspectives, context, and deeper layers of learner experience.

The selection of evaluation models is far from incidental; each brings certain strengths and limitations, shapes the questions that are asked, and frames the kind of evidence that is collected and valued. While some models emphasise predetermined objectives and measurable outcomes, others encourage attention to stakeholder needs, programme context, process fidelity, or even the unintended consequences of curriculum change. In practice, many institutions draw on a combination of models to address different evaluation purposes - using, for example, Tyler for accountability, CIPP for programme improvement, and Stake or Scriven for responsive and participatory evaluation.

By considering a range of models, educators, leaders, and policymakers are better equipped to engage with the complexity of curriculum evaluation - choosing and combining approaches that best fit their local context, aims, and values. This section introduces and situates several major and emerging models, establishing a solid foundation for understanding and critically applying curriculum evaluation in diverse educational settings

Tyler's objectives model of curriculum evaluation

Ralph Tyler's objectives model, developed in the 1940s, remains one of the foundational frameworks for curriculum evaluation across all educational stages, from primary to higher education (Tyler, 1949). Central to this model is the idea that curriculum evaluation should assess how well educational objectives - clearly stated and carefully designed in advance - have been achieved. This approach emphasises a logical and systematic process linking objectives, instruction, and assessment, aimed primarily at determining whether intended learning outcomes have been attained.

In practice, Tyler's objectives model tends to be outcome-focused, privileging clearly articulated, measurable objectives as the primary criteria for evaluating success. In primary education, this translates into setting specific learning targets - for example, pupils should be able to read a particular list of words or solve certain types of mathematical problems by the end of a term - and using assessment data to evaluate progress against these criteria (Alexander, 2021). The model supports careful alignment between stated objectives, teaching sequences, and assessment tasks.

In secondary schools, where curricula are often subject-specific and compartmentalised, Tyler's approach provides a useful framework for ensuring that schemes of work and assessment regimes coherently measure the attainment of syllabic objectives. For instance, GCSE and A-level specifications naturally lend themselves to objective-based evaluation, with exams testing achievement against defined learning outcomes (Whitty, 2010). However, there is an ongoing debate over the extent to which an overly rigid application of objectives might narrow curriculum breadth or restrict pedagogical creativity (Wiggins & McTighe, 2011).

In further education (FE), Tyler's model continues to underpin many vocational qualifications and competency frameworks, where the focus lies on demonstrable skills and competencies aligned to industry standards. The clear articulation of learning objectives enables targeted assessment and efficient recognition of prior learning, which is essential for diverse FE cohorts with varying prior experiences. Yet, practitioners often stress the importance of complementing objectives with an emphasis on learners' broader developmental needs and employability skills, which Tyler's model may insufficiently capture.

Within higher education (HE), the model's influence persists predominantly in programme specification and module design, where intended learning outcomes provide a scaffold for curriculum development and quality assurance (Barnett & Coate, 2005). However, HE increasingly integrates more expansive evaluations, considering not only the attainment of cognitive outcomes but also aspects such as critical thinking, research engagement, and graduate attributes. This expansion reflects critiques of purely objectives-based approaches as overly reductionist for complex, higher-level learning (Knight & Yorke, 2003).

Despite critiques, Tyler's objectives model remains valuable for its clarity and structure. It emphasises accountability and intentionality, helping educators systematically link intended outcomes with instruction and assessment. Nonetheless, modern curriculum evaluation increasingly combines Tyler's logically sequenced framework with more flexible and formative approaches to address the dynamic and contextual nature of learning (Priestley & Biesta, 2013).

Stake's Countenance Model

Stake's Countenance Model, developed by Robert Stake in the late 1960s, is a prominent and influential framework for curriculum evaluation used across educational contexts. Renowned for its comprehensive and holistic perspective, the model addresses the complexities and nuances of curriculum processes by using both systematic description and critical judgment. Unlike models that focus solely on objectives and outcomes, such as Tyler's, Stake's model incorporates context, process, and stakeholder perspectives, allowing for a richer evaluation of educational programmes.

Core Structure: Description and judgment

At its heart, the Countenance Model distinguishes between two principal dimensions or "countenances": *description* and *judgment*. In the descriptive phase, evaluators gather detailed information about the curriculum as planned (intent) and as enacted (observed) across three domains:

- *Antecedents*: The conditions or inputs prior to implementation. In a primary context, this might include teacher background, resources, student readiness, or school culture. In HE, antecedents might encompass institutional mission, entry requirements, and available infrastructure.

- *Transactions*: The actual processes and activities during implementation - the teaching methods, student interactions, and learning experiences. For example, classroom dynamics, modes of instruction, and assessment methods.

- *Outcomes*: The results or consequences of the curriculum, including measurable achievements, skills, attitudinal changes, and broader educational impacts.

After mapping these descriptive elements, the model introduces a *judgmental matrix* (Table 7.1).

Dimension	Description / Intent	Observed Implementation	Quality Standard / Criteria	Sample Judgments / Comments
Antecedents	Pre-conditions, resources, teacher readiness, student characteristics	Accessibility and adequacy of resources, teacher qualifications, student readiness evident in practice	National curriculum requirements, institutional policies, staff training norms	Adequate materials; staff need further training for EAL learners
Transactions	Pedagogical methods, engagement strategies, learning interactions	Classroom observations, student engagement, use of learning activities	Best practice pedagogy, inclusive teaching strategies	Mostly effective use of hands-on activities, but inconsistent differentiation
Outcomes	Learning results, skills acquisition, attitudes	Assessment results, pupil work, student feedback	Achievement benchmarks, expected skill development	Student progress strong in literacy; numeracy lags in some groups

Table 7.1 - Stake's judgmental matrix

Using the matrix, evaluators assess the degree of congruence between what was intended and what actually occurred, and apply relevant standards to make judgments about quality or success. This twofold approach helps ensure evaluations are not only rich in data but also meaningful in their implications for improvement.

Application in context

In primary settings, Stake's model can be employed to evaluate how well a new literacy programme is being implemented. Evaluators might examine the initial resources and teacher expertise (antecedents), observe how lessons are delivered and how students interact with new materials (transactions), and then assess changes in reading fluency or attitudes to books (outcomes). Judgments are made regarding how closely observed practices and outcomes match the educator's or policymakers' intentions, as well as accepted educational standards.

In secondary schools and FE, the model is used to track both process and outcome. For instance, when a new science curriculum is introduced, antecedents might include prior student attainment and resource allocation; transactions involve classroom experiments and teaching style; outcomes are seen in knowledge gains, exam performance, and student engagement. As FE provision is often more diverse, involving adult and vocational learners, the model's flexibility for stakeholder input (including employers, teachers, and learners) is especially valued.

In HE, Stake's model is applicable when evaluating degree programmes or modules. Antecedents include programme specifications and staff qualifications, transactions comprise modes of delivery (lectures, seminars, practical work), and outcomes span degree results, skills acquisition, and employability measures. The model's particular strength here lies in accommodating both quantifiable outcomes and qualitative experiences, such as student satisfaction or learning community development.

Qualitative and responsive orientation

A hallmark of Stake's Countenance Model is its *responsive orientation*. Evaluation includes the concerns and perspectives of multiple stakeholders, often using interviews, observations, and documentary analysis to capture diverse voices (e.g., students, teachers, leaders, employers). This approach fosters a more participatory and democratic evaluation, where findings are not only reported but actively shared and contextualised for practical use.

Strengths

- *Accommodates complexity*: Suitable for diverse, multi-layered curricula.
- *Stakeholder involvement*: Gives voice to those directly affected by curriculum changes.
- *Balance of data*: Integrates qualitative and quantitative information, enabling richer interpretation of congruence and discrepancy.

- *Practicality*: Useful for formative as well as summative evaluation, supporting continuous improvement.

Limitations

- Can be demanding in terms of time, data collection, and analytic expertise.
- The subjective element in interpretive judgment means evaluations can be influenced by evaluator bias unless carefully managed.

Stufflebeam's CIPP curriculum evaluation model

Stufflebeam's curriculum evaluation model, also known as the CIPP model, provides a comprehensive framework for systematically assessing educational programmes at all levels - from primary education to higher education (Stufflebeam & Shinkfield, 2014). Distinct from traditional product-oriented approaches that focus primarily on outcomes, the CIPP model (Figure 7.3) embraces a holistic view concerned with *Context*, *Input*, *Process*, and *Product*, making it highly adaptable and practical across diverse educational settings.

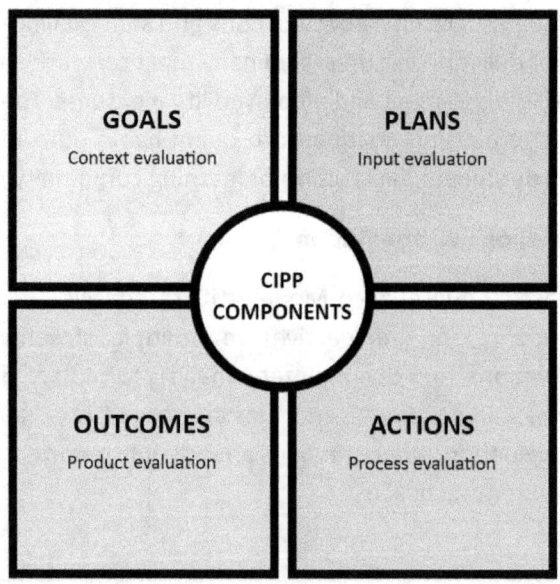

Figure 7.3 - Stufflebeam's curriculum evaluation model (CIPP)

The *Context* component involves assessing the environment in which the curriculum operates. This includes analysing the needs of learners, institutional conditions, socio-economic factors, and policy frameworks that shape curriculum design. For example, in a primary school, context evaluation might explore pupil demographics, community resources, and national curriculum mandates. In higher education, it could include analysing disciplinary standards, student diversity, and market demands for graduate skills (Barnett & Coate, 2005; Kelly, 2009).

The *Input* evaluation focuses on the resources, strategies, and plans used to implement the curriculum. This phase assesses the adequacy of teaching materials, staff qualifications, funding, and infrastructural support, as well as curriculum structure and design. For instance, in FE, input evaluation might involve reviewing vocational training resources, employer partnerships, and formal qualification documentation. In secondary education, this could mean determining if departments have sufficient expertise and sequencing strategies to deliver the curriculum effectively.

Process evaluation examines the actual implementation of the curriculum - how teaching and learning unfold in practice. This includes observing classroom dynamics, instructional methods, assessment procedures, and learner engagement. Process data inform whether planned activities are realised as intended and identify potential obstacles or innovations as they occur. Within HE, process evaluation might comprise peer reviews of teaching or analysis of blended learning approaches, while in primary settings, it might involve looking at teaching of literacy skills or differentiation strategies (Alexander, 2021; Priestley & Biesta, 2013).

Finally, the *Product* evaluation considers the outcomes of the curriculum. This goes beyond just test scores or final grades to include wider measurements of impact such as learner progression, skills development, attitudes, and long-term readiness for further education or employment. For example, product evaluation in secondary schools includes GCSE outcomes but also considers personal development and engagement. In FE, progression rates into apprenticeships or employment provide crucial data, while in HE, graduate employability, research outputs, and student satisfaction surveys contribute to understanding product effectiveness (Barnett & Coate, 2005; QAA, 2024).

A key strength of Stufflebeam's model lies in its *formative and summative utility*: it not only facilitates ongoing feedback for improvement (formative) but also informs high-stakes decisions about curriculum efficacy and accountability (summative) (Stufflebeam & Shinkfield, 2014). By engaging multiple stakeholders - including learners, teachers, administrators, and external partners - the model fosters a participatory and inclusive evaluation culture. This characteristic makes it particularly suitable for complex educational environments where contextual factors and process dynamics are critical.

In practice, educational institutions often customise the CIPP model to their unique settings. For instance, primary schools may emphasise context and process evaluation to monitor inclusivity and engagement, while higher education providers might focus more on input quality and product impact, aligned with academic standards and employability frameworks. Further education colleges frequently integrate employer feedback into both input and product evaluation phases to ensure vocational relevance.

Despite its comprehensive nature, challenges using the CIPP model include the intensive data collection and analysis it demands and the requirement for evaluators to synthesise diverse data forms into coherent judgments, calling for skilled leadership and collaborative effort (Priestley & Biesta, 2013).

Overall, Stufflebeam's CIPP model offers a flexible, robust framework for curriculum evaluation that promotes continuous improvement and stakeholder engagement. Its emphasis on multiple dimensions - from situational analysis through implementation to outcomes - makes it highly relevant for exploring curriculum quality in varied educational contexts, supporting practitioners and policymakers in making informed, context-sensitive decisions.

The Kirkpatrick model of curriculum evaluation

The Kirkpatrick model, initially developed in the 1950s by Donald Kirkpatrick, remains one of the most widely recognised frameworks for evaluating training and educational programmes. Although originally conceived to assess corporate training effectiveness, it has since been adapted successfully across educational sectors (Kirkpatrick & Kirkpatrick, 2016). The model (Figure 7.4) provides a systematic, four-level approach that enables educators and leaders to evaluate both immediate and longer-term effects of a curriculum or learning intervention.

The Kirkpatrick model, originally developed by Donald Kirkpatrick and updated in 2016, provides a systematic, multi-level framework for evaluating the effectiveness of training and educational programs beyond end-of-course assessments. It is structured around four levels: learner reactions, knowledge and skill acquisition, observable behavioural change, and ultimate results or impact at organisational or individual level.

This hierarchy highlights how satisfaction and engagement facilitate meaningful learning and practical skill application. The model connects immediate gains to longer-term outcomes - including academic achievement, workplace performance, and employability—and is widely adopted for capturing both short- and long-term learning impacts.

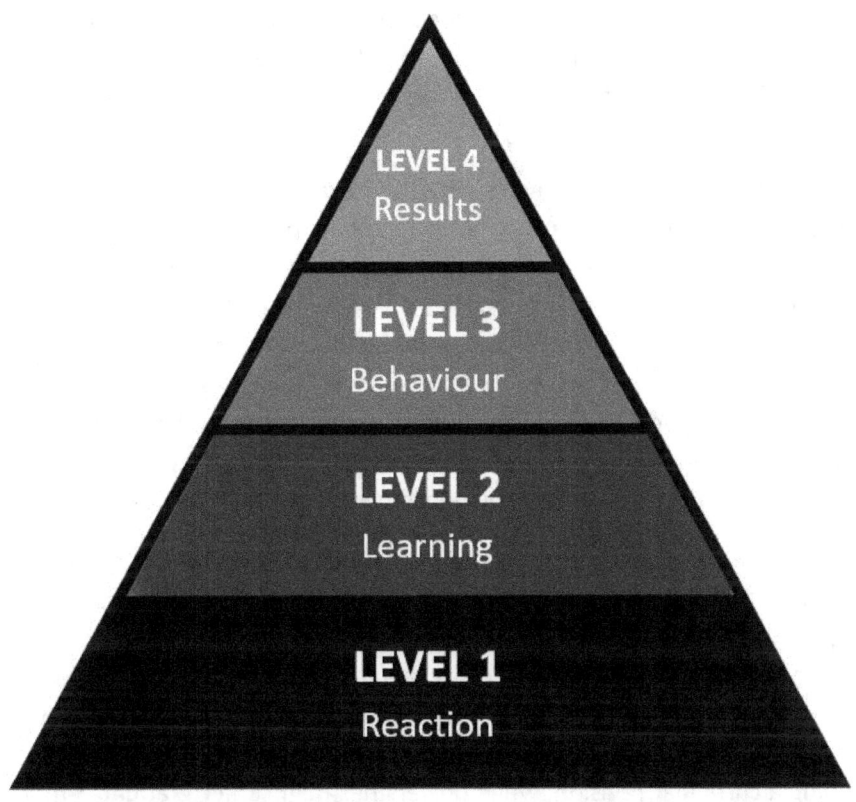

Figure 7.4 - Kirkpatrick's four level approach to curriculum evaluation

Overview of the four levels

Level 1 - Reaction: The first level concerns learners' immediate responses to their educational experience. It gauges how learners perceive the curriculum or training - whether they find it engaging, relevant, and well delivered. Reaction data are typically collected via surveys, focus groups, or informal feedback. In primary education, for example, pupil enjoyment and interest in a literacy programme might be assessed through age-appropriate questionnaires or teacher observations. In HE, student evaluation of teaching surveys (SETs) serve a similar purpose, providing insight into learner satisfaction (Kirkpatrick & Kirkpatrick, 2016; Barnett & Coate, 2005).

Level 2 - Learning: This level evaluates the degree to which learners have acquired the intended knowledge, skills, attitudes, or competencies. Assessment methods range from formative quizzes and tests in schools to practical demonstrations in FE and comprehensive academic assessments in HE. Learning evaluation focuses on whether the curriculum has equipped students with the capabilities necessary to meet its intended objectives. For instance, in secondary science, pre- and post-tests in data interpretation might reveal gains attributable to a new module. In FE, successful completion of competency-based units can serve as learning evidence (Black & Wiliam, 2009; Kelly, 2009).

Level 3 - Behaviour: Level 3 assesses whether learners apply what they have learned when they return to their learning or professional environments. This behavioural change dimension is crucial in bridging the gap between learning and performance. In a primary school setting, this may involve examining whether pupils can transfer newly learnt mathematical reasoning to problem-solving in different contexts. In FE and HE, it concerns assessing whether students apply skills - such as communication, teamwork, or technical proficiencies - in placements, internships, or further courses (Kirkpatrick & Kirkpatrick, 2016). Observations, interviews, and workplace supervisor reports often form the evidence base for behaviour change.

Level 4 - Results (Impact): The final level examines the broader outcomes or results stemming from curriculum implementation. This includes indicators such as improved examination results, progression rates, graduate employability, and institutional reputation. At this level, evaluators attempt to link the educational intervention to organisational goals, community benefits, or student empowerment. For example, a secondary school might analyse GCSE statistics over multiple years following a curricular revision, while universities might track graduate employment or postgraduate study uptake. This level is the most challenging to isolate causally, given the multitude of influencing factors, yet it remains vital for strategic decision-making (Kirkpatrick & Kirkpatrick, 2016; QAA, 2024).

Application across educational sectors

Primary Education: Kirkpatrick's model emphasises the initial levels of reaction and learning to ensure that young learners find the curriculum engaging, accessible, and developmentally appropriate. Assessment of pupil behaviour and progress involves a combination of teacher-led formative assessments, standardised national tests, and monitoring of developmental milestones. This ongoing formative monitoring throughout the academic year allows for timely adjustments, while high-stakes assessments at key stages provide cumulative data that inform broader evaluations of curriculum impact (Ofsted, 2019; Alexander, 2021).

Secondary Education: All four levels apply distinctly. Learner reaction is gauged via pupil voice surveys and classroom observations, learning assessed through regular testing, behavioural changes monitored by transferability of skills and classroom application, and results measured through public examinations, attendance, and progression data. The model's comprehensive scope aligns well with inspection regimes and departmental quality reviews (Whitty, 2010; Kelly, 2009).

Further Education (FE): FE's vocational and diverse learner populations benefit significantly from Kirkpatrick's model, especially Levels 3 and 4. Reaction data include learner satisfaction with relevance and delivery, learning verified through competency assessments, behaviour evidenced in workplace placements, and results shown by employment rates or progression to further study. Employers' feedback often contributes to capturing real-world behavioural outcomes.

Higher Education (HE): In HE, Level 1 evaluations commonly take the form of module evaluations or SETs, Level 2 involves explicit assessment of learning outcomes, Level 3 indexes students' application of knowledge in complex academic tasks or internships, and Level 4 tracks long-term graduate success and societal contribution. The model complements other quality assurance frameworks, such as those advocated by the Quality Assurance Agency (QAA) (Barnett & Coate, 2005; QAA, 2024).

Strengths and limitations

The Kirkpatrick model's key strength lies in its intuitive, staged approach that connects learner experience directly with organisational impact. It encourages multifaceted data collection and links short-term learning to sustained change. Moreover, its adaptability across sectors and contexts enhances its usefulness as a common evaluative language.

However, the model has been critiqued for assuming a linear progression between levels, which may oversimplify complex educational dynamics. Challenges also arise in reliably measuring behaviour and results, particularly attributing long-term impact causally to curriculum changes alone. Additionally, focusing heavily on learner reaction risks overemphasising satisfaction over learning quality (Scriven, 1991; Whitmore, 1998).

The Kirkpatrick model remains a foundational framework for curriculum evaluation across educational sectors despite some critiques. Its multi-layered approach evaluates immediate learner reactions, ongoing learning, behavioural changes, and broader institutional outcomes. This comprehensive structure provides educators and leaders with a practical guide to assess curriculum effectiveness holistically. When integrated with qualitative insights and adapted to specific educational contexts, the model facilitates responsive, nuanced, and comprehensive curriculum improvement, supporting continuous enhancement aligned with learners' needs and institutional goals. This flexible application makes it a valuable tool in diverse settings.

Eisner's educational connoisseurship

Elliot Eisner's model of educational connoisseurship and criticism offers a distinctive, arts-based approach to curriculum evaluation that emphasises the qualitative, experiential, and interpretive dimensions of educational practice. Developed initially in the context of arts education, Eisner's framework has since informed curriculum evaluation across all educational contexts, particularly where understanding the subtleties of classroom life, pedagogy, and learning environment is valued alongside measurable outcomes (Eisner, 2017).

Theoretical basis and key concepts

Central to Eisner's model is the metaphor of the 'connoisseur' - an individual who, through education, training, experience, and heightened perception, can notice, appreciate, and interpret the complex qualities present in a given situation. Just as an art connoisseur discerns subtle distinctions in a painting, the educational connoisseur observes, recognises, and values the nuances of curriculum enactment, pedagogical interactions, and classroom culture (Eisner, 2017).

Proponents argue that connoisseurship is not merely subjective opinion; instead, it is grounded in refined discrimination, disciplined observation, and professional judgement. This mode of curriculum evaluation assumes that much of what is meaningful in education - creativity, classroom atmosphere, learner motivation, and subtle acts of teaching - is not easily captured by checklists or test scores (Greene, 2013). Instead, evaluation must attend to qualitative textures and broader educational values.

Accompanying connoisseurship is the idea of 'educational criticism', which involves not just noticing and interpreting, but sharing these insights with others through thick, evocative description and reflection. In this way, educational criticism aims to make the "invisible visible", helping educators, leaders, and stakeholders see what is otherwise overlooked and engage in richer conversation about quality and values (Eisner, 2017).

Application in different educational contexts

Primary education: In primary settings, Eisner's model is particularly suited to the evaluation of learning experiences that are holistic, creative, and affective. A connoisseur might enter a classroom to observe the tone of a story-telling session, the quality of student interactions during art projects, or the way teachers respond to spontaneous curiosity. Rather than counting how many students met a set objective, the evaluator describes the atmosphere, engagement, and subtle learning signals that may indicate deep understanding or inclusion (Eisner, 2017).

Secondary education: At the secondary level, educational connoisseurship can illuminate complex aspects of classroom dynamics or curricular richness, such as how teachers blend subject knowledge with passion, or how school culture is conveyed through routines and relationships. For example, it might be used to evaluate the climate of a geography department, or the sense of belonging fostered in a literature class, which standard metrics may ignore.

Further education (FE): In FE, where vocational and adult learning contexts prevail, connoisseurship recognises the value of context-sensitive, relational teaching and the often-tacit transmission of skills and attitudes within workshops or work placements. Evaluators using Eisner's approach notice not only technical skill mastery but also emerging professional identity, social integration, and the authenticity of practical experiences - elements vital for holistic learner development.

Higher education (HE): In higher education, Eisner's model is especially valuable for evaluating teaching and learning in disciplines where interpretive, creative, or dialogic processes are central - for instance, the studio critique in fine art, discussion-based seminars in literature, or immersive fieldwork in anthropology (Barnett & Coate, 2005). Educational connoisseurship enables evaluators to capture the nuance and quality of teaching practices that are not easily quantified. It supports rigorous peer review, informed teaching observation and curriculum innovation, fostering a deeper appreciation for the rich pedagogic diversity and cultural vibrancy found within academic communities.

Process and practicalities

Eisner recommends a four-step process for educational criticism:

1. *Description:* Rich, textured narrative capturing the environment, process, and interactions.

2. *Interpretation:* Explaining the significance of what is observed, drawing on educational theory and professional judgement.

3. *Evaluation:* Making informed judgements about quality, value, or effectiveness in relation to educational aims and values.

4. *Thematics:* Identifying broader lessons, themes, or implications for policy, practice, or further inquiry (Eisner, 2017).

 A primary school evaluator may describe a classroom's democratic ethos during inquiry-based science, interpret how this shapes inclusivity, evaluate its alignment with school values, and discuss themes pertinent to other classrooms or policy levels.

Strengths and critiques

Eisner's model is praised for recognising that curriculum evaluation is not solely about what can be measured but also about what can be meaningfully understood, celebrated, or improved. It values professional artistry and the moral, creative, and affective elements of education that are too often 'lost in translation' in data-driven accounts (Biesta, 2015).

Critics caution that connoisseurship risks subjectivity or elitism if not anchored in transparency and critical collegial dialogue (Kelly, 2009). Eisner responds that robust connoisseurship involves explicit demonstration of interpretive processes and invites multiple perspectives, making professional judgement open to scrutiny and shared improvement.

Overall, educational connoisseurship invites curriculum evaluators to embrace the complexity, subtlety, and artistry of teaching and learning - across all educational sectors - complementing quantitative models with a rich, contextual, and humane form of curriculum evaluation.

Comparison of evaluation models

Table 7.2 offers a concise comparison of the five prominent evaluation models - Tyler's Objectives Model, Stake's Countenance Model, Stufflebeam's CIPP Model, the Kirkpatrick Model, and Eisner's Educational Connoisseurship. This comparison highlights their principal focus, evaluation approach, data types typically used, main strengths, key limitations, and common use cases across primary, secondary, further, and higher education.

Each curriculum evaluation model embodies distinct theoretical foundations and practical purposes, influencing how evaluation is approached across educational contexts. Models like Tyler's focus on the precise definition, articulation, and measurement of objectives, favouring quantifiable and outcome-driven evidence to ascertain curriculum success. In contrast, Eisner's and Stake's models embrace qualitative, interpretive methods that prioritise the richness and complexity of real educational experiences and contexts. Stufflebeam's CIPP and the Kirkpatrick Model offer expansive, multi-layered frameworks that track the entire evaluation process - from initial learner engagement through to broader institutional or societal impact.

Understanding these differences equips educators and leaders to select, tailor, or integrate evaluation models according to their specific goals, settings, and stakeholder priorities.

Model and focus	Approach	Data types	Main strengths	Limitations	Typical use
Tyler's Objectives Model Clear, measurable objectives and achievement	Linear and rational	Quantitative, mainly - test results, assessments	Provides clear linkage between objectives, instruction, outcomes	Can be rigid and reductionist, less suited to complex learning	Primary to HE for assessing attainment
Stake's Countenance Model Description and judgment of curriculum and context	Responsive, mostly qualitative	Qualitative & quantitative - observations, interviews, "thick descriptions"	Captures complexity and context, involves stakeholders	Time-consuming, potential subjective bias	Broad use in all educational stages for holistic evaluations
Stufflebeam's CIPP Model Context, Input, Process, Product	Systematic, comprehensive	Mixed methods - surveys, stats, qualitative data	Addresses multiple phases, supports formative & summative use	Resource intensive, complexity in data integration	Comprehensive institutional and programme evaluation
Kirkpatrick Model Learner Reaction, Learning, Behaviour, Results	Hierarchical and outcome oriented	Quantitative and qualitative - surveys, performance data	Links satisfaction to learning and real-world application	Assumes linear progression; challenging to attribute impact	Training, professional development, and curriculum impact assessment
Eisner's Educational Connoisseurship Qualitative connoisseurship and criticism	Artistic, interpretive	Predominantly qualitative - rich narratives and observations	Illuminates nuanced, often overlooked learning experiences	Potentially subjective, difficult to standardise	Useful for arts, creative disciplines, reflective professional development

Table 7.2 - Comparison of evaluation models

This comparison underlines that no single model suffices for all situations. Rigorous curriculum evaluation often requires a combination of approaches, enabling both accountability through measurable objectives and meaningful improvement through rich, context-sensitive understanding. Selecting the appropriate model - or blend of models - should reflect the purposes, values, and unique challenges of each educational setting.

Phases of evaluation

Whatever the model, evaluation tends to be carried out in a number of phases (Figure 7.5).

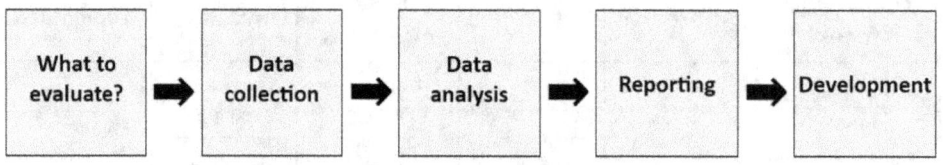

Figure 7.5 - Five phases of evaluation

1. Aspects of the curriculum to be evaluated

The evaluator determines what is to be evaluated. This may be an institute-wide or departmental evaluation, though it is more likely to be a particular programme, a particular course or a particular subject.

2. Data collection

Identify the information to be collected and the tools for collecting the data. This may involve interviews, questionnaires, tests, collection of documents and so forth. The evaluator also identifies the people from whom data is to be collected.

3. Data analysis

The data collected is analysed and presented in the form of tables and graphs. Statistical tools are often used to compare significant differences, and to establish correlation or relationship between variables.

4. Reporting

Reports are written describing the findings and interpretation of the data. Based on the findings, conclusions are made on the effectiveness of curriculum implementation efforts. Recommendations are made to reconsider certain aspects of the curriculum.

5. Development

The curriculum / objectives are modified to address any issues raised by the data analysis, and to make improvements based on the recommendations.

Periodicity of evaluation

The periodicity of evaluation depends upon the stage of development. During initial implementation, evaluation tends to be more frequent. Checks and balances applied at monthly, 3-monthly and 6-monthly intervals are not uncommon. Once the curriculum becomes established, evaluation usually takes place cyclically. A typical cycle will be yearly or each time a programme / course is delivered.

Continuing improvement

Evaluation that follows a regular cycle will likely bring about 'continuing' improvement to the curriculum and to the teaching, learning and assessment processes associated with it. However, periodic evaluation is not without its problems. It can prove difficult to reflect back on the issues encountered over an extensive period, and feedback from students and staff is often reactive because it is elicited under pressure and within a short timescale.

Continuous improvement

An alternative is to bring about improvements as soon as possible, and continuously, as a programme or course progresses. Whilst it may not be possible to change course objectives in this way, it is entirely possible to effect changes to teaching, learning, resources and environments. Improvement of this nature is said to be 'continuous'. The advantage of continuous improvement is that it is proactive and stems from progressive feedback and observation. It brings about incremental change which has immediate benefit and is more likely to be enduring.

Evaluation documents

Effective curriculum evaluation depends fundamentally on a well-organised and coherent system of evaluation documents. These documents form the backbone of the evaluation process by providing necessary structure, clear guidance, and reliable evidence to inform decision-making at multiple levels. They ensure that quality assurance is continuous and systematic, foster transparency throughout the institution, and promote meaningful engagement among stakeholders such as teachers, students, leaders, and external reviewers.

Evaluation documents play a critical role in helping institutions meet regulatory and inspection requirements mandated by bodies like Ofsted and the Quality Assurance Agency (QAA). Due to the multifaceted nature of curriculum evaluation, education providers typically maintain a comprehensive suite of documentation, including detailed evaluation procedures, data collection instruments such as questionnaires and checklists, and formal reports designed to address particular phases and audiences within the curriculum review cycle.

Evaluation procedures and quality assurance frameworks

Most educational institutions embed curriculum evaluation within their broader quality assurance frameworks, often mandated by governmental or sector-specific regulatory bodies such as Ofsted, the Quality Assurance Agency for Higher Education (QAA), and Training Standards Offices. These frameworks require formal documentation that defines the evaluation cycle, responsibilities, timelines, and criteria for success (Ofsted, 2019; QAA, 2024).

For example, a primary school might have a documented evaluation policy specifying annual curriculum review dates, roles of the Deputy Head Teacher and subject leaders, and processes for collecting evidence including lesson observations and pupil voice. Similarly, universities typically empower Vice Principals or Directors of Curriculum and Quality to administer evaluation procedures, ensuring alignment with institutional academic standards and external benchmarks (Barnett & Coate, 2005).

The formal procedure documents typically include:

- **Evaluation policy statements** describing scope, objectives, and guiding principles.
- **Evaluation cycles and timetables** defining key phases, such as planning, data collection, analysis, reporting, and action.
- **Roles and responsibilities matrices** clarifying leadership, staffing, and committee involvement in the process.
- **Communication protocols** to keep stakeholders informed and engaged throughout.

Such procedural documents ensure that evaluations are systematic, transparent, and action-oriented, helping institutions shift from reactive to proactive quality management.

Self-evaluation documents and tools

Self-evaluation has become a central feature of curriculum evaluation, especially in environments valuing professional agency and continuous improvement (QAA, 2024; Ofsted, 2019). Self-evaluation documents and instruments enable teachers, lecturers, and course teams to critically assess their curricula, teaching strategies, and student outcomes using institutional frameworks.

Key self-evaluation documents include:

- **Self-evaluation frameworks or rubrics,** which provide criteria and scales for judging curriculum quality across aspects such as intent, implementation, and impact. These rubrics often reflect national standards and institutional priorities.

- **Self-assessment questionnaires or surveys**, typically administered online, allow educators to reflect on their own practices and gather evidence on perceived strengths and areas for development.

- **Reflective logs or evaluation diaries** record ongoing observations, insights, and decisions related to curriculum delivery and student learning.

- **Peer review checklists** facilitate structured feedback between colleagues, fostering collaborative evaluation culture.

These documents help build ownership and reduce anxieties associated with external inspection by promoting honest, formative critique aimed at improvement. For instance, a secondary school department may complete a self-evaluation report every term to prepare for external reviews, highlighting curriculum effectiveness, innovative teaching approaches, student response and identifying topics needing refinement.

Evaluation instruments

Institutions use a range of standardised evaluation instruments to collect both quantitative and qualitative data efficiently and systematically. These documents function as tools to operationalise curriculum evaluation and transform abstract criteria into measurable or describable indicators.

Interview schedules

Semi-structured interviews with staff, students, or external stakeholders help capture nuanced insights beyond standardised forms. Interview guides or schedules ensure relevant topics - such as perceptions of curriculum relevance or barriers to implementation - are consistently explored. For example, FE providers may interview workplace mentors to evaluate vocational curriculum effectiveness.

Questionnaires and surveys

Widely used for gathering perspectives from learners, teachers, parents, and employers, questionnaires are often delivered online for ease of distribution and data analysis. Examples include student satisfaction surveys, teacher confidence inventories, and employer feedback forms in FE or HE. Well-designed questionnaires integrate Likert scales, open-ended questions, and demographic filters to balance data richness and comparability (Priestley & Biesta, 2013).

Checklists

Checklists support evaluators in observing curriculum components such as resource availability, lesson delivery, or assessment alignment. For example, an Ofsted school inspection checklist might include items on curriculum breadth, inclusion of SEND pupils, and integration of cross-curricular skills (Ofsted, 2019). Checklists foster consistency by standardising what observers attend to and record. Checklists are also valuable for guiding systematic observation and ensuring reliability across multiple evaluators. However, they can sometimes constrain observer judgments, reducing rich, contextual insights to tick-box exercises. Training observers to interpret checklist items flexibly while maintaining standards is crucial to prevent overly mechanistic evaluation.

Together, these instruments provide triangulated evidence: quantifiable data from questionnaires, direct observations from checklists, and rich narrative from interviews allow for comprehensive evaluation. This triangulation strengthens validity by cross-verifying findings across methods and perspectives, which is critical in capturing the complex realities of curriculum implementation and impact.

Evaluation reports and documentation of findings

The culmination of an evaluation cycle is the production of evaluation reports that collate findings, draw conclusions, and recommend actions. These reports vary in format and level of detail depending on the context and audience but usually include:

- **Executive summaries**: Concise overviews highlighting key findings and prioritised recommendations.

- **Context and methodology**: Description of the curriculum evaluated, evaluation purpose and methods, and stakeholder involvement.

- **Detailed findings**: Results organised around evaluation criteria such as curriculum intent, implementation fidelity, learner outcomes, and areas for development.

- **Evidence appendices**: Samples of student work, quantitative data tables, observation notes.

- **Improvement plans**: Actionable and time-bound recommendations supported by identified resources and responsibilities.

In schools, reports might feed into whole-school development plans and be shared in staff meetings and governor committees. In FE and HE, they often contribute to annual course review documentation, academic board papers, and accreditation submissions (Barnett & Coate, 2005; QAA, 2024).

Electronic report templates and document management systems assist institutions in maintaining consistency and transparency. Increasingly, reports incorporate visual data representations (charts, dashboards) to support readability and stakeholder engagement.

Balancing documentation demands and practical effectiveness

While comprehensive documentation serves to strengthen accountability and communication, it can also generate burdensome, "document heavy", bureaucracy. To mitigate this, institutions strive to streamline documentation by:

- Embedding evaluation in existing workflows (e.g., integrating self-evaluation reports with professional development records).
- Using digital platforms for automated questionnaire delivery and data analysis.
- Focusing reports on actionable insight rather than exhaustive detail.
- Encouraging collaborative report-writing to distribute workload and increase buy-in.

The aim is to maintain rigour in evaluation without stifling professional judgement or innovation.

Ofsted's role in curriculum evaluation

Ofsted's role in curriculum evaluation spans primary schools, secondary education, further education (FE) providers, and beyond. Although Ofsted does not inspect higher education (HE) directly, its inspection frameworks and published guidance significantly influence evaluation approaches throughout the education pipeline.

Ofsted's evolving position underscores the importance of assessing not only curriculum intent and implementation but also the critical *impact* of education on learners' knowledge, skills, and preparedness for future stages. This approach advocates a balanced and comprehensive view of educational quality, emphasising that impact cannot be judged by exam results alone; instead, the entire learner journey, including progress at all stages and readiness for next steps, must be considered. Across all sectors, the triangulation of quantitative and qualitative evidence facilitates rich and actionable evaluation. Self-evaluation, leadership oversight, and responsive improvement cycles are essential to fostering a culture where curricular impact drives continuous enhancement, ensuring education is equitable, coherent, and ambitious.

Curriculum evaluation in Ofsted's inspection framework

Since the introduction of the Education Inspection Framework (EIF) in 2019, Ofsted has explicitly positioned curriculum evaluation and impact as central to its judgement of educational effectiveness (Ofsted, 2019). The EIF requires inspectors to evaluate how well the curriculum prepares pupils for subsequent phases of education and life beyond school, thereby focusing on outcomes achieved rather than solely on inputs or teaching practices. Curriculum impact, in this sense, is understood as the extent to which learners acquire the essential knowledge, skills, behaviours, and cultural capital expected at each stage.

Ofsted's methodology involves triangulating quantitative evidence - such as assessment results and progression data - with qualitative evidence gathered through work scrutiny, lesson observations, and interviews with pupils and staff. This multidimensional approach fosters a holistic understanding of impact, emphasising that exam results and test scores, while important, are only part of the wider picture (Ofsted, 2019).

Expectations across educational phases

Primary education

In primary schools, Ofsted takes a keen interest in the quality and impact of curriculum delivery, particularly in foundational subjects like reading, writing, and mathematics (Ofsted, 2019). Inspection considers whether pupils gain solid knowledge that builds progressively over time and whether the curriculum includes opportunities to develop wider skills and dispositions. Impact evaluation involves assessing pupils' academic progress as well as their engagement, curiosity, and readiness to transition to the next stage.

Formative assessments and teacher judgments are central to the ongoing monitoring of pupil progress, with inspection teams looking for evidence that such assessments are effectively used to identify gaps and tailor instruction. In addition, inspectors consider how schools support pupils with Special Educational Needs and Disabilities (SEND), English as an Additional Language (EAL), and those from disadvantaged backgrounds, ensuring equitable progress and inclusion (Ofsted, 2019; Alexander, 2021).

Secondary education

Secondary school inspections increasingly emphasise curriculum breadth, sequencing, and cumulative impact over a pupil's five or seven years of study through Key Stages 3 and 4. Ofsted scrutinises the design and delivery of the curriculum and how these lead to substantive learning gains, not just progress in externally assessed qualifications (Ofsted, 2019).

Inspectors evaluate whether pupils remain engaged with a broad spectrum of subjects for as long as possible and whether the curriculum equips them with the depth of knowledge and critical thinking skills required for post-16 education or training. The impact is judged through multiple data points including GCSE and other examination results, but also through qualitative indicators such as pupils' ability to articulate learning, demonstrate higher-order skills, and show preparedness for future study or employment (Whitty, 2010).

Differentiation within and across classes or streams is examined as part of impact evaluation, with particular attention paid to how well lower-attaining pupils catch up and how more able pupils are extended. This reflects Ofsted's commitment to reducing achievement gaps and raising overall standards (Ofsted, 2019).

Further education (FE)

For FE colleges and providers, Ofsted's inspection framework similarly underscores curriculum impact on learners' development and destination outcomes (Ofsted, 2019). Here, the curriculum spans academic, vocational, and apprenticeship pathways, demanding evaluation of a wider set of learning outcomes beyond formal qualifications.

Ofsted evaluates how effectively further education (FE) providers prepare learners for employment, higher education, and independent living. This involves detailed scrutiny of curricula to ensure they foster the development of industry-relevant skills, essential employability attributes, and broader personal growth. Impact assessment encompasses various key indicators, including learner retention and achievement rates, progression into employment or continued education, and feedback from both learners and employers. Additionally, Ofsted's inspections pay close attention to how FE providers accommodate diverse learner needs, particularly supporting adult learners and those participating in flexible or part-time programmes, ensuring equitable access and meaningful outcomes for all students.

Higher education (HE)

While Ofsted does not inspect HE institutions, its broader quality assurance expectations influence curriculum evaluation practices within HE delivered alongside FE or regulated by bodies such as the Quality Assurance Agency for Higher Education (QAA). The QAA's Quality Code complements Ofsted's focus on impact by expecting institutions to demonstrate that curricula facilitate student achievement of specified learning outcomes, development of graduate attributes, and employability skills (QAA, 2024).

HE institutions conduct extensive internal curriculum evaluations supported by student feedback (e.g., the National Student Survey) and external review processes, mirroring Ofsted's principles on triangulating data and considering both academic and personal development outcomes. This alignment underscores the growing importance of impact evaluation beyond traditional academic results, reinforcing inclusivity, academic rigour, and graduate readiness.

Ofsted guidance on self-evaluation and improvement

Ofsted strongly advocates for robust self-evaluation practices within educational institutions as a foundation for curriculum evaluation and impact monitoring. The self-evaluation process enables schools and providers to critically review curriculum effectiveness regularly, identify strengths and weaknesses, and drive strategic improvements ahead of external inspections (Ofsted, 2019).

Schools are expected to maintain clear evaluation documentation demonstrating how impact data is gathered and used. Effective self-evaluation embraces a wide range of evidence, from pupil work and attainment data to stakeholder feedback and lesson observations, fostering a culture of reflective practice and continuous development.

Leadership's role in sustaining effective evaluation is emphasised, with senior and middle leaders responsible for ensuring that evaluation leads to timely actions that enhance curriculum quality and outcomes for all pupils (Ofsted, 2019).

Challenges highlighted by Ofsted in curriculum evaluation and impact

Inspection reports frequently identify recurrent challenges in curriculum evaluation and impact realisation, including:

- A disproportionate focus on high-stakes examinations at the expense of broader curriculum goals.

- Inconsistencies in tracking long-term pupil progress and readiness for future education or employment.
- Limited use of qualitative evidence such as pupil voice or work scrutiny in evaluating impact.
- Weak or irregular self-evaluation processes that fail to inform improvement.
- Insufficient focus on outcomes for vulnerable groups such as SEND or disadvantaged pupils (Ofsted, 2019).

Addressing these challenges is repeatedly positioned as vital for schools and providers seeking to improve inspection outcomes and, more importantly, learner success.

 **Activity: Curriculum implementation audit and reflection**

1. Select a curriculum, module, or programme from your professional context (or one with which you are familiar).
2. Map out the intended learning outcomes and key success criteria for this curriculum.
3. Collect evidence of impact using a range of approaches (e.g., student work samples, achievement data, feedback surveys, observations).
4. Apply a chosen evaluation model(s) (such as Tyler's Objectives model, Stufflebeam's CIPP, or Scriven's Goal-Free) to critique curriculum effectiveness.
5. Identify at least two strengths and two areas for improvement, considering both summative outcomes and formative processes.
6. Propose an action plan or recommendations to address identified weaknesses or to build on strengths, justifying your reasoning with reference to theory or evidence from this chapter.
7. Optional: Share and compare your findings with colleagues to explore different perspectives on evaluating curriculum impact.

Summary

Curriculum evaluation provides the lens through which aspirations, implementation, and outcomes are aligned and improved. It is a dynamic, multi-phased process, supporting both summative judgments and continual professional reflection. By drawing on robust models, diverse forms of evidence, and clarity about both aims and values, educational providers can ensure their curricula genuinely serve learners' needs and societal demands. Understanding Ofsted's stance and aligning internal evaluation practices to recognised standards help maintain rigour while remaining responsive to context. Ultimately, effective curriculum evaluation underpins a culture of critical enquiry, adaptive improvement, and sustained educational impact.

8 DESIGNING ONLINE LEARNING

Introduction

Designing online learning is a complex, evolving endeavour that goes far beyond simply transferring face-to-face content to digital platforms. It demands deliberate attention to learner engagement, interaction, accessibility, and the alignment of objectives, content, learning activities, and assessment in virtual formats. Online learning environments require specific pedagogical approaches that recognise diverse learner needs and utilise multimedia and interactivity effectively. This chapter explores key theories and principles underpinning good online course design, strategies for maintaining instructor presence and student motivation, and methods of ensuring inclusivity and quality. It also introduces cutting-edge themes such as activity-led design and the use of artificial intelligence tools, equipping educators across primary, secondary, further, and higher education with practical insights to develop compelling online learning experiences.

This chapter

- Examines foundational theories and principles of online learning design.
- Discusses alignment of learning outcomes, content, and assessments in virtual environments.
- Explores strategies for learner engagement, interaction, and motivation online.
- Analyses the role and optimisation of multimedia and interactive content.
- Reviews approaches to assessment and feedback tailored for online delivery.
- Highlights the importance of instructor presence and facilitation in digital contexts.
- Considers accessibility and inclusive design for diverse learner populations.
- Reviews platforms and technologies supporting online and blended learning.
- Investigates emerging trends such as AI-assisted course design and activity-led development.

Introduction to online learning

Online learning has emerged as a core mode of education across all stages, fundamentally transforming teaching and learning from primary schools to higher education (HE). Once regarded as supplementary or alternative, online learning is now firmly established - driven by advances in internet connectivity, digital technology, and changing societal demands (Alexander, 2021). Its evolution can be traced from early correspondence courses and broadcast-based distance education, through computer-based training innovations of the late twentieth century, to the dynamic, interactive platforms and blended delivery models we see today (Kentnor, 2015; QAHE, 2022).

Origins and evolution

The origins of online learning are rooted in nineteenth-century correspondence education, such as the University of London's External Programme, and later, educational radio and television broadcasting. Computer-based education expanded in the 1960s and 1970s with systems like PLATO at the University of Illinois, which enabled users to interact with educational material and peers remotely (QAHE, 2022; Kentnor, 2015). The growth of the internet in the 1990s enabled the rise of virtual learning environments, online universities, and the early use of learning management systems. Recent decades have been shaped by the rise of Massive Open Online Courses (MOOCs), micro-credentials, the rapid expansion triggered by the COVID-19 pandemic, and ongoing integration of artificial intelligence and adaptive learning technologies (Kentnor, 2015; QAHE, 2022).

Comparisons with face-to-face (f2t) learning

A defining characteristic separating online from f2f learning is the flexibility of access. Online learning enables asynchronous study - individuals can engage with content and complete assessments at their own pace, from any location (Ofsted, 2019). Unlike traditional classrooms that rely on fixed times and real-time, co-located interactions, digital environments accommodate a range of life circumstances, including those with geographical constraints, disabilities, or work commitments (QAHE, 2022). Synchronous features, such as live webinars and interactive forums, also permit real-time engagement while retaining the option for recorded access and review.

Technological affordances in online education enable educators to utilise a wide array of multimedia resources, interactive assessments, adaptive learning pathways, and advanced digital communication tools. Unlike f2f teaching - where feedback is often instant and social cues are readily apparent - online environments require careful course structuring, explicit instructions, and robust digital support systems to guide learners. These platforms also produce granular analytics, capturing data on student engagement and progress. This allows educators to monitor participation closely, identify emerging learning needs, and implement timely, personalised interventions that enhance both learner support and academic outcomes (QAHE, 2022).

Sector-specific applications

- **Primary education:** Online approaches use gamified, age-appropriate resources and family engagement to promote foundational skills. Interactive content and adaptive assessment support motivation and differentiated progress.

- **Secondary education:** Online platforms expand curriculum access, support varied pacing, and encourage collaborative digital projects. Self-directed modules allow students to consolidate knowledge or pursue enrichment.

- **Further education (FE):** Blends academic and vocational content, linking digital instruction with real-world, work-based learning. Learner progress is tracked through digital portfolios and workplace feedback (QAHE, 2022).

- **Higher education:** Online and blended learning greatly expand flexibility for part-time, mature, and remote students. Degree programmes, CPD courses, and research projects use video lectures, virtual seminars, discussion boards, and advanced analytics (QAHE, 2022; McKinsey, 2023).

Unique advantages and persistent challenges

The principal advantages of online learning include accessibility, personalised pacing, diverse content formats, and scalable delivery. Data-driven insights enable targeted support and course improvement. Adaptive technologies and AI continue to personalise pathways, automate content creation, and support instant feedback (QAHE, 2022; 13).

However, challenges remain. Unequal digital access - the digital divide - risks excluding disadvantaged learners, as not all students have reliable internet, devices, or digital literacy (OECD, 2025). Learner isolation, reduced immediacy in feedback, and barriers to building a strong sense of community are recurring concerns (QAHE, 2022). Teachers and students both require new digital competencies, while curriculum design must be reimagined - simply transferring classroom content online often fails to create engaging or effective learning experiences (Greenhow et al., 2022).

Blended and hybrid approaches

In practice, many settings now blend online and in-person experiences, seeking flexibility and accessibility while retaining the benefits of social interaction, direct feedback, and classroom community (QAHE, 2022; Stavredes & Herder, 2014). Such hybrid models are anticipated to define the future, aligning digital innovation with pedagogical best practice and inclusivity at every educational stage.

Key principles of online course design

Designing effective online learning demands more than the mere transfer of classroom content to digital platforms. It is an intentional process, shaped by foundational learning theories and robust instructional design models that together underpin high-quality course structure across educational contexts, from primary to higher education (QAHE, 2022). This section explores the key principles, theoretical underpinnings, and best practice models necessary for creating engaging, equitable, and impactful online learning experiences.

Foundational theories for online learning design

1. **Behaviourism, cognitivism, and constructivism**

   - **Behaviourism** posits that learning occurs through responses to external stimuli. In online learning, this translates to the use of video, audio, quizzes, modelling, response tracking, token systems, simulation, automated feedback, and reinforcement strategies (Stavredes & Herder, 2014; Edge Education, 2020).

   - **Cognitivism** focuses on how learners process and organise information. Online courses, guided by cognitivism, prioritise logical sequencing, chunked content, scaffolding, and cognitive load management - for instance, using multimedia to support memory and understanding.

   - **Constructivism** emphasises that learners actively construct knowledge through experience and social interaction. Digital environments support this through activity-led content, collaborative tasks, problem-based projects, and discussion forums, all of which enable students to co-create meaning and build communities of inquiry (QAHE, 2022).

2. **Situated and connectivist theories**

   - **Situated learning** highlights learning as inherently social and contextual. Online design, informed by this theory, embeds learning in authentic tasks and real-world scenarios, encouraging peer interaction and application of knowledge.

- **Connectivism** - a learning theory of the digital age - focuses on the development of networks and the capacity to access and navigate diverse information sources. This is operationalised online through hyperlinking, branching resources, and fostering learners' digital literacy (Siemens, 2005).

3. **Community of Inquiry framework**

   A widely cited model, the Community of Inquiry (CoI), underscores the interplay between cognitive presence (deep thinking), social presence (connection and belonging), and teaching presence (design and guidance). Courses structured with Community of Inquiry in mind intentionally build dialogue, collaboration, and instructor engagement into every stage of learning (Garrison et al., 1999; QAHE, 2022).

Core instructional design models for digital learning

1. ADDIE Model (Analysis, Design, Development, Implementation, Evaluation)
ADDIE (Figure 8.1) is a systematic, iterative model that remains central to online course development (Digital Learning Institute, 2023).

Figure 8.1 - ADDIE model for digital learning

- **Analysis:** Examining learners' profiles, needs, and context.
- **Design:** Setting learning outcomes, sequencing content, selecting activities and technologies.
- **Development:** Creating and assembling digital resources (videos, quizzes, forums).
- **Implementation:** Launching the course and supporting students' navigation and participation.
- **Evaluation:** Using analytics, feedback, and learner performance to review and enhance design.

The ADDIE model's cyclical design fosters continuous improvement by integrating evaluation at every stage, ensuring that insights from feedback are systematically used to refine and enhance instructional materials, delivery methods, and learner support, promoting ongoing refinement and responsiveness (Digital Learning Institute, 2023).

2. Backward Design

This model begins with the end in mind - identifying desired learning outcomes before designing assessments and learning activities (Wiggins and McTighe, 2011). Used widely across sectors, it ensures clear alignment between aims, course structure, and assessment, avoiding activities or assignments that keep students occupied but do not meaningfully contribute to their achievement, and focusing on meaningful progressions. Online, backward design helps teachers select technology and interaction formats that directly support outcome achievement.

3. Other instructional design frameworks

- *SAM (Successive Approximation Model):* Emphasises rapid prototyping and iterative feedback, making it well suited to agile course design in fast-evolving sectors.

- *Dick and Carey Model:* Focuses on systematic analysis of goals, learner needs, instructional strategies, and formative evaluation at each phase (Calibr, 2025).

All these models emphasise careful analysis, alignment, and iteration, making them adaptable across all sectors.

Good practice design principles for online courses

1. Structure and clarity

Courses should be highly structured, organised, and easy to navigate. Clear modules, learning paths, and instructions reduce cognitive load and help learners self-regulate. Visual course roadmaps or checklists support orientation and progress tracking (Taylor Institute, 2024).

2. Alignment

Every component of a course - content, learning activities, interactions, and assessment - must be deliberately aligned with clearly defined learning outcomes to ensure coherence and purpose throughout the learning experience. This principle, known as *constructive alignment* (Wiggins and McTighe, 2011), facilitates meaningful engagement and helps learners achieve intended goals. It also enables systematic measurement of progress and effectiveness, fostering transparent and accountable educational practice (Biggs, 2022).

3. Engagement and motivation

Effective online courses use hooks, anticipatory sets (stimulating introductions), and a variety of interactive tasks to promote motivation (Digital Learning Institute, 2023). Technologies should support polling, quizzes, discussion, and multimedia exploration. Social and cognitive engagement is fostered through collaboration, authentic challenges, and regular instructor presence (Garrison et al., 1999).

4. Feedback and interaction

Timely, targeted feedback (automated or instructor-led) supports progression and corrects misunderstandings. Opportunities for peer assessment and group discussion build understanding and foster community.

5. Accessibility and inclusion

Online design must anticipate and accommodate SEND, EAL, and other diverse needs. Principles include use of plain language, consistent layout, alternative text, captions for video, keyboard navigation, and compatibility with screen readers (QAHE, 2022).

6. Scaffolding and support

Courses should provide supports that propel learners from initial orientation to increasing independence - such as worked examples, scaffolding prompts, clear rubrics, and low-stakes practice before major assessments. Tying support to analytics (identifying struggling students) further personalises guidance.

7. Community building

Effective course design cultivates a strong sense of belonging and active engagement among learners by incorporating interactive activities, synchronous live sessions, collaborative group projects, and regular instructor-led communication. These elements work together to create an online learning community that nurtures student participation, builds resilience in facing challenges, and encourages persistence towards achieving academic goals (Garrison et al., 1999).

8. Evaluation and continuous improvement

Embedding regular opportunities for reflection, feedback, and evaluation within online course design fosters continuous, iterative refinement. By using digital data such as usage analytics, learning analytics, and pulse surveys, educators can monitor learner engagement and performance in real time, enabling informed decisions for immediate enhancements and longer-term strategic improvements.

Application across educational contexts

Primary education: Prioritise age-appropriate structure, interactivity, scaffolds, and communication with parents. Use gamification, visual cues, and chunked videos to support sustained engagement.

Secondary and FE: Blend synchronous and asynchronous elements, emphasise self-management skills, collaboration, and formative feedback. Scaffold more complex, project-based work and offer varied assessment types.

HE: Structure for flexibility and independent learning at scale. Use peer-to-peer learning, research-led activities, virtual seminars, and reflective assignments. Support digital literacy and offer analytics-based interventions for at-risk students (QAHE, 2022).

Defining learning outcomes and objectives

Defining clear and measurable learning outcomes and objectives is fundamental to the design of any effective educational programme, particularly in online learning environments where clarity and structure are paramount.

Learning outcomes are learner-focused and describe what a student is actually expected to know, understand, or be able to demonstrate by the end of an instructional unit. They are broad-based, reflecting a long period of learning (Marsh, 2009). Outcomes define the measurable achievements or competencies the learner will show, such as "Analyse the causes of World War I" or "Demonstrate the process of photosynthesis through diagram labelling". Outcomes are evidence-based targets of learning and used for assessment and quality assurance.

Learning objectives tend to be teaching-focused, describing what the instructor plans to teach or cover during a lesson, module, or programme. They are a sub-set of learning outcomes and are often framed as the goals that guide instructional activities. For example, an objective might be: "Introduce students to the causes of World War I" or "Explain the concept of photosynthesis". Objectives are commonly narrower and are about the intentions of teaching.

When designing courses for online delivery, a central question often arises: Should the learning outcomes and objectives differ from those set for the equivalent face-to-face (f2f) course? Current educational research and sector guidance consistently indicate that the fundamental learning outcomes and objectives for a course or module delivered online can - and frequently are - exactly the same as those for the corresponding face-to-face version. It is the means by which these outcomes and objectives are achieved that differs (Stavredes & Herder, 2014; Stack, 2015).

Learning outcomes and objectives have been covered in Chapter 3.

Why alignment is both possible and desirable

Learning outcomes (what students should know, understand, or be able to do by the end of a course) and learning objectives (stepwise goals set by instructors) are statements of intended achievement that focus on the knowledge, skills, and competencies a course develops - regardless of the delivery medium. Research comparing online and f2f courses repeatedly finds no statistically significant differences in student achievement of course learning outcomes when the content, assessment standards, and instructor expectations are matched (Stack, 2015; Ortiz et al., 2022).

What *does* change between online and face-to-face teaching is how learning is supported - through different activities, technologies, and interactions. Online courses use digital forums, multimedia content, asynchronous discussions, and virtual assessments, while f2f classes may rely more on real-time discussion and hands-on classroom engagement. The method of delivery adapts, but the academic standards and intended outcomes remain constant (QAHE, 2022).

Practical implications

- Universities and educational bodies encourage parity of outcomes to ensure consistency and fairness for all students, regardless of learning mode (QAHE, 2022).

- Quality assurance agencies draw on the same outcome frameworks and benchmarks when accrediting online and in-person modules, ensuring students meet equivalent expectations (QAA, 2024).

- Studies show that, with careful design and adequate support, students achieve the same learning outcomes online as they do in traditional classrooms - sometimes even exceeding them depending on context and instructional quality (Stack, 2015; Mastour et al., 2023).

Key considerations

While the outcomes themselves may be unchanged, course design for online learning places greater explicit emphasis on clarity, structure, and alignment due to the self-directed nature of the digital environment (Stavredes & Herder, 2014). Activities, resources, and assessments must be thoughtfully selected and adapted to ensure students can realistically achieve the same objectives online. Nonetheless, educators should feel confident that the goals and standards students are working towards remain stable, equitable, and academically robust across both online and face-to-face courses.

Course structuring

Effective course structuring is fundamental to facilitating coherent, progressive, and engaging learning experiences across all educational phases. In online and blended environments especially, organising content into well-defined modules, units, and lessons supports learner autonomy, clarity, and motivation.

Logical sequencing

Logical sequencing is the deliberate ordering of learning content and activities to build knowledge and skills progressively. Well-sequenced curricula enable learners to connect new information to prior knowledge and form deeper conceptual understanding (Alexander, 2021; Biggs, 2022).

- **Spiral and cumulative approaches:** Particularly at primary and secondary levels, content revisits key themes and concepts at increasing levels of complexity over time. For instance, in mathematics, learners might first understand simple number bonds in Year 1, progressing through fractions in Year 3, then ratio and proportion in Year 6. Spiral curricula ensure concepts become embedded and transferable (Bruner, 1960).

- **Prerequisite relationships:** Effective sequencing identifies foundational skills and knowledge required before advancing. In FE and HE, this is evident in modular degree programmes where students must complete introductory modules before undertaking specialised or advanced topics. Clear prerequisites support cognitive scaffolding and prevent learner frustration (Oakley et al., 2004).

- **Cohesion across disciplines:** Cross-disciplinary sequencing allows content to be integrated horizontally as well as vertically. For example, science and history modules might align to explore the industrial revolution's technological and social dimensions, providing richer, interconnected learning (Drake, 2012).

- **Chunking content:** Breaking down material into manageable segments facilitates cognitive processing. Online courses commonly divide modules into units and lessons that can be completed in shorter, focused timeframes, helping reduce cognitive overload and maintain engagement (Sweller, 2011).

Navigation

Clear navigation within online courses is essential to enable learners to move easily through content, locate resources, and understand their progress. Intuitive and user-friendly navigation underpins learner self-efficacy and reduces anxiety, especially where students manage study independently.

- **Consistent structural design:** Using uniform layouts and navigation menus across modules helps learners predict where to find materials and activities. Standardised icons, buttons, and menus foster familiarity and efficient exploration (Moreno-Ger et al., 2014).

- **Visual roadmaps and progress indicators:** Offering visual cues such as course maps, breadcrumbs, or completion bars enhances orientation. Learners can see what they have accomplished and what remains, promoting motivation and time management (Reeves, 2016).

- **Multiple access routes:** Providing several ways to access content - linear navigation, thematic menus, search functions - accommodates diverse learner preferences. Some may prefer stepwise progression; others might jump to particular topics needing review or interest.

- **Accessibility and device responsiveness:** Navigation systems must be designed to function seamlessly across devices (computers, tablets, smartphones) and conform to accessibility standards for learners with disabilities (W3C, 2018).

- **Embedded help and orientation materials:** Tutorials, FAQs, glossaries, and contact options support learners in resolving navigational difficulties and maintaining momentum.

Scaffolding

Scaffolding refers to instructional supports that assist learners as they develop new skills and knowledge, gradually withdrawn as learners gain independence (Wood, Bruner and Ross, 1976). In online contexts, scaffolding is often digitally mediated and critical to bridging the gap between learner preparedness and course demands.

- **Cognitive scaffolding:** Course design incorporates tools such as worked examples, guided questions, and interactive simulations to model problem-solving and exemplify outcomes. For example, a science module might include a virtual lab demonstrating data collection before expecting students to conduct assessments independently (Quintana et al., 2018).

- **Metacognitive scaffolding:** Activities encouraging self-reflection, planning, and monitoring of learning aid development of autonomy. Journals, self-assessment checklists, and prompts help learners appraise their progress and adjust strategies (Jonassen et al., 2008).

- **Social scaffolding:** Collaborative forums, peer feedback, and instructor facilitation foster interaction and community, allowing learners to articulate reasoning, question assumptions, and receive affirmation (Garrison, Anderson and Archer, 1999).

- **Technical scaffolding:** Clear instructions on using technologies, as well as just-in-time guidance within platforms, reduce extraneous cognitive load and prevent technical barriers from undermining learning (Kay, 2011).

- **Adaptive scaffolding:** Learning analytics can pinpoint learner difficulties and trigger personalised supports or alternative resources, ensuring timely intervention (D'Mello and Graesser, 2015).

- **Gradual release:** Effective scaffolding applies a gradual release model allowing learners to progressively assume greater responsibility for their learning (Pearson and Gallagher, 1983).

Applications across educational phases

- **Primary education:** Scaffolding is critical given learners' developmental stages. Sequenced units build foundational skills, utilising multimedia stories, games, and interactive activities paired with parent/family engagement to reinforce learning. Navigation tends to be highly guided, with visual cues and prompts prominent (Richards et al., 2015).

- **Secondary education:** Greater cognitive demands necessitate more explicit scaffolding around abstract concepts and independent study skills. Courses often blend synchronous and asynchronous components, offering group work, formative assessments, and extensive feedback to maintain scaffolds.

- **Further education:** FE courses often require scaffolding targeted at vocational skills alongside academic learning. Digital portfolios, workplace simulations, and scaffolds supporting reflection and professionalism are commonplace, integrated with clear navigation of modular units (Prins et al., 2017).

- **Higher education:** Independent learning is emphasised, with scaffolding focusing on research skills, critical thinking, and reflective practice. Navigation must balance freedom and structure, enabling access to vast resources and networking opportunities. Advanced adaptive scaffolding through analytics supports timely, targeted interventions (Rienties & Toetenel, 2016).

Challenges and best practices

Balancing adequate scaffolding is essential to support learners while avoiding dependency or oversimplification, as excessive scaffolding can undermine motivation and autonomy (Pea, 2018). Logical sequencing within curricula requires continuous review and adaptation to maintain relevance and coherence in the face of evolving knowledge and diverse learner needs (Drake, 2012). Additionally, navigation design should account for the varied digital literacy levels among learners; therefore, inclusive and minimalistic interfaces are often the most effective in accommodating diverse audiences (Seale & Cooper, 2010). Together, these elements foster meaningful, accessible, and engaging learning experiences.

Successful scaffolding depends on instructor presence and responsiveness, requiring professional development and platform features enabling timely interaction and feedback.

Learner engagement strategies

Learner engagement is essential to the success of any educational experience, but it assumes particular importance in virtual environments where the absence of physical co-presence poses unique challenges. Research consistently shows that engaged learners are more likely to persist, achieve higher levels of understanding, and develop key transferable skills across all sectors of education (Martin & Bolliger, 2018; Bond et al., 2021).

The nature of engagement in virtual learning

Engagement in virtual education is a multi-dimensional construct, encompassing cognitive, behavioural, and emotional domains that together influence the quality and depth of student learning. Cognitive engagement refers to the learner's psychological investment in understanding material, demonstrating curiosity, and sustaining effort to master challenging concepts. Behavioural engagement encompasses visible actions like regular attendance, active participation in discussions, and completion of assignments or activities on time. Emotional engagement reflects positive feelings about learning, such as interest, enthusiasm, and a strong sense of belonging within the online community (Fredricks et al., 2004). Without the cues and accountability of physical presence, sustaining all three forms of engagement requires deliberate, varied, and well-scaffolded strategies tailored to virtual settings (Bond & Bedenlier, 2019).

Strategies to foster interaction

1. Structured synchronous activities

Synchronous sessions - such as live video classes, webinars, or instant messaging - provide real-time interaction mirroring some facets of face-to-face conversation. Breakout rooms, polls, and live collaborative documents can be used to stimulate small group discussion and peer-to-peer learning (Martin & Bolliger, 2018; Major, 2015). For example, in school settings, "show and tell" sessions allow young learners to present to classmates, fostering oral skills and digital confidence.

2. Asynchronous discussion forums and peer review

Asynchronous tools such as discussion boards, blogs, and journals enable learners to contribute at their own pace and reflect more deeply. These are particularly beneficial for students who may be reticent in live settings or who need extended time to process information (Hrastinski, 2008). In secondary and higher education, peer review tasks - where students give feedback on each other's work - both deepen understanding and build community (Nicol et al., 2014).

3. Social presence and community building

Creating opportunities for informal connection can be as important as academic interaction. Ice-breaker activities, *virtual cafés*, and interest-based groups help establish trust and rapport. Educational research demonstrates that fostering a sense of social presence - where instructors and peers are perceived as 'real' and approachable - predicts higher engagement and persistence (Richardson et al., 2017). In FE and HE, regular tutor check-ins and the use of authentic instructor video messages have shown to increase motivation and retention.

4. Collaborative projects and team-based learning

Collaborative assignments - such as group projects, debates, or case study analysis - require learners to coordinate efforts, negotiate roles, and co-construct understanding, fostering valuable communication and teamwork skills. The use of shared digital workspaces (for example, Google Docs, Padlet, or Miro) supports both real-time and asynchronous collaboration, accommodating diverse schedules and participation styles. For younger learners, clearly defined team roles and structured guidance are especially beneficial, while older students can engage with more complex, open-ended problem-solving activities that promote both independence and critical thinking (Laal & Ghodsi, 2012; Bond et al., 2021).

5. Prompt, personalised communication

Timely, tailored feedback is critical for maintaining momentum and helping learners feel valued. Automated quizzes offer instant results; handwritten or audio comments on assignments add a personal touch. Personalised messaging - such as acknowledging a contribution or congratulating improvement - strengthens the relationship between educator and learner (Martin & Bolliger, 2018).

Strategies to enhance motivation

1. Relevance and authenticity

Making learning relevant to students' lives and aspirations increases engagement (Ryan & Deci, 2000). In virtual settings, this might involve using real-world scenarios, workplace simulations, or inviting guest speakers. Primary and secondary pupils engage more when tasks connect to their experiences or community issues, while FE and HE students value assignments that mirror professional contexts (Bryson & Hand, 2007).

2. Autonomy and learner choice

Allowing learners to exercise control - such as choosing topics, formats for projects, or the order of tackling tasks - can enhance intrinsic motivation (Patall et al., 2008). Online environments make it easier to offer differentiated pathways or optional challenge activities to suit different interests and abilities.

3. Goal setting and progress tracking

Clear expectations, goal setting, and visible progress bars or checklists help learners monitor their advancement and sustain motivation. Gamified elements - like badges or levels - can also provide a sense of achievement (Dichev & Dicheva, 2017). In primary education, simple sticker charts or digital certificates are effective, whereas older learners may respond to milestones tied to assessment or awards.

4. Scaffolding and timely support

Motivation can decline rapidly when learners experience overload or uncertainty in virtual environments. Thoughtfully designed scaffolding - breaking complex tasks into clear, manageable steps, providing explicit instructions, and offering timely, just-in-time hints - helps sustain active engagement and effort. In higher education, integrating dedicated academic skills tutorials within modules supports students in bridging knowledge or skill gaps, maintaining their confidence and promoting ongoing motivation throughout their studies.

5. Recognising and celebrating achievements

Highlighting good work - through displays, e-newsletters, or virtual 'walls of fame' - boosts morale and reinforces a culture of success. For younger learners, praise from teachers or peers is powerful; for older students, public recognition in online seminars or academic events has similar benefits (Bond et al., 2021).

Strategies for active participation

1. Interactive content and active learning

Videos with embedded quizzes, simulations, branching scenarios, and drag-and-drop exercises require learners to do more than passively absorb information. In primary and secondary phases, adaptively designed games or puzzles raise engagement; in HE, virtual labs and scenario-based assessments immerse students in decision-making and analysis (Bates, 2015).

2. Flipped classroom approaches

Providing pre-recorded lectures, readings or videos for independent study, then using synchronous time for discussion or problem-solving, capitalises on the flexibility of the online environment (O'Flaherty & Phillips, 2015). This encourages preparation and active participation in live classes across age groups.

3. Mobile and micro-learning

Short, focused learning activities accessible via mobile devices fit learners' varied schedules and attention spans. These might include quiz questions, prompts, or mini-videos that can be completed 'on the go', benefiting working adults in FE/HE or supporting revision for primary and secondary students (Crompton & Burke, 2018).

4. Real-time polling and Q&A

Live polls, word clouds, and question upvoting technology (e.g., Mentimeter, Slido) make large-group sessions interactive and give instant feedback to teachers about understanding, while allowing all voices to be heard - including those of quieter or remote students.

5. Peer teaching and mentoring

Opportunities for learners to teach each other, create resources, or act as digital mentors deepen understanding and foster engagement (Topping, 2005). In primary contexts, 'buddy' systems promote inclusion; in HE, peer support forums reduce isolation and promote retention.

Supporting engagement across diverse contexts

It is essential to adapt strategies to the context and learner cohort. For example, primary-aged learners may benefit from shorter session lengths, more physical movement breaks, and visual prompts. Secondary and FE learners require scaffolding for independent study and explicit guidance on digital study skills. HE students increasingly expect flexible, self-paced learning but still require encouragement to participate actively and avoid isolation (Bond et al., 2021; Martin & Bolliger, 2018).

Barriers such as digital poverty, language differences, and additional needs must be anticipated and addressed through targeted support, differentiated activities, and inclusive design (Ofsted, 2021).

Instructor presence and modelling

Instructor presence is one of the strongest predictors of both engagement and success in online courses across educational levels. Beyond providing academic content or assessment, the visible and consistent involvement of instructors helps establish a sense of community, reduces feelings of isolation, and fosters trust within virtual classrooms (Richardson et al., 2017; Martin et al., 2018). Effective instructor presence means being available and responsive: posting regular announcements, engaging in discussion forums with personalised replies, and promptly addressing questions or technical issues. These actions signal to students that their participation is valued and that help is accessible, enhancing motivation and persistence.

Equally important is modelling expected behaviours. Instructors who actively demonstrate how to engage - by thoughtfully replying to forum posts, sharing resources, posing reflective questions, and providing constructive feedback - set explicit standards for communication, courtesy, and academic rigour. For example, modelling how to support peers, give feedback, or ask clarifying questions encourages learners to replicate these behaviours, gradually building a collaborative and supportive learning culture. In synchronous sessions, teachers can show active listening, acknowledging diverse perspectives and celebrating contributions, which has been shown to increase participation and social presence.

Ultimately, instructor presence and modelling contribute to the creation of a safe, motivating, and inclusive online learning environment where students feel empowered to engage, take risks, and persist in their studies (Garrison et al., 2010).

Use of multimedia and interactive content

Multimedia and interactive content have become essential tools for enriching online and blended learning. These technologies support engagement, accommodate diverse learning styles, and promote deeper understanding and skill development. This section explores key types of multimedia - videos, simulations, quizzes, and branching scenarios - and highlights their applications and benefits across educational contexts.

Videos

Videos are one of the most pervasive and effective multimedia tools in education. In primary education, short, engaging videos help bring stories and concepts to life, capturing the attention and imagination of younger learners. For example, animated explanations of scientific phenomena or story-readings develop foundational understanding. In secondary education, videos support complex explanations in subjects such as mathematics, science, and literature, often using real-world examples and animated graphics to clarify abstract concepts. Further education (FE) benefits particularly from videos that demonstrate workplace practices, vocational techniques, or customer interactions. In higher education (HE), recorded lectures, expert interviews, and seminar recordings cater to flexible, self-paced study and revision. Video content encourages repeated viewing and accessibility - captions, multiple languages, and playback controls make learning more personalised and inclusive (Bates, 2015; Martin & Bolliger, 2018).

Sourcing educational videos

A vast ecosystem of pre-existing educational videos is now available for educators:

- *Curated educational video libraries:* Platforms such as ClickView (widely used in UK schools) and Boclips offer vast libraries of curriculum-aligned, rights-cleared videos. These are specifically designed or selected for classroom use, ensuring content is safe, ad-free, and mapped to relevant educational frameworks. ClickView, for example, provides resources tailored to primary, secondary, and all-through school contexts, as well as FE and HE, including documentaries, original filmed series, animations, and studied films that can be integrated with minimal preparation. Boclips supports seamless licensing for over 1.7 million educational videos from hundreds of reputable publishers, ensuring content provenance and simplifying digital learning design for institutions and educators.

- *Public repositories and open resources:* Other established sources include TED-Ed, Khan Academy, National Geographic, TeacherTube, Teachers TV, YouTube, and the BBC Bitesize collection. These platforms cater for a wide array of ages and subjects, from science animations for young children to advanced topic explainer videos for sixth form and HE. University content teams and trusted open educational repositories also regularly share high-quality lectures and expert interviews.

Best practice in sourcing

When sourcing videos, it is vital to ensure that they are:

- Rights-cleared and free from copyright or licensing risks.
- Aligned to the curriculum or module's intended learning outcomes.
- Age-appropriate, culturally sensitive, and accessible (including subtitles, multiple languages, and audio description as required).

Platforms such as ClickView and Boclips allow educators to filter by subject, age group, academic level, and even specific learning objectives, making integration efficient.

Creating bespoke educational videos

While sourced videos offer breadth and convenience, bespoke video creation enables exact alignment with local teaching aims, context, and institutional culture.

- *Why create custom videos?*
  - Tailor content to specific courses, cohorts, languages, or learner needs.
  - Embed precise terminology, references, or examples relevant to local curriculum priorities.
  - Humanise courses with authentic staff or student voices (e.g. welcome videos or personal introductions in HE).
- *Production practices and tools:*
  - *Script and planning:* Start with a clear learning objective and script. Focus each video tightly on a small set of concepts, and keep it concise (ideally under 6 minutes for most learning segments). Use storyboarding to map visuals, narration, and supporting media.
  - *Filming essentials:* Good lighting, clear audio (lapel microphones are strongly recommended), and considered framing significantly enhance student engagement. Three-point lighting setups and professional, yet authentic, delivery help videos connect.
  - *Editing and accessibility:* Quality editing ensures clarity and pacing. Add captions for accessibility, translations if serving multilingual cohorts, and visual cues to guide attention.
  - *Animation and AI tools:* Platforms like Synthesia or educational animation services can generate consistent, brand-aligned animated sequences and

avatar-led videos. These are especially useful for abstract topics, language neutrality, or where live filming is difficult.

- o *Engagement features:* Consider embedding questions, interactive segments, or summary slides to make videos more participatory and reinforce active learning.

- *Collaboration and workflow:* Professional video production services (e.g. Digital Finch, Creamy Animation) offer full-cycle creation, from scripting and filming to post-production, often involving educators at every stage. For smaller-scale, in-house projects, educators can use widely available tools (e.g. smartphones, Zoom, Panopto, or Powtoon) with a focus on authenticity over perfection.

- *Types of bespoke videos:* In education, bespoke production may include explainer videos, live demonstrations, staff/stakeholder interviews, animated explainers, scenario-based training (such as branching decision-making), and video feedback for assignments.

Simple methods of creating video

Here are some simple ways to create videos, suitable for educators or learners at all levels, using accessible technology and user-friendly platforms:

1. *Using your laptop or device camera*

- *Built-in camera apps:* Most laptops and tablets come with a built-in camera and an app (e.g., Camera on Windows, Photo Booth on Mac) that lets you record video straight away. This option is quick, requires no additional software, and saves videos directly to your device (Riverside Blog, 2025).

- *QuickTime Player (Mac):* Use your webcam to record directly. This method also allows you to choose different cameras or microphones if you have them connected.

2. *Online tools and free software*

- *Clipchamp (Windows or browser):* Clipchamp is a free, browser-based video creator and editor now integrated into Windows 10 and 11. You can record with your webcam, edit clips, trim, add text, transitions, music, and export your final video - all in one place. It supports built-in or external cameras and microphones.

- *Online webcam recorders:* Websites like Webcamera.io or Canva's online video recorder allow recording through your web browser with just a few clicks, no installation needed. These tools are ideal for quickly capturing talking-head videos or activity demonstrations.

- *CapCut and FlexClip:* Both are free, browser-based video editors where you can upload clips, trim, add music, text, and effects, then export your finished video.

CapCut includes extra tools like auto-captioning, background removal, and trendy templates to polish your work.

3. *Creating more professional recordings*

- *OBS Studio:* A free, cross-platform software that lets you record video from your laptop camera and even your screen at the same time. While it has more features and a learning curve, it is popular for high-quality video lectures, demonstrations, or blended content creation (YouTube tutorial, 2024).

- *Phone or tablet:* Don't overlook smartphones and tablets! Most feature excellent HD cameras and free apps for recording and basic editing. Transfer your clip to your laptop if you want to use a more advanced editor afterwards.

Simulations

Simulations offer immersive, interactive experiences where learners can manipulate variables, experiment, and view the consequences of their decisions without real-world risks. In primary classrooms, simulations are often embedded in games that teach maths or science through virtual manipulatives. Secondary pupils might use simulations for virtual chemistry experiments, geography field trips, or language immersion environments. In FE, learners in technical or vocational fields such as engineering or health care can practise key skills in a safe, controlled digital environment. HE students encounter sophisticated simulations in disciplines like medicine, business, or economics, where complex, scenario-based tasks support the development of decision-making and professional judgement. Simulation-based learning has been shown to enrich motivation, retention, and practical competence (Gredler, 2008).

Quizzes

Quizzes - especially those that embed multimedia and interaction - enhance knowledge reinforcement, self-assessment, and formative feedback. In primary and secondary settings, quizzes assess reading comprehension, numeracy, or subject content in fun, accessible ways, often using gamification techniques such as badges and progress bars.

For FE, quizzes aligned with vocational standards or regulatory content facilitate incremental mastery. In HE, quizzes range from quick polls in large virtual lectures to full-scale e-assessments offering instant, diagnostic feedback. Gamified quizzes with leaderboards and challenges have proven to increase motivation, promote healthy competition, and support knowledge retention. Importantly, digital quizzes generate data that help instructors tailor support and adapt curriculum delivery for maximum impact (Stavredes & Herder, 2014; Martin & Bolliger, 2018).

Branching scenarios

Branching scenarios present learners with choices that influence subsequent events or outcomes, offering personalised learning paths and inviting complex problem-solving. In primary education, branching digital stories teach decision-making, empathy, and consequence-awareness. In secondary and FE, more challenging scenarios - such as medical triage, business strategy, or customer service cases - spark higher-order thinking, ethical analysis, and practical skill development. In HE, branching is extensively used for professional and ethical training, such as clinical reasoning in medicine or dilemma casework in law and management. These scenarios increase engagement, deepen learning through reflection on consequences, and allow learners to safely encounter and learn from errors (eLearning Industry, 2024).

Cross-sector considerations

When integrating multimedia and interactive content, designers and educators must attend carefully to learner age, cognitive development, digital skills, and accessibility. For young learners, content should be visually rich, explicitly scaffolded, and simple to navigate. In secondary, FE, and HE, multimedia must be appropriately challenging, supporting autonomy and critical engagement. Accessibility - including captions, alternative text, and clear navigation - is highly recommended to ensure all students benefit. Regular feedback and evaluation enable continuous improvement, and institutional investment in training and technical support is critical for effective, equitable integration of these tools (Bond et al., 2021; Martin & Bolliger, 2018).

Assessment and feedback in online learning

Online learning environments introduce distinct opportunities and challenges for assessment and feedback that differ significantly from traditional face-to-face (f2f) settings. While the fundamental purposes of assessment remain consistent - measuring achievement, guiding learning, and certifying outcomes - the digital context demands adapted design, delivery, and feedback strategies to ensure validity, engagement, and equity across education sectors.

Designing formative assessment for online learning

Formative assessment in online learning environments plays a crucial role in supporting and guiding continuous learner development by offering frequent, low-stakes opportunities for practice, reflection, and adjustment. Unlike face-to-face settings, online formative assessments benefit from automation features, comprehensive data capture, and flexible timing and formats that accommodate diverse learning schedules. However, to maintain learner motivation and prevent disengagement - often caused by social isolation or technical difficulties - these assessments require thoughtful and intentional design that fosters interaction, timely feedback, and accessibility.

Use of quizzes and interactive tasks

Digital platforms can provide immediate feedback through auto-graded quizzes, drag-and-drop activities, polls, and multimedia assignments. These interactive formats promote active retrieval and self-assessment, fostering metacognitive awareness (Boud & Molloy, 2013). Primary learners engage well with gamified quizzes that include rewards or progress badges, while older learners use self-tests to identify gaps before summative evaluation (Nicol, 2014).

Peer and self-assessment tools

Online environments facilitate structured peer review workflows, enabling students to critique each other's work using rubrics and guided questions (Topping, 2017). Self-assessment journals and blogs encourage reflective practice. These formats develop critical thinking and foster ownership of learning but depend on clear guidance and moderation to ensure reliability (Nicol & Macfarlane-Dick, 2006).

Continuous analytics and dashboards

Learning management systems (LMS) provide real-time dashboards that track engagement, quiz attempts, and assignment progress, helping learners and instructors identify needs for intervention (Arnold & Pistilli, 2012). Analytics can highlight patterns of behaviour indicating misconceptions or disengagement, which can trigger supportive feedback or adaptive remediation.

However, formative assessment in online settings faces risks of low participation if not well integrated into overall course design and of over-reliance on automated feedback, which can lack depth or developmental insight (Wiliam, 2011).

Summative assessment in a digital context

Summative assessment online largely serves to certify competency or achievement upon course or module completion. The shift from paper-based to digital submission necessitates new considerations for security, authenticity, and accessibility.

Online submission platforms: Tools like Turnitin, Moodle assignments, Canvas submissions, and Microsoft Teams enable seamless uploading of written work, presentations, or multimedia projects. These platforms support multiple file formats and versions while timestamping submissions for tracking. Familiarity and reliability of the interface are essential to reduce learner frustration and technical issues, which disproportionately affect vulnerable groups (Kear, 2013).

Originality and plagiarism checking: Digital submission allows use of sophisticated originality checking software (e.g., Turnitin, Urkund) that compare work against vast databases and flag potential unoriginal text. This protects academic integrity in online learning, where opportunities for collusion or contract cheating may increase (Newton, 2018). However, educators must balance detection with pedagogical approaches that educate students about citation practices and ethical scholarship.

Remote proctoring: For timed, high-stakes exams, online proctoring technologies monitor candidates through webcams, screen recording, and AI-driven behaviour analysis. This ensures exam security but raises concerns about privacy, equity (due to variable home environments), and accessibility. Many institutions are exploring open-book or alternative assessments to mitigate these issues.

Diverse assessment formats: Online summative assessments often utilise a broader range of formats beyond written essays or exams, such as e-portfolios, video presentations, case study analyses, or simulations. These alternatives accommodate varied learning styles and professional skill demonstration, especially in higher education and vocational settings (Boud & Soler, 2016).

Harnessing AI in assessment and feedback

Artificial intelligence technologies are transforming online assessment and feedback in multiple ways, offering both efficiency gains and new pedagogical possibilities.

Automated grading and feedback: AI algorithms can now assess objective items (e.g., multiple-choice) and increasingly open-ended responses like short answers or essays, providing instant scoring and formative comments (Shermis & Burstein, 2013). Chatbots and virtual tutors offer on-demand, clarifying support for student queries (Heffernan & Heffernan, 2014).

Adaptive assessment: AI enables dynamic testing where question difficulty adapts in real-time based on learner responses, offering personalised challenge and mapping nuanced proficiency levels (Conati & Kardan, 2013). This enhances validity and learner motivation by reducing frustration or boredom.

Plagiarism and contract cheating detection: Beyond text matching, emerging AI tools analyse writing style, source use, and metadata patterns to detect sophisticated misconduct attempts. Institutions are developing combined human-AI systems to ensure accuracy and fairness in integrity assurance.

AI-generated feedback: Natural language processing tools can generate tailored feedback leveraging large corpora of expert commentary, fostering detailed learner reflection and targeted improvements (Nikolova et al., 2022). However, ethical and transparency issues arise, requiring careful implementation and human oversight.

While AI offers promising advancements in automating and enhancing educational assessment and feedback, it also raises significant challenges. These include the potential for algorithmic biases that may unfairly affect certain learner groups, ongoing privacy concerns related to data usage, and the risk that AI-generated feedback becomes overly generic or formulaic, reducing its meaningfulness and pedagogical value (Zawacki et al., 2019).

Providing timely and actionable feedback online

Feedback is critical to learner development, arguably even more so in online settings where direct, in-person contact is limited.

Timeliness: Quick turnaround supports learners in correcting misconceptions and sustaining motivation. Online platforms facilitate rapid dissemination via annotated documents, voice notes, or video feedback. Primary and secondary learners benefit from frequent, bite-sized feedback aligned to scaffolded activities; HE students expect comprehensive, formative comments supporting independent revision (Nicol, 2014).

Clarity and actionability: Feedback must clearly identify strengths and areas for improvement, linked directly to learning outcomes and assessment criteria. Rubric-based commentary helps quantify expectations while personalised comments engage learners (Jonsson & Svingby, 2007).

Multimodal feedback: Combining written, audio, and video comments caters to diverse preferences and enhances emotional connection (Carless & Boud, 2018). Video feedback can replicate some social presence lost online, encouraging dialogue and deeper engagement.

Dialogic feedback: Platforms encouraging learner response to feedback (via comments or reflection journals) foster sustained two-way communication rather than one-off judgments. Peer feedback further enriches perspective and ownership (Boud & Molloy, 2013).

Challenges: Despite digital convenience, feedback quality may suffer if rushed, generic, or disconnected from learning activities. Educator workload and digital literacy influence effectiveness; hence, training and institutional support are essential (Gikandi et al., 2011).

Differences and challenges compared to f2f assessment and feedback

Lack of immediate, non-verbal cues means online feedback requires greater explicitness and opportunities for dialogue.

Risk of technical difficulties and digital divide can hamper participation and timely submission or feedback access.

Potential for depersonalisation, especially with automated systems, makes intentional instructor presence critical.

Scaling feedback in large, asynchronous cohorts challenges traditional one-to-one models, calling for creative uses of technology and peer support.

Monitoring academic integrity is more complex, requiring technology-supported approaches beyond in-person proctoring.

Technology platforms and learning management systems

Technology platforms and learning management systems (LMS) have become indispensable components of education across all sectors of education. Their role in organising, delivering, and enhancing digital learning experiences is critical for both educators and learners.

Virtual learning environments (VLEs)

Virtual learning environments are software platforms designed to support online teaching and learning by providing a cohesive digital space where content, communication, assessment, and collaboration occur (Conole, 2013). VLEs aim to replicate many pedagogical functions of the classroom while capitalising on the affordances of technology such as flexibility, multimedia integration, and data tracking.

In primary education, VLEs often provide intuitive interfaces with gamification elements, animations, and interactive activities tailored to younger learners' cognitive and motivational needs. Popular platforms such as Seesaw and Google Classroom offer secure, parent-inclusive environments that facilitate communication between teachers, pupils, and families. They support personalised learning pathways and allow younger learners to submit work digitally with minimal complexity.

Secondary schools employ VLEs that provide subject-specific resources, discussion boards, and calendar-driven assignment management. Platforms like Microsoft Teams and Google Classroom allow teachers to assign differentiated tasks, monitor engagement analytics, and communicate securely with larger cohorts. These VLEs often integrate with national exam boards or school management systems, streamlining curriculum delivery and assessment processes (Ofsted, 2019).

In further and higher education, VLEs grow more sophisticated, facilitating independent study, research collaboration, and professional development. Moodle, Blackboard, and Canvas are widely adopted systems enabling features such as forum discussions, peer review, multimedia content hosting, e-submissions, and adaptive learning paths aligned with programme outcomes (Guri-Rosenblit, 2011). Advanced analytics dashboards within these platforms enable educators to identify at-risk students and adapt instructional strategies proactively. The integration of synchronous tools (Zoom, Collaborate Ultra, TEAMs) enhances real-time engagement within predominantly asynchronous environments.

Managed learning environments (MLEs)

Managed learning environments refer to broader institutional systems that integrate several components of educational administration alongside VLE functions, creating a unified ecosystem for teaching, learning, and school/university management (Marshal & Williams, 2020). MLEs combine curriculum planning, attendance, behaviour tracking, communication portals, and assessment workflows in addition to learning content delivery.

In primary and secondary schools, MLEs such as SIMS (School Information Management System) and Capita integrate VLE features with data management, enabling holistic tracking of pupil progress, pastoral care, and parental communication. This integration supports data-driven planning and targeted intervention strategies. MLEs foster collaboration among teachers, support staff, and leaders, with centralised access to pupil records, lesson resources, and assessment data.

In FE institutions and universities, MLEs extend to enrolment management, timetabling, feedback collection, and quality assurance systems. Platforms like Tribal and Unit-e provide end-to-end solutions that incorporate VLEs alongside administrative functions, simplifying regulatory compliance and enhancing learner support. This comprehensive infrastructure supports complex programme delivery requirements, modular course structures, and multi-campus operations (QAA, 2024).

Selecting and using digital tools to optimise learning experiences

Choosing appropriate digital tools within VLEs or MLEs is key to creating engaging, accessible, and effective online learning experiences. The selection process must consider pedagogical fit, ease of use, interoperability, inclusivity, and scalability (Hodges et al., 2020).

Pedagogical alignment: Tools should support curriculum objectives, accommodate diverse learning styles, and promote active learning. For younger learners, interactive apps and multimedia storybooks aligned with literacy and numeracy goals are vital. Secondary, FE and HE contexts benefit from collaborative platforms, simulation software, and critical thinking tasks, while vocational learners require practical assessment and workplace communication tools (Biggs, 2022).

Ease of use and accessibility: User-friendly interfaces are essential to minimise cognitive load, particularly for SEND and EAL learners. Platforms and tools complying with accessibility standards (WCAG 2.1) ensure equitable participation and legal compliance (W3C, 2018). For example, captioned video players, screen readers, and colour contrast options enhance inclusivity.

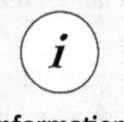

Information: WCAG 2.1 stands for the Web Content Accessibility Guidelines version 2.1, a set of internationally recognised recommendations published by the World Wide Web Consortium (W3C) to make web content more accessible for people with disabilities. These guidelines help ensure that websites and digital resources are usable by a wider range of people, including those with blindness or low vision, deafness or hearing loss, physical disabilities, cognitive or learning disabilities, and photosensitivity.

Interoperability and integration: Tools that seamlessly integrate with core LMS functions (gradebook, calendar, authentication) reduce administrative burden and provide learners with unified access. Open standards (LTI, SCORM) facilitate embedding external applications such as interactive quizzes, virtual labs, or adaptive learning modules (Selwyn, 2021).

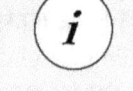

Information: LTI (Learning Tools Interoperability) and SCORM (Sharable Content Object Reference Model) are two widely used standards in e-learning. LTI enables seamless integration of third-party tools and apps into a learning management system (LMS), streamlining single sign-on and secure data exchange, but does not itself track learner progress in detail. SCORM is used to package, deliver, and track e-learning courses within an LMS, recording data such as completion rates and scores. LTI focuses on tool connectivity and interoperability, while SCORM centres on content packaging and progress tracking

Scalability and support: Institutions should consider the capacity of platforms to support varying cohort sizes, peak usage times, and technical support resources. Cloud-based systems offer flexibility and resilience, essential as demand fluctuates.

Data use and privacy: When selecting digital tools, ensuring compliance with data protection legislation (such as GDPR in the UK/EU) and institutional policies is critical. Tools must handle personal data securely, and transparency regarding data use enhances trust among learners and staff.

Professional development and community: Successful adoption depends on staff training and support structures. Institutions are increasingly investing in digital pedagogical frameworks, peer networks, and workshops to empower educators in effective tool integration (Whalen, 2020).

Activity: Designing an online learning module

1. Select a subject, course, or module relevant to your educational context (primary, secondary, FE, or HE).
2. Define two or three clear, measurable learning outcomes suitable for online delivery.
3. Sketch an outline of an online learning module structured into logical units or lessons, incorporating a variety of content types (texts, videos, quizzes, discussions).
4. Identify at least three interactive or activity-based elements that actively engage learners and promote deeper understanding.
5. Choose assessment methods appropriate for the online environment and aligned to your learning outcomes.
6. Reflect on accessibility considerations, noting how you would support diverse learners including SEND and EAL students.
7. Optional: Explore AI tools or prompt techniques you could use to assist in designing or refining your online module.
8. Share your design plan with colleagues or peers for feedback and propose one improvement based on their input.

Summary

The shift to online learning transforms education, offering flexible, accessible, and personalised experiences across all levels. Effective online course design integrates clear learning outcomes, aligned content, and appropriate assessment. Engagement is fostered through interactive multimedia and collaborative activities that support diverse learner needs. Instructors maintain presence and provide timely feedback, enhancing motivation and learning quality. Accessibility and inclusivity are paramount, incorporating universal design principles and accommodations for disabilities and language diversity. Technologies such as Learning Management Systems (LMS) and standards like SCORM enable smooth delivery and tracking. Emerging innovations include AI-assisted course creation and activity-based module design, supporting adaptability and personalisation. Successful online learning balances structure with flexibility, ensuring a coherent, engaging curriculum that prepares learners for current and future challenges in a digitally connected world.

9 ASSESSMENT, GRADING AND REPORTING

Introduction

Assessment is not only a core element of educational practice but also a fundamental part of the curriculum itself. It shapes how learners engage with the conceptual and practical aims of study and how educators plan, adapt, and deliver their teaching to ensure those aims are met. Far from being merely a technical or administrative procedure, assessment reflects the underlying intent, coherence, and values of a curriculum - serving as the principal bridge between what is planned, what is taught, and what is learned.

When assessment is thoughtfully embedded within curriculum design, it becomes a dynamic mechanism to promote deep learning, equity, and continual improvement. Assessment aligned to curriculum intent and learning outcomes helps clarify expectations, supports progression, and ensures that reporting on attainment is both meaningful and actionable for learners, teachers, and institutional leaders.

This chapter:

- Examines the fundamental principles and cycle of assessment within curriculum design.
- Discusses key assessment design decisions, implementation, and fit-for-purpose approaches.
- Explores communicating assessment results, grading practices, and providing effective feedback.
- Reviews evaluation and continuous improvement of assessment practices in curriculum contexts.
- Differentiates product and process assessment, domains of learning, and adapting assessment to learner needs.
- Investigates group assessment and various assessment formats across educational phases.
- Analyses assessment application, impact on learner progression, and curriculum quality assurance.
- Highlights the role of technology-enhanced assessment tools and digital platforms in modern curricula.

The principles of assessment

Assessment is a critical component embedded within the educational curriculum, influencing both the design and enactment of teaching and learning processes. It functions not only as a means of measuring students' progress and achievements but also as a mechanism that shapes instructional decisions and curriculum development. Effective assessment practices help ensure that curricular aims and learning outcomes are realised in practice and support continuous refinement of the curriculum to meet learner needs.

What is assessment?

Assessment is the systematic process of collecting, interpreting, and using evidence about learners' achievements to inform educational decisions. Within UK education, assessment spans formal examinations, coursework, observations, and formative feedback, serving the dual purposes of gauging performance and supporting learning development (Black & Wiliam, 2009). Crucially, assessment must be aligned with the curriculum's intended outcomes to accurately reflect students' acquisition of knowledge, skills, and competencies.

Why do we assess?

Within a curriculum framework, assessment serves as both a monitoring and developmental tool. For learners, it identifies strengths and areas requiring further support, thus guiding their educational journey in alignment with curricular goals. For educators, assessment data provide essential feedback on the effectiveness of instructional strategies, enabling adjustments to content sequencing, pedagogical approaches, and differentiation to better support diverse learner profiles. At system levels, assessment ensures that curriculum standards are maintained and offers transparent, actionable insights for stakeholders - including students, parents, educators, and policymakers - promoting accountability and informed progression decisions (Murchan & Shiel, 2024). National and qualification-level assessments such as GCSEs and A-levels function within a curriculum quality and progression framework, certifying attainment relative to defined standards.

The connection between curriculum and assessment

Curriculum and assessment are fundamentally interconnected elements of effective education, each shaping and reinforcing the other, a principle known as *constructive alignment* or *congruence* (Figure 9.1). The curriculum articulates the intended learning outcomes and specific objectives that define what learners should know, understand, and be able to do by the end of a course or programme. Assessment serves as the practical mechanism for evaluating the extent to which these outcomes and objectives have been achieved.

Figure 9.1 - Curriculum and assessment interconnected

In a well-designed curriculum, assessment is not an add-on or afterthought but is integrated throughout the learning process. Every learning activity, where feasible, should provide an opportunity to gather evidence about learner progress, helping to determine whether the intended outcomes are being met. This alignment ensures that assessment is meaningful, valid, and supportive of learning rather than merely evaluative.

By linking assessment explicitly to curriculum aims, educators can provide clear guidance to learners about expectations and success criteria, enhancing motivation and focus. Moreover, ongoing formative assessment embedded within the curriculum allows for timely feedback and instructional adjustments, facilitating deeper understanding and continuous development.

Assessment rubrics

The linkage between learning and assessment is often expressed in assessment rubrics that provide a set of performance statements differentiated across levels of proficiency. These descriptors articulate what constitutes excellent, competent, and developing work relative to each learning outcome, offering transparency and consistency in judgements.

These rubrics support learner self-assessment, peer evaluation, and instructor grading, and align formative and summative assessment practices within the curriculum. This comprehensive approach ensures that assessment is not an isolated event but a coherent component of the curriculum, guiding learners through a structured progression toward mastery and enabling educators to refine teaching based on formative evidence. Ultimately, effective rubric design enhances educational equity by setting clear, shared standards, fostering learner agency, and promoting valid, reliable assessment across diverse educational contexts.

A sample assessment rubric can be found in Appendix 8.

Principles of effective assessment

To genuinely support curriculum intent, assessment must uphold several foundational principles that ensure fairness, validity, and inclusivity, while fostering learning progress:

- **Suitability:** Assessments should be coherent with the curriculum's purpose and tailored to the subject matter, learner developmental stage, and intended learning outcomes. For example, diagnostic assessments identify knowledge gaps to inform curriculum pacing, whereas summative assessments confirm mastery of programme-level objectives.
- **Reliability, validity, and objectivity:** Alignment with curriculum standards demands that assessments yield consistent, accurate, and unbiased measures of specified learner outcomes. Clear assessment criteria and standard procedures enhance trustworthiness across cohorts and contexts.
- **Inclusivity:** Curriculum-embedded assessment must accommodate learner diversity, ensuring accessibility for students with SEND, EAL, or other needs. This is achieved through plain language, alternative formats, and culturally sensitive content, thereby safeguarding equitable curriculum participation.
- **Ongoing evaluation:** Regular analysis of assessment data across multiple methods helps identify and address potential biases or inequities within curriculum delivery and assessment practices, promoting fairness and continuous improvement.
- **Feedback:** A curriculum-integrated approach emphasises timely, specific, and constructive feedback. This guides learners toward mastery of curricular objectives, fostering self-regulation and motivation. Effective feedback supports the learning process rather than focusing solely on grades.

Informing instruction and curriculum design through assessment evidence

Assessment provides vital evidence about learner knowledge, skills, and understanding, informing the ongoing development and adaptation of curriculum content, teaching methods, and learning activities. Since no single test can capture the full breadth of curriculum attainment, triangulating multiple forms of assessment evidence promotes a more nuanced and accurate picture of achievement and progression. Embedded formative assessment cycles within curriculum delivery ensure responsiveness to learner needs and support differentiated instruction aligned to curriculum goals.

Integrated and transparent assessment communication

Assessment should not be a standalone procedure separate from teaching and curriculum implementation. Instead, it must be seamlessly integrated within the learning cycle to inform both learners and educators continuously. Transparent communication of assessment outcomes - through clear reports and dialogue with learners and their families - fosters trust, clarity of expectations, and active engagement with curricular objectives.

Types of assessment and their curricular roles

As outlined in Table 9.1, assessment methods can be broadly categorised into various types, each serving distinct but complementary functions within the curriculum. These include formative assessments that support learning progression, summative assessments that evaluate achievement, diagnostic tools to identify learners' prior knowledge and needs, and other specialised forms such as synoptic and value-added assessments. Together, these diverse approaches enable a comprehensive understanding of learner development and inform curriculum planning and delivery.

Assessment type	Curricular role
Summative assessment *(Assessment of learning)*	Conducted at authorised points to evaluate the extent to which curriculum objectives have been achieved. Summative assessments provide final judgements on attainment, essential for certification and progression, e.g., GCSEs and A-levels in the UK (Murchan & Shiel, 2024).
Formative assessment *(Assessment for learning)*	Embedded within curriculum delivery, formative assessments provide ongoing feedback supporting learner development, enabling curriculum and instructional adjustments. Approaches include quizzes, peer review, and teacher observation, which have demonstrably improved outcomes when well aligned to learning goals (Black & Wiliam, 2009).
Baseline assessment	Establishes learners' starting points relative to curriculum expectations. Used to tailor subsequent instruction and curricular pacing. For example, assessing reading levels in early primary education informs early literacy programming.

Diagnostic assessment	Identifies prior knowledge, misconceptions, and skills gaps before introducing new content, guiding responsive curriculum modification and differentiated teaching strategies.
Dynamic assessment	Combines evaluation and intervention and aligns strongly with Vygotsky's *Zone of Proximal Development*, focusing on learners' potential to progress with support. This encourages curriculum approaches that are flexible and reflective of learner readiness and developmental stages (Vygotsky, 1978).
Synoptic assessment	Evaluates learners' ability to synthesise and apply knowledge and skills across multiple curriculum areas, particularly relevant for integrated or interdisciplinary curricula often found in higher education.
Criterion referenced	Measures student performance against fixed curriculum criteria or learning outcomes, ensuring transparent and consistent standards across diverse cohorts.
Norm referenced	Compares learners against a peer group, often used in standardised testing environments for selection purposes.
Value-added assessment	Focuses on learner progress over time relative to starting points, emphasising curriculum effectiveness in promoting advancement and addressing inequalities (Rivkin et al., 2005).

Table 9.1 - Assessment types

The assessment cycle

The assessment cycle (Figure 9.2) is a foundational framework within curriculum planning and implementation, encompassing key phases of baseline, formative, and summative assessment. While often associated with school settings, its principles apply broadly across all education and training sectors.

This cycle's strength lies in its structured approach to embedding assessment within the curriculum, supporting coherent learner progression and informed instructional decision-making. It begins by establishing learners' starting points through baseline assessment, continues with ongoing formative assessment linked directly to curriculum content and objectives, and culminates in summative assessment that evaluates cumulative learning against standards or benchmarks.

Baseline assessment, sometimes called *placement* or *initial* assessment, is undertaken at the start of instructional programmes to identify prior knowledge, skills, and attitudes relative to the curriculum's intended outcomes. This information allows educators to position learners accurately within the curriculum's sequence, ensuring that teaching is appropriately targeted and developmentally appropriate. In a curriculum context, baseline data inform both initial differentiation and the effective allocation of learning pathways that maximise progression.

Formative assessment occurs throughout the learning process and is integral to curriculum enactment. It provides timely, actionable feedback to learners and instructors, enabling the dynamic adjustment of teaching to meet evolving learner needs and ensuring alignment with curriculum aims. As described by Black & Wiliam (1998), formative assessment is a critical mechanism for enhancing educational standards by actively engaging learners with their progress and supporting deep, sustained understanding. Within curriculum design, formative assessment also informs continuous review of curricular content and pacing to better scaffold student learning.

Summative assessment takes place at key milestones - such as the end of units, modules, or programmes - and serves as an evaluative measure of learner achievement against specified curriculum standards. Typically associated with high stakes - like end-of-year exams or final project submissions - summative assessment provides evidence for awarding qualifications and benchmarking institutional effectiveness. While summative assessment offers comprehensive snapshots of attainment, its role within the curriculum is complemented and balanced by formative approaches to avoid overly prescriptive or fragmented learning experiences. The classic distinction articulated by Stake (1967) - "When the cook tastes the soup, that's formative; when the customer tastes the soup, that's summative" - illustrates the complementary functions these assessments play in curriculum delivery and evaluation.

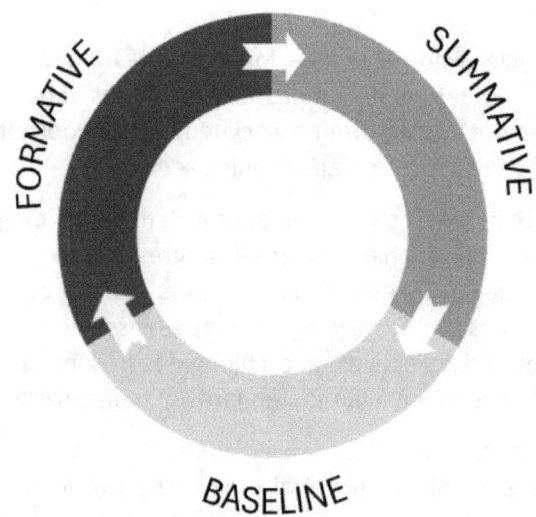

Figure 9.2 - The assessment cycle

>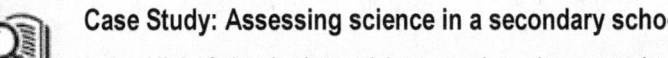
> **Case Study: Assessing science in a secondary school**
>
> Ireby High School, situated in a semi-rural community and serving a diverse range of student abilities, implements a robust and comprehensive assessment framework within its science department. This strategy is carefully aligned with the national curriculum to promote both conceptual understanding and the development of practical scientific skills. Throughout Key Stage 3, the department integrates baseline, formative, and summative assessments systematically to monitor learner progress, inform teaching, and ensure effective preparation for the academic and practical demands of Key Stage 4 science courses.
>
> **Baseline assessment:**
>
> At the beginning of Year 7, science teachers administer a diagnostic test covering fundamental scientific knowledge such as basic biological concepts, introductory physics, and chemistry ideas. This assessment identifies gaps in understanding related to prior learning from primary science education. Results inform differentiated grouping and personalised lesson planning, ensuring that foundational misconceptions are addressed early and that teaching is pitched appropriately.
>
> **Formative assessment:**
>
> Throughout the year, formative assessment practices include frequent classroom quizzes, hands-on laboratory observations, and concept-mapping exercises. Teachers routinely use peer and self-assessment during collaborative experiments, promoting metacognitive awareness. Real-time feedback informs ongoing curriculum pacing. Digital platforms provide instant quiz feedback and track individual progress, enabling timely instructional adjustments.
>
> **Summative assessment:**
>
> At the end of each term, students undertake a summative assessment consisting of written tests with a combination of multiple choice, structured short answers, and extended questions requiring application of scientific reasoning. These assessments contribute to formal reporting and support evaluations of both individual attainment and curriculum effectiveness. Analysis of results guides curriculum review to emphasise areas needing reinforcement or enrichment.

Assessment design

Designing assessment is a deliberate and systematic process that involves multiple carefully planned steps. It requires thoughtful consideration and informed decision-making at every stage to ensure alignment with clearly defined learning objectives, relevant curriculum frameworks, and the diverse needs of learners. As outlined by Bearman et al. (2014), effective assessment design encompasses six distinct stages, each crucial for establishing the validity, reliability, and overall quality of the assessment approach, ultimately supporting meaningful evaluation and enhanced learning outcomes.

Step 1: Purpose of assessment

Assessment serves multiple functions including supporting student learning, aiding achievement of learning goals, contributing to final grades, and fostering learners' ability to self-evaluate. Although all these roles are important, assessment design often prioritises summative grading over promoting learning or enhancing self-assessment capabilities.

Example: Peer assessment in a writing or design course encourages learner reflection and critical evaluation. While it may influence final marks, its main aim is to support student learning and self-appraisal.

Step 2: Context of assessment

Assessment design is inseparable from its educational context, influenced by factors such as learners' characteristics, teaching staff, institutional policies, and disciplinary conventions. Vocational standards, departmental culture, and learners' backgrounds all shape how assessments are crafted and delivered. Collaboration and clear communication among educators and learners are key to tailoring assessment appropriately.

Example: Group projects in business studies reinforce teamwork skills typical of the discipline, preparing students for professional practice and aligning with programme objectives and learner development.

Step 3: Learning outcomes

Assessments must be closely matched to the intended learning outcomes to verify that students meet course and external standards. Assessment tasks support learning development throughout the course - introducing new skills via formative assessment and validating mastery with summative evaluation. Assessments can also promote broader competencies, such as academic writing or scientific reasoning, extending beyond specific outcomes to support holistic development.

Example: In healthcare or business, case studies require application of theory to practice. Formative discussions and feedback develop critical thinking, while summative case reports confirm attainment of learning goals and cultivate transferable skills.

Step 4: Assessment format

The format chosen - essay, presentation, observation, etc. - is essential to effective assessment design. Formats should enable learners to demonstrate knowledge, build skills, and receive formative feedback. Each assessment aligns with curriculum goals and outcomes, featuring explicit criteria and rubrics that describe performance levels.

Example: Portfolios in creative arts or education courses showcase continuous development, encourage reflection, and allow iterative feedback rather than relying on a one-off exam, supporting alignment with learning outcomes.

Step 5: Feedback processes

Feedback is an ongoing dialogue where students submit work, receive constructive input, and refine their efforts. Effective assessment design encourages learners to engage actively with feedback. Multiple submission opportunities and involvement of peer feedback enhance development over the course duration.

Example: For project-based assessments, formative feedback might include suggestions for deeper analysis, while summative comments provide an overall evaluation, highlighting strengths and areas to enhance.

Step 6: Interactions

Assessment design is an ongoing, iterative process that involves continuous interaction among educators, students, and stakeholders. This collaborative approach ensures assessments remain relevant, clear, and aligned with the overall programme goals. By working together, educators can establish shared evaluation criteria, gather diverse perspectives, and incorporate feedback effectively - thus promoting continual improvement and enhancing the quality and fairness of assessments.

Example: Designing presentations as a method of assessment involves dialogue with peers and learners to clarify structure, provide formative feedback, and adapt tasks responsively to performance evidence.

Information

Not all assessments require original design. Standardised, statutory assessments such as SATs, GCSEs, and A-Levels follow government-mandated frameworks with prescribed formats and scoring, limiting local adjustment.

Assessment implementation

After design, implementation involves organising logistics such as scheduling submissions, arranging invigilation, coordinating moderators and markers, and preparing venues or digital platforms. Piloting assessments on smaller scales helps identify difficulties, improve clarity, and validate reliability and fairness. For example, testing a new rubric for critical thinking in one class before wider use ensures alignment with outcomes and supports buy-in from stakeholders.

During evaluation, coordinators ensure consistent grading standards and manage reporting processes for accountability and quality assurance. Ongoing review of results informs future refinements (Winstone & Boud, 2019).

Communicating assessment results

Clear, fair, and timely communication of outcomes is vital. Feedback should be actionable to guide improvement (Bloxham & Boyd, 2007). External reporting may be required for accreditation or regulatory compliance.

Evaluating and improving assessment practices

Continuous review is essential to keep assessment relevant and aligned with learning outcomes. Regular programme evaluations and feedback from faculty and students identify strengths and areas for development (Ramsden, 2003). Benchmarking against peer institutions and sector standards promotes best practices (Biggs & Tang, 2022). These data inform evidence-based enhancements in assessment design, grading, and feedback processes, fostering a culture of continuous improvement (Torrance, 2012).

Designing fit-for-purpose assessments

Over the past decade, educational assessment design has increasingly emphasised creating assessments that are valid, reliable, and responsive to the diverse needs of learners. This involves developing fit-for-purpose assessments that balance product-oriented evaluation with process-focused approaches, addressing various learning domains such as cognitive, affective, and psychomotor skills. Aligning assessments with learners' individual needs and contexts has become a priority, including effective strategies for group assessment. Importantly, the *Accreditation of Prior Experiential Learning* (APEL) has gained recognition, stressing the value of flexible, inclusive assessment practices that acknowledge and validate learners' prior knowledge and experiences, thereby promoting equity and lifelong learning.

Product and process assessment

Product assessment evaluates the end result of learning, typically through summative methods such as final exams or essays. These assessments focus on the output of the learning process, measuring how well learners have achieved the intended outcomes. This aligns with the *Tyler Rationale* of curriculum design and assessment (Tyler, 2009).

Process assessment, on the other hand, concentrates on how learners engage with the learning journey, often using formative assessment methods like portfolios, projects, and observations. Process assessments provide ongoing feedback to both students and educators, helping to guide the learning process and allowing for adjustments to be made in real-time. This aligns with *Stenhouse's Process Model* of curriculum design and assessment (Stenhouse, 1975) and *Dewey's Progressive Education Philosophy* (Dewey, 1986).

Both types of assessment are essential for a comprehensive evaluation of student learning. While product assessments are often used to judge the final outcomes of educational programmes, process assessments enable the tracking of progress and the development of skills over time (Nicol & Macfarlane-Dick, 2006). A balanced assessment strategy that integrates both product and process assessments ensures that the full scope of student achievement is captured, promoting continuous improvement and more accurate learning outcomes.

The product-process dilemma

The final grade for an educational course is often determined by a single, end-of-course assessment. Such assessments are deemed to measure the extent to which learners have achieved the intended learning outcomes for the course. This is all well and good provided that the learning outcomes are detailed and comprehensive.

Question

Consider the following learning outcomes for a course.
1. Develop an understanding of design principles and technology.
2. Students will apply their knowledge to create design solutions.
What do you think is the title of this course?
Could the learning outcomes alone be used as assessment criteria?

You would be correct to have identified the course as Design & Technology. However, the learning outcomes are quite broad and lack specific details about what exactly students should learn or how they should demonstrate their understanding and skills.

Hopefully, the course specification would include more detailed objectives such as:

1. Students will demonstrate an understanding of key design principles, including form, function, and aesthetics, by analysing existing products and identifying how these principles are applied.
2. Students will research and evaluate different materials and their properties (e.g., strength, durability, sustainability) and explain how these influence material selection in design.
3. Students will use sketching and computer-aided design (CAD) software to create detailed design proposals for a product, showing an understanding of scale, proportions, and design specifications.
4. Students will plan and construct a prototype using appropriate tools and techniques, applying knowledge of manufacturing processes and safety procedures.
5. Students will conduct testing of their prototype, evaluating its performance against design criteria such as functionality, usability, and durability, and suggest improvements based on their findings.
6. Students will reflect on the environmental and ethical implications of product design, demonstrating an understanding of sustainable design practices and considering factors such as resource efficiency and lifecycle impact.
7. Students will communicate their design ideas effectively through written reports, presentations, and visual diagrams, demonstrating the ability to explain the rationale behind their design choices to a range of audiences.
8. Students will collaborate in teams to solve a design problem, applying problem-solving skills, critical thinking, and effective teamwork strategies to develop and refine a design solution.
9. Students will analyse the impact of technological advancements on the design process, exploring how new tools, materials, and technologies can be incorporated into modern design solutions.
10. Students will critique and evaluate their own designs and those of peers, using relevant design terminology and providing constructive feedback for improvement.

These learning objectives are more specific and measurable, ensuring that students can demonstrate both their theoretical understanding and practical skills gained during the course. Therefore, the objectives themselves should be used as the basis for the assessment criteria rather than just the learning outcomes.

Information

Assessing learning objectives progressively throughout a course is generally more effective. This method provides regular feedback, offering a comprehensive view of student progress. It enhances motivation, reduces the pressure associated with final exams, and allows for clearer, more transparent grading based on specific assessment criteria, ultimately supporting continuous learning and improvement.

Domains of learning

The domains of learning refer to different areas in which learners develop during the educational process. *Bloom's Taxonomy*, originally divided learning into three primary domains: *cognitive*, *psychomotor*, and *affective* (Gershon, 2015) (Appendix 2). Understanding these domains is essential for designing assessments that are aligned with the diverse nature of learning.

Cognitive domain: This domain involves intellectual skills and knowledge acquisition. It is traditionally the primary focus of academic assessments, where learners demonstrate their ability to recall information, analyse concepts, and apply learned material to new contexts. Cognitive assessments are designed to measure the depth and breadth of understanding in a particular subject (Anderson, 2001).

Psychomotor domain: This domain encompasses physical skills and the ability to perform tasks that require coordination and fine motor skills. Assessing psychomotor abilities is critical in subjects like physical education, vocational training, and healthcare, where practical performance is an essential part of learning (Viscione et al., 2017). Psychomotor assessments often involve observation of skills in action, as well as practical tests and demonstrations.

Affective domain: This domain relates to the emotional aspects of learning, including attitudes, values, and motivation. Assessing affective learning requires different methods than cognitive and psychomotor assessments, as it focuses on measuring students' personal growth, self-awareness, and emotional intelligence. While difficult to assess with traditional methods, educators can measure affective outcomes through self-reports, peer assessments, and reflective writing (Krathwohl, 2009).

To design fit-for-purpose assessments, it is crucial to ensure that all three domains of learning are considered. In the UK, where vocational education, practical skills, and personal development are increasingly emphasised, educators must use a range of assessment methods to capture progress in all three areas (Boud & Falchikov, 2007).

Fitting assessment to learners' needs

In today's educational context, assessments must be thoughtfully designed to accommodate the diverse abilities, backgrounds, and learning styles of all students. By employing *individualisation*, educators tailor assessment tasks to meet each learner's unique needs, while *differentiation* ensures variations in complexity, support, and format across groups. Together, these approaches promote fairness, equity, and inclusivity in assessment, providing every student with a genuine and accessible opportunity to demonstrate their understanding and skills fully.

Differentiation and individualisation

Differentiation and individualisation are crucial strategies for meeting the unique needs of learners.

Differentiation involves tailoring the content, process, and assessment methods to accommodate the varying learning styles, abilities, and interests of students. For instance, students with additional learning needs, such as dyslexia, might benefit from extended time for assessments or alternative formats, such as oral presentations instead of written exams (Tomlinson, 2001).

Individualisation goes one step further, allowing students to have a more personalised learning and assessment experience, often involving the use of learning plans or adaptive technologies.

By designing assessments that provide options for students to demonstrate their knowledge in various formats, educators can ensure that all learners have a fair chance to succeed (Guskey & Bailey, 2010).

Equality and inclusivity

Equality and inclusivity are central to ensuring that assessments are accessible to all learners, regardless of their background or abilities. According to the *UK Equality Act 2010*, educational institutions are required to provide reasonable adjustments for learners with disabilities or specific learning needs, ensuring that assessments are not discriminatory (UK Government, 2010). For example, students with visual impairments may require assessments to be provided in braille or audio formats. Similarly, students from different cultural backgrounds may benefit from assessments that are mindful of linguistic diversity, avoiding bias in question design.

Inclusive assessment practices also promote a fairer representation of students' achievements and competencies, especially in diverse classrooms. Ensuring that assessments do not disadvantage particular groups is a key component of fit-for-purpose assessment design (Race, 2019).

Group assessment

Group assessments have become increasingly prevalent in educational settings due to their ability to foster collaborative learning and develop essential teamwork skills among students. These assessments typically involve collective projects, presentations, or problem-solving tasks that require individuals to coordinate, communicate effectively, and share responsibility to achieve a common goal. Such formative and summative tasks promote interpersonal skills and reflect real-world working environments.

Benefits and challenges

The main benefit of group assessments is that they simulate real-world work environments, where collaboration is often necessary for success. Additionally, group assessments encourage students to engage with peers, which can deepen understanding and foster a sense of community within the classroom (Cohen, 1994). However, group assessments come with challenges, particularly in the fair distribution of effort among group members. Often, some students contribute less than others, which can lead to inequities in the final grades (Boud & Falchikov, 2007). This can be problematic in ensuring that all students are held accountable for their learning.

Strategies for fair assessment of group work

To address the challenges of group assessments, educators can implement strategies to ensure fairness and equity. These include the use of peer evaluations, where students assess each other's contributions to the project, and the provision of individual assessments alongside group tasks (Topping, 2009). Clear guidelines and expectations, along with structured group roles, can also help ensure that all students contribute meaningfully to the assessment.

Accreditation of Prior Learning and Experience (APEL)

Accreditation of Prior Learning (APL) and *Accreditation of Prior Experiential Learning* (APEL) are processes that recognise the value of knowledge and skills acquired outside formal education. APEL is especially relevant in lifelong learning contexts, where learners bring diverse experiences to their studies.

Through APEL, learners can gain academic credit for their prior experiences, which can then contribute to their progression in formal qualifications. This process involves the assessment of non-academic achievements such as work experience, volunteering, or informal learning. APEL requires the use of clear, structured assessment criteria and can involve the submission of reflective portfolios or assessments designed to match the learner's previous experiences with curriculum requirements.

Assessment formats

Educators utilise a diverse and comprehensive array of tools and techniques to assess students effectively across various educational stages. This wide-ranging approach integrates conventional, well-established assessment methods with emerging, innovative practices. Together, these strategies support a holistic evaluation of students' academic progress, engagement, and skill development, tailored to each phase of learning.

Assessment instruments

Observations

Observation is a qualitative assessment tool used to monitor and evaluate student behaviour, participation, and skill application in real-time settings. It is particularly effective in early years education, where structured and unstructured observation techniques help assess developmental milestones (Tickell, 2011). Observational frameworks, such as those outlined by Ofsted (2019), provide guidance for assessing aspects like social interaction and practical skills. While observation offers rich contextual insights, its subjective nature necessitates standardised criteria to ensure reliability and validity.

Example

An example of standardised criteria in a primary school setting is the use of an observation rubric to assess pupils' participation in collaborative group work during a structured activity (Figure 9.3).

	Participation
4	Actively engages in discussion and tasks, contributing ideas and solutions.
3	Participates consistently but with occasional prompting or guidance.
2	Engages minimally, with little initiative or contribution.
1	Rarely participates or disrupts the group's efforts.

Figure 9.3 - Observation rubric
(Where: 4=Excellent, 3=Good, 2=Fair, 1=Needs improvement)

The teacher systematically observes each group in action, recording scores against pre-determined criteria that ensure consistency and fairness in assessment. Following the activity, detailed feedback is provided to each group and to each individual pupil, highlighting their strengths and pinpointing areas for growth. This feedback not only fosters self-awareness but also encourages skill development in key areas.

In practice, the rubric might encompass a range of essential competencies such as effective communication, constructive cooperation, and timely task completion, ensuring a holistic evaluation of the pupils' collaborative skills.

Questioning techniques and taxonomies

Questioning is a ubiquitous assessment technique, and frameworks like *Bloom's Taxonomy* remain foundational in designing questions that target various cognitive levels. Recent adaptations, such as Anderson & Krathwohl's (2001) revision, emphasise higher-order thinking skills like analysing and creating.

Effective questioning strategies, including Socratic questioning and diagnostic questioning, are central to formative assessment practices (Wiliam, 2011). They encourage deeper engagement with subject matter but require skilful implementation to avoid superficial responses. Table 9.2 illustrates Bloom's Taxonomy along with examples of questions that might be asked at each level.

Level	Examples of assessment questions
6. Create	Can you design an experiment to test the effects of sunlight on plant growth? Can you write a short story that incorporates the themes we discussed in class.
5. Evaluate	Do you agree with the author's argument? Why or why not? Which solution to the problem do you think is the most effective? Justify your answer. How would you assess the credibility of this news source?
4. Analyse	What evidence supports the character's decision in the story? Can you compare and contrast the roles of the legislative and executive branches of government? Why do you think this experiment produced these results?
3. Apply	How would you use what you've learned about fractions to double this recipe? Can you apply the laws of motion to explain how a car accelerates? How would you solve this math problem using the formula we learned?
2. Understand	Can you describe the main idea of the story? How would you explain photosynthesis in your own words? What's the difference between a democracy and a monarchy?
1. Remember	What are the key points discussed in today's lesson? Can you list the steps in the water cycle? Who wrote *Romeo and Juliet*?

Table 9.2 - Bloom's taxonomy and associated question types

Oral assessments and interviews

Oral assessments, including viva voce and structured interviews, allow students to articulate knowledge and reasoning verbally. They are frequently employed in disciplines like language learning and professional training (Reimann & Yates, 2020). These methods assess not only content knowledge but also communication skills and critical thinking. Challenges include ensuring standardisation and minimising examiner bias, which recent studies address through rubrics and digital recording for moderation (Boud & Falchikov, 2019).

Portfolios, journals, and log books

Portfolios are versatile tools that showcase a learner's progress, achievements, and reflections. They can include academic work like essays, reports, and presentations, as well as creative outputs such as artwork, creative writing, or multimedia projects. Practical and vocational evidence, like photographs of tasks or skill checklists, can also be included. Reflections, self-evaluations, and feedback responses highlight personal growth, while certificates, awards, and professional skills documentation demonstrate competencies. Portfolios may also feature collaborative work, prior learning evidence, digital projects, and learning plans, offering a comprehensive view of a learner's journey and achievements. They are widely used in creative disciplines and professional qualifications (Quality Assurance Agency, 2024).

Journals and logbooks encourage reflective learning, allowing students to document their experiences and analyse their development. These tools foster autonomy and metacognition but require clear guidelines to ensure consistency in content and assessment criteria (Moon, 2013).

Essays, reports, and objective tests

Essays and reports are traditional assessment tools used to evaluate critical thinking, synthesis, and academic writing skills. They remain integral to summative assessments, particularly in higher education.

Objective tests, such as multiple-choice questions, provide an efficient way to assess factual knowledge and application skills. Advances in automated marking technology have enhanced the scalability and reliability of objective tests (Nicol, 2020). However, these tools must balance assessing surface-level knowledge with deeper learning outcomes.

Seminars and presentations

Seminars and presentations assess students' ability to research, organise, and communicate information effectively. These methods are especially valuable in fostering soft skills like public speaking and teamwork. Peer evaluation during presentations can enhance engagement but must be managed carefully to ensure fairness and constructive feedback.

Role-play and problem-solving tasks

Role-playing and problem-solving tasks engage students in experiential learning, simulating real-world scenarios to assess practical skills and decision-making abilities. These methods are particularly relevant in professional training programmes, such as teacher education and healthcare (Boud et al., 2021). They foster creativity and collaboration but require significant preparation and facilitation to be effective.

Digital simulations and games

Technology-enhanced assessments, including digital simulations and serious games, have gained traction in recent years. Simulations, such as virtual labs and case studies, allow students to practise skills in a controlled environment (Laurillard, 2012). Games engage learners through interactive and immersive experiences, promoting problem-solving and critical thinking (Gee, 2007). In the UK, initiatives like JISC's *Digital Capabilities Framework* encourage the integration of such tools in higher education (JISC, 2023). Challenges include ensuring accessibility and aligning these methods with learning outcomes.

Peer and self-assessments

Peer and self-assessments involve students evaluating their own or their peers' work, fostering a deeper understanding of assessment criteria and promoting reflective practices. These methods align with constructivist theories of learning, emphasising active participation (Vygotsky, 1978). Peer assessment is widely used in collaborative projects, while self-assessment supports personal goal-setting and accountability (Boud et al., 2018). Recent studies highlight the importance of providing clear rubrics and training to enhance the reliability of these approaches (Tai et al., 2018).

Application and impact

Integrating multiple methods

Effective assessment strategies often combine multiple tools to address diverse learning objectives and student needs. For instance, a programme might use observations for formative feedback, essays for summative evaluation, and digital simulations for skill development. Integrating traditional and innovative methods ensures a comprehensive assessment framework that caters to cognitive, affective, and psychomotor domains.

Addressing equity and inclusivity

Assessment design must thoughtfully integrate principles of equity and inclusivity, ensuring that every learner is afforded a fair opportunity to demonstrate their knowledge and skills. While digital tools offer innovative possibilities, they must be carefully selected and adapted to remain accessible to students with disabilities and those from disadvantaged backgrounds, avoiding the risk of widening existing gaps. Inclusive assessment practices - such as accommodating diverse learning needs, providing alternative formats, and embedding cultural relevance - are not just supplementary measures but essential components of a supportive and empowering learning environment. These practices promote not only fairness but also a sense of belonging, enabling all students to engage fully and succeed (Hockings, 2010).

Adapting to evolving educational needs

The COVID-19 pandemic significantly accelerated the adoption of online and hybrid assessment methods, compelling educators worldwide to re-evaluate and transform traditional approaches to evaluation (Crawford et al., 2020). This abrupt shift illuminated the vast potential of technology to introduce greater flexibility, enhance student engagement, and expand access to innovative assessment practices. However, it also exposed critical challenges, such as the pressing need for robust digital infrastructure, equitable access to devices and connectivity, and comprehensive digital literacy for both educators and students. These insights have reshaped the discourse on assessment, emphasising the importance of preparedness and inclusivity in using technology for education.

Grading and feedback

Grading and feedback are essential components of the educational process, providing mechanisms for evaluating student performance, maintaining standards, and fostering learning. These elements must be thoughtfully designed and implemented to ensure they are equitable, valid, and effective in enhancing student outcomes.

Developing grading systems

Grading systems provide a structured framework for assessing and communicating student achievement within the curriculum. This process includes the careful design of marking schemes and rubrics that outline clear criteria for performance, as well as the development of explicit level and grade descriptors to promote transparency and consistency in measurement and reporting.

Marking schemes and rubrics

Marking schemes and rubrics are foundational tools for grading. A marking scheme provides specific criteria for evaluating an assignment, while rubrics (Appendix 8) offer a detailed breakdown of performance levels for each criterion. Research highlights the effectiveness of rubrics in promoting transparency and fairness (Brookhart, 2013). For instance, a rubric for an essay might assess clarity of argument, evidence use, and writing mechanics, assigning distinct descriptors for performance levels ranging from "excellent" to "needs improvement". By aligning grading with clear criteria, rubrics reduce subjectivity and enhance reliability.

Level and grade descriptors

Level and grade descriptors articulate the expectations for student performance at different stages of education. These descriptors align with national frameworks, such as the UK's *Regulated Qualifications Framework* (RQF), ensuring consistency across institutions (Ofqual, 2020). For example, a Level 3 descriptor might specify that students must demonstrate analytical skills, while a Level 6 descriptor might require critical evaluation. Clear descriptors help students understand what is required to achieve specific grades, promoting self-directed learning.

Maintaining assessment standards

Ensuring validity, reliability, standardisation, and moderation are key to maintaining high assessment standards. These processes uphold the integrity of grading and ensure that outcomes are fair and meaningful.

Validity

Validity refers to the extent to which an assessment accurately measures what it is intended to measure. It ensures that the content and objectives of the assessment align with the intended learning outcomes. For example, if a mathematics test is designed to assess problem-solving skills, including an excessive number of language-heavy word problems could reduce its validity for non-native speakers or students with reading difficulties. This is because the assessment might inadvertently test language comprehension rather than mathematical reasoning.

There are several types of validity to consider:
- **Content validity:** Ensures the assessment content adequately represents the subject matter. For instance, an English literature exam that focuses only on poetry would lack content validity if the curriculum also covers novels and plays.
- **Construct validity:** Refers to how well the assessment aligns with the theoretical constructs it aims to measure. For example, a test designed to measure critical

thinking skills should include tasks that require analysis, evaluation, and synthesis, rather than just recalling facts.
- **Criterion-related validity:** Indicates how well an assessment correlates with an external criterion. For instance, a vocational skills test's results should align with actual performance in a real-world work environment.

An assessment with poor validity can lead to misleading results, potentially disadvantaging learners or failing to identify gaps in knowledge and skills accurately. To improve validity, educators should align assessments closely with learning objectives, review test items for bias, and pilot assessments with diverse groups of students.

Reliability

Reliability refers to the consistency of assessment outcomes over time, across different assessors, or within the same test. A reliable assessment yields stable and consistent results, minimising the influence of external factors such as variations in marking or test conditions.

Key factors influencing reliability include:

- **Clear criteria**: Detailed rubrics or marking schemes help ensure consistency in grading. For example, a rubric for evaluating student essays might specify criteria for coherence, evidence use, grammar, and structure, with clear descriptors for each performance level.
- **Assessor training**: Ensuring that all assessors have a shared understanding of the grading criteria enhances reliability. For instance, in GCSE English exams in the UK, assessors undergo standardised training to ensure consistency in marking.
- **Test-retest reliability**: Refers to the stability of assessment results over time. If students take the same test under similar conditions on two occasions, their scores should be comparable, barring significant changes in their knowledge or skills.
- **Inter-rater reliability**: Ensures consistency between different assessors grading the same work. This can be achieved through moderation processes, where multiple assessors review and discuss a sample of work to align their grading standards.

Balancing validity and reliability

While both validity and reliability are essential, they can sometimes conflict. A highly reliable multiple-choice test may lack validity if it only measures recall, while an open-ended project may offer high validity but be harder to grade reliably. To strike a balance, educators can use mixed methods - such as combining multiple-choice questions for factual knowledge with essays to assess critical thinking and argumentation.

Improving validity and reliability requires careful design, regular review, and iterative testing of assessments. Incorporating feedback from students, peer reviews, and expert consultations can further enhance the quality of assessment tools, ensuring they meet the diverse needs of learners and the intended educational goals.

Standardisation and moderation processes

Standardisation and moderation processes are vital mechanisms for ensuring consistency, fairness, and credibility in assessment practices. These processes address potential discrepancies in grading that may arise due to subjective interpretations, diverse institutional practices, or contextual differences in how assessments are administered.

Standardisation refers to the development and application of consistent procedures, grading criteria, and benchmarks to ensure uniformity in assessment outcomes across assessors and settings. It typically involves creating detailed rubrics, conducting training sessions for assessors, and establishing clear guidelines for marking. In schools, standardisation might include aligning teachers' understanding of national curriculum standards through professional development workshops or collaborative meetings. For example, in primary education, teachers may engage in moderation meetings to compare and standardise the grading of writing samples using agreed rubrics.

In higher education, standardisation ensures that assessments across modules and programmes reflect comparable levels of academic rigor and learning outcomes. For instance, a university offering similar courses across multiple campuses might use standardised marking guides and grading policies to ensure that students' work is assessed consistently, regardless of location.

Moderation refers to the quality assurance processes used to review and verify assessment decisions to uphold standards and address any inconsistencies. Moderation can occur at various stages, including pre-assessment (e.g., reviewing the validity of assessment tasks), during assessment (e.g., collaborative marking), or post-assessment (e.g., reviewing grading outcomes). Moderation techniques include:

- **Cross-marking:** Work is independently graded by multiple assessors to compare and align interpretations. For example, in teacher education programmes, two assessors might independently grade a student teacher's lesson observation to ensure a consistent evaluation of teaching competencies. In higher education, a student dissertation will likely be graded by moderating the scores of two independent markers.
- **Moderation through sampling:** A moderator selects a sample of student submissions that is representative of the entire cohort. The size of the sample

often follows a statistical model, such as the square root of the total number of submissions, ensuring that the sample is neither too small to miss significant discrepancies nor too large to become inefficient. This process allows moderators to focus on identifying patterns of inconsistency or bias rather than reviewing every individual submission.

- **Review panels:** Panels of experts or educators meet to discuss and agree on the grading of a sample of assessments. In vocational training, for example, industry professionals might join educators to moderate assessments to ensure they align with workplace standards.
- **External reviews:** Independent external examiners or auditors evaluate assessment practices and grading to ensure they meet institutional or national standards. In UK higher education, the external examiner system plays a crucial role in this process. External examiners review samples of graded work, assessment tasks, and marking criteria to verify that academic standards are being upheld and applied consistently across institutions (Quality Assurance Agency, 2024).

In further education (FE), moderation processes might include partnerships with awarding bodies, which require standardisation meetings and external verification visits to maintain the credibility of vocational qualifications. Similarly, in adult education settings, moderation helps ensure that assessments for non-formal certifications are fair and aligned with recognised standards.

In international contexts, such as *International Baccalaureate* (IB) schools or institutions delivering transnational education, moderation processes are essential for ensuring consistency across diverse cultural and linguistic contexts. For instance, IB teachers worldwide participate in moderation activities coordinated by the IB Organisation, including the review of coursework and examinations by global panels to maintain equity across regions (IBO, 2024).

Moderation fosters confidence in the fairness and credibility of assessments for all stakeholders. For students, it reassures them that their grades reflect equitable standards. For educators, it provides a framework to ensure their judgments align with best practices. For external stakeholders, such as employers or accrediting bodies, moderation enhances the trustworthiness of qualifications and certifications.

Assessing group work

Group work is increasingly used in education to develop collaborative skills, but assessing group work presents unique challenges. Key approaches include shared group grades and peer review mechanisms.

Shared group grades

Assigning a shared grade for group work can encourage collective responsibility and collaboration, as it reflects the output of the group as a whole. However, this approach often raises concerns about fairness, particularly when individual contributions are unequal. Disputes over effort and participation can affect group dynamics and outcomes. Recent research advocates for hybrid approaches that combine group grades with individual assessments to address these challenges (Chiriac, 2014). For example, a group project might be graded on the overall quality of the final product, such as a report or presentation, while individual contributions are assessed separately. This could involve reflective reports, self-assessments, peer evaluations, or individual presentations that highlight each member's role and input. Rubrics that clearly define expectations for both group and individual components can help manage discrepancies and ensure transparency in grading.

Hybrid approaches are particularly beneficial in diverse educational contexts. For instance, in vocational education, group projects may simulate workplace tasks, and individual performance is often evaluated to ensure alignment with professional competencies. In online learning environments, individual assessments can help monitor engagement and contribution in virtual teams. These methods recognise the value of teamwork while mitigating potential conflicts, leading to fairer and more comprehensive evaluations of students' skills and efforts.

Peer review and assessment

Peer assessment enables students to evaluate their peers' contributions, fostering accountability, self-regulation, and critical thinking. When students assess each other's work, they engage more deeply with assessment criteria and develop a better understanding of quality standards. Tools like online peer evaluation platforms, such as *Peergrade* and *FeedbackFruits*, have enhanced the feasibility of implementing peer review in group assessments by streamlining the process and providing anonymity. These tools allow instructors to collect, review, and integrate peer feedback effectively, even in large classes.

To ensure fairness and reliability in peer assessments, it is crucial to provide students with training on giving constructive feedback and using the assessment criteria appropriately. Clear guidance on how to evaluate peers, examples of effective feedback, and calibration exercises can improve the quality of peer reviews (Topping, 2017). Anonymous mechanisms, where students do not know whose work they are evaluating or who has evaluated their work, can reduce bias and alleviate concerns about interpersonal conflicts.

In practice, peer assessment is widely used across disciplines. For example, in engineering education, students might evaluate each other's contributions to a design project, providing feedback on technical accuracy and teamwork. In creative disciplines, such as arts or media studies, students may assess peers' portfolios or performances, offering critiques that contribute to iterative improvement. However, peer assessment requires careful implementation, as students may lack the expertise or confidence to provide accurate evaluations. Combining peer feedback with instructor moderation can address these limitations and enhance the overall assessment process.

Feedback strategies

Feedback is a powerful tool for learning, but its effectiveness depends on how it is delivered. Strategies for providing timely, constructive feedback and managing feedback in high-stakes contexts are critical for supporting student growth.

Timely and constructive feedback

Timeliness is crucial for feedback to be effective. Research indicates that feedback is most impactful when provided soon after the assessment, allowing students to act on it while the learning experience is still fresh (Hattie & Clarke, 2019). Constructive feedback should focus on specific strengths and areas for improvement, using clear language to guide students toward actionable steps. For example, instead of stating, "This argument is unclear", feedback might specify, "Clarify your argument by providing more evidence to support your claim ".

Managing feedback in high-stakes contexts

High-stakes assessments, such as final exams or capstone projects, pose additional challenges for feedback delivery. In these contexts, feedback should not only address performance but also support emotional resilience and future learning. Studies highlight the importance of balancing critical and positive comments to maintain motivation and self-efficacy (Carless, 2020). Additionally, institutions should provide opportunities for follow-up, such as one-to-one meetings or workshops, to help students interpret and apply feedback effectively.

Technology-enhanced assessment

Technology-Enhanced Assessment (TEA) has transformed educational evaluation by integrating digital tools to enhance assessment design, implementation, and feedback. This evolution has been particularly significant in online and blended learning environments, where traditional assessment methods may not fully capture student learning and engagement. While TEA offers significant opportunities to enrich educational evaluation through innovative methods that cater to diverse learning environments, it also presents challenges that require careful consideration to ensure accessibility, validity, and ethical use. Ongoing research and thoughtful implementation are essential to harness the full potential of TEA in enhancing student learning outcomes.

Technology in assessment design

Online and blended learning contexts: In online and blended learning settings, technology facilitates diverse assessment strategies that accommodate various learning styles and provide immediate feedback. The increasing adoption of online assessments has highlighted the need for valid, reliable, and fair evaluation methods in virtual environments. Research on technology-enhanced assessment emphasises the importance of selecting appropriate online assessment formats to maintain educational standards (Khan & Jawaid, 2020).

Digital portfolios and e-assessments: Digital portfolios and e-assessments enable students to showcase their work and reflect on their learning over time. These tools support formative assessment by allowing continuous monitoring of student progress and providing opportunities for self-assessment. Research in higher education indicates that digital technologies in assessment can enhance student engagement and provide more comprehensive evaluations of student competencies (Nkomo et al., 2021).

Methods in tech-based assessment

Automated testing and AI tools: Artificial Intelligence (AI) has introduced automated testing systems capable of evaluating complex student responses efficiently. AI-driven assessments can provide instant feedback, adapt to individual learning needs, and reduce the grading burden on educators. A systematic review highlighted the potential of AI in automating the assessment of text-based responses, enhancing the scalability and consistency of evaluations (Gao et al., 2024).

Interactive learning activities: Interactive assessments, such as simulations and gamified quizzes, engage students actively, promoting deeper learning and retention. These activities can be tailored to individual learner profiles, providing personalised learning experiences. The integration of interactive assessments in technology-enhanced learning environments has been shown to improve student motivation and achievement (Duterte, 2024).

Synchronous and asynchronous assessments: Technology enables both synchronous (real-time) and asynchronous (time-independent) assessments, offering flexibility to accommodate diverse student schedules and learning paces. Synchronous assessments, such as live quizzes, facilitate immediate feedback and interaction, while asynchronous assessments, like discussion boards and recorded presentations, allow thoughtful reflection and self-paced learning. The choice between synchronous and asynchronous assessment methods should align with learning objectives and student needs.

Challenges and opportunities

Ensuring accessibility: While technology-enhanced assessments offer numerous benefits, ensuring accessibility for all students remains a critical challenge. Factors such as internet connectivity, digital literacy, time zones, and accessibility must be considered to provide equitable assessment opportunities. Institutions need to implement inclusive design principles and provide necessary support to address these disparities.

Balancing innovation with validity: Innovative assessment methods must maintain validity and reliability to ensure that they accurately measure intended learning outcomes. The rapid integration of AI and other technologies in assessments raises concerns about academic integrity and the potential for misuse. Educators are advised to develop clear guidelines and ethical frameworks to govern the use of AI in assessments, ensuring that technology serves as a tool for learning enhancement rather than a shortcut for students.

Future trends in assessment

The evolution of assessment practices is increasingly shaped by advancements in technology, the growing emphasis on personalised learning, and the interconnectedness of the global community, alongside ethical imperatives. Emerging trends indicate a paradigm shift toward adaptive systems that are globally relevant and grounded in principles of equity, integrity, and sustainability. Personalised learning and adaptive assessments hold the potential to enhance learner engagement and outcomes, while global frameworks stress the importance of skills relevant to a connected world. Addressing ethical and sustainability challenges remains crucial to ensuring that these innovations uphold principles of equity. As these trends continue to evolve, collaborative efforts among educators, policymakers, and technologists will be essential to shape assessment practices that are both innovative and responsible.

Personalised learning and adaptive assessments

One significant trend is the rise of personalised learning, underpinned by adaptive assessments. These assessments utilise artificial intelligence (AI) and data analytics to tailor questions and feedback to individual learners' abilities, ensuring a customised learning experience. Adaptive assessments can identify gaps in knowledge more efficiently than traditional methods, allowing educators to provide targeted interventions. These systems use algorithms that adjust the difficulty level of questions in real-time, promoting both engagement and mastery.

Personalised assessments are transforming formative and summative evaluations. Platforms such as *Duolingo* and *Khan Academy* demonstrate the efficacy of adaptive tools in assessing language proficiency and mathematical skills. These innovations are not confined to academics but extend to professional training, where competency-based assessments align with industry standards. However, the widespread adoption of adaptive assessments requires careful calibration to avoid biases embedded in algorithms, necessitating ongoing research and monitoring. Relying too heavily on AI in assessments poses a risk, highlighting the need for human oversight to guarantee a fair evaluation process (Vorecol, 2024).

Global trends in assessment practices

Globally, assessment practices are shifting to emphasise skills relevant to the 21st century, such as critical thinking, creativity, collaboration, and digital literacy. Organisations like the *Organisation for Economic Co-operation and Development* (OECD) have pioneered frameworks such as the *PISA for Schools* initiative, which evaluates problem-solving and global competencies alongside traditional academic skills.

Cross-national assessments are increasingly incorporating technology to ensure scalability and inclusivity. The transition to digital platforms enables seamless administration, scoring, and reporting across borders. In higher education, micro-credentials and digital badges are gaining traction as alternative forms of assessment that recognise specific skills and competencies. These credentials align with lifelong learning paradigms, allowing learners to showcase their achievements in a flexible, modular manner (Brown et al., 2021).

Ethical considerations and sustainability

As assessment practices evolve, ethical considerations and sustainability are becoming central to their design and implementation. Ethical challenges include ensuring data privacy, preventing algorithmic biases, and maintaining transparency in automated scoring systems. As Williamson (2021) argues, the increasing reliance on data-driven assessments necessitates robust governance frameworks to protect student rights and ensure accountability.

Sustainability in assessment encompasses both environmental and social dimensions. Digital assessments reduce the environmental impact associated with paper-based testing but raise concerns about electronic waste and energy consumption. Social sustainability requires that assessment systems be equitable and accessible, addressing disparities in technology access and digital literacy.

> **Information** *i*
> Electronic waste (e-waste) is unwanted or broken electronic devices, like old computers, laptops, iPads, phones, or TVs. It can harm the environment if not recycled properly.

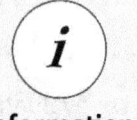

> **Activity: Assessment review and redesign**
>
> Select a curriculum, programme, or course from your setting across primary, secondary, FE, or HE. Using the following prompts as a guide, conduct a structured review of its assessment, evaluating alignment with learning outcomes, fairness, inclusivity, and balance of formative and summative methods. Reflect on strengths and improvements.
>
> 1. Identify the stated or implied learning outcomes and objectives associated with the assessment strategy. How clearly are they articulated and aligned with curriculum aims?
> 2. Analyse the balance and integration of formative and summative assessment within the curriculum. Are there sufficient opportunities for ongoing feedback and learner adjustment?
> 3. Evaluate how well the current grading and reporting methods communicate learner progress in ways that support curriculum intent, equity, and motivation.
> 4. Consider the appropriateness and inclusivity of assessment formats for the learner group, including adaptations for diverse needs.
> 5. Propose at least two concrete improvements to better align assessment and reporting with curriculum design principles to enhance learner engagement and progression.
>
> Prepare a brief reflective summary of your findings and redesign proposals. If possible, share and discuss your insights with colleagues to explore variations and common challenges in curriculum-aligned assessment.

Summary

Assessment is a vital, integrated element of curriculum design and delivery. It serves as both a measure and a driver of learning, shaping how learners engage with and achieve curriculum aims. When aligned effectively with curriculum intent and learning outcomes, assessment supports meaningful progression, equity, and transparency across educational contexts - from primary to higher education.

Thoughtfully designed assessment practices inform teaching strategies, guide curriculum adaptation, and foster shared understanding among learners, educators, and stakeholders. Grading and reporting, rooted in robust assessment, provide critical feedback loops that sustain learner motivation and educational improvement.

As digital tools evolve, technology-enhanced assessment offers new opportunities to deepen engagement and refine curriculum impact, making assessment a pivotal mechanism for ensuring curriculum quality and relevance.

10 MANAGING THE CURRICULUM

Introduction

Strong curriculum leadership plays a fundamental role in ensuring institutional effectiveness and student success. It involves overseeing the strategic design, delivery, and continuous evaluation of the curriculum to maintain its relevance, coherence, and quality. Effective leadership shapes the organisation's trajectory and directly affects the experiences of staff and learners. This relies on robust leadership from principals, middle managers and a range of curriculum leaders with the critical objective of aligning curricular decisions with the wider aims of the institution.

This chapter

- Highlights the importance of aligning curriculum management decisions with institutional vision, priorities, and the evolving needs of learners and society.
- Examines the process of curriculum change across primary, secondary, further, and higher education, highlighting key stages and drivers.
- Discusses the management cycle and strategic approaches for planning, implementing, and sustaining curriculum change within educational institutions.
- Explores the roles, duties, and leadership models of principals and other curriculum leaders, including collaborative leadership approaches.
- Reviews practical strategies for engaging stakeholders, navigating barriers, and addressing challenges in curriculum management.
- Examines effective frameworks and models for ongoing curriculum evaluation and review, including quality assurance and accountability requirements.
- Investigates ways leaders can build professional capacity and foster collaborative, reflective practice among staff.

Planning curriculum change

Curriculum change is an essential and ongoing feature within educational institutions across all sectors, driven by the evolving needs of learners, policy shifts, advancing knowledge, and changing societal expectations. However, for curriculum change to lead to real and lasting improvement, it must be guided by careful planning, strong and strategic leadership, and responsive management practices that support staff and engage stakeholders throughout the process of implementation and evaluation.

Understanding the process of curriculum change

At its core, curriculum change involves deliberate modifications to the intended learning content, pedagogical approaches, assessment methods, or organisational structures that define the educational experience. Fullan (2016) emphasises that change is a process, not an event, characterised by implementation over time, iterative refinement, and adaptation to contextual realities. This perspective is critical when managing curriculum change in diverse educational settings.

Key stages in curriculum change

Various models exist to conceptualise curriculum change, but a common feature is a cyclical, phased approach encompassing diagnosis, planning, implementation, evaluation, and consolidation (Guskey, 2002). These stages are depicted in Figure 10.1.

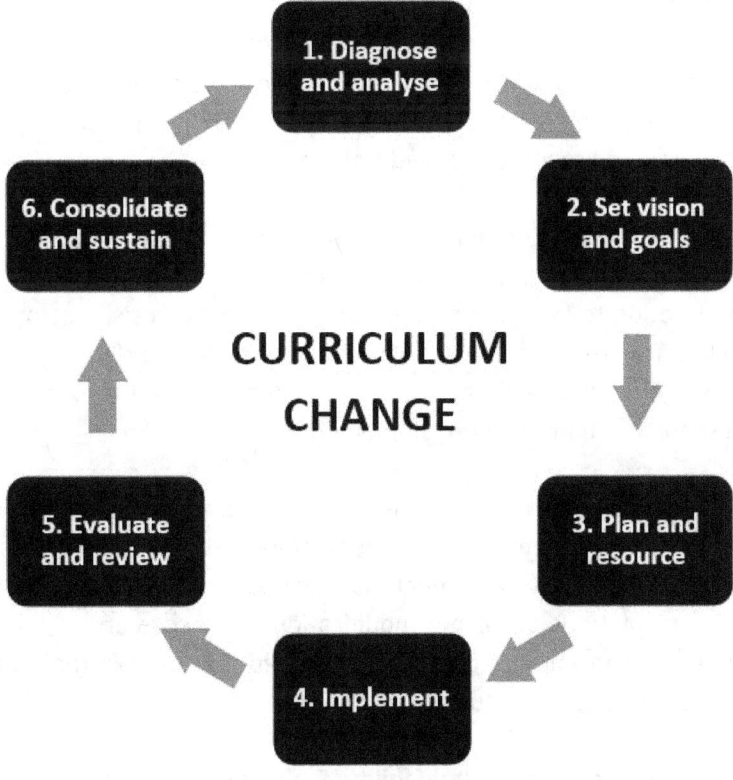

Figure 10.1 - Curriculum change

1. **Diagnosis and needs analysis:** Identifying drivers for change, such as curriculum review findings, policy updates, learner feedback, or external requirements (Alexander, 2021). For example, in FE colleges, emerging labour market demands may necessitate curriculum realignment to new qualifications or skills frameworks (Ofqual, 2023). In HE, changing research priorities or graduate attributes can prompt programme redesign.

2. **Vision and goal setting:** Establishing a clear and shared vision for the intended change, articulating precise objectives aligned with institutional priorities and learner needs. Effective communication of this vision is vital to gaining staff and stakeholder buy-in across all sectors (Leithwood & Louis, 2012). In primary settings, this might involve articulating the rationale for including new cross-curricular themes such as digital literacy or wellbeing.

3. **Planning and resource allocation:** Developing detailed action plans covering curriculum content, pedagogy, assessment, staff development, and necessary resources. This includes scheduling, budgeting, and staff roles, ensuring adequate professional development for those involved (Fullan, 2016). For example, secondary schools introducing a new GCSE subject must coordinate timetabling, acquire materials, and train teachers.

4. **Implementation:** Carrying out the planned changes, while monitoring progress and challenges. This phase requires strong leadership and ongoing communication to keep the momentum and address resistance or unforeseen obstacles. Theories like Lewin's (1947) three-step model - unfreeze, change, refreeze - offer useful frameworks for understanding the psychological and organisational dynamics during implementation.

5. **Evaluation and review:** Systematically assessing the impact of curriculum changes through a combination of qualitative and quantitative data, including learner achievement, engagement, and feedback (Stiggins, 2002). This informs whether adaptations or further modifications are necessary. Higher education institutions often employ curriculum committees and external examiners to uphold quality assurance during this phase.

6. **Consolidation and sustainability:** Embedding successful changes into routine practice, ensuring they become part of the institutional culture, curriculum documentation, and staff expectations (Fullan, 2016). Sustained change is more likely when supported by ongoing leadership, continuous

professional learning, and participative decision-making across organisational levels (Hargreaves & Fink, 2006).

Reasons for curriculum change

Curriculum change in education is typically driven by three overarching categories: adaptation, innovation, and transformation.

Adaptation
Curriculum adaptation occurs in response to external pressures such as policy reforms, changes in funding, demographic shifts, or significant events. Educational institutions adapt their curricula to comply with new statutory requirements, survive in a changing environment, or remain relevant to learners' needs and societal expectations. Examples include responding to Ofsted recommendations, revising curriculum to meet new national curriculum frameworks, or altering curriculum delivery modes due to unforeseen circumstances.

Innovation
Curriculum innovation involves the introduction of new ideas, technologies, teaching strategies, or assessment practices designed to enhance learning and better meet contemporary demands. Innovation is typically internally motivated - driven by a desire to improve student outcomes, modernise the curriculum, or incorporate findings from educational research and technological advances. This may include periodic updates to curriculum content, piloting novel interdisciplinary projects, integrating AI-assisted learning tools, or redesigning assessment to foster creative thinking. Often, such changes start as small-scale initiatives within departments before wider adoption.

Transformation
Curriculum transformation extends beyond incremental improvements or adaptations; it represents fundamental, systemic rethinking of educational purpose, structure, or culture. Transformative curriculum change might involve shifting from subject-based to competency-based frameworks, developing entirely new curricular philosophies, or restructuring assessment to better support holistic learner development. Such changes are rare, often requiring visionary leadership or arising out of crisis. For instance, the Curriculum for Wales, introduced by the Welsh Government in 2022, is a notable example of national, transformative curriculum reform, aiming to build a more inclusive and learner-centred education system (Evans, 2022).

These three categories can be viewed as a continuum: curriculum adaptation is typically reactive, responding directly to external prompts; curriculum innovation is proactive, seeking to improve or modernise existing practice; and curriculum transformation is strategic and long-term, fundamentally altering the educational landscape.

Table 10.1 compares these key drivers of curriculum change:

Driver	Commonality	Typical source	Examples
Adaptation	Very common	External pressures.	Responding to Ofsted; implementing new curriculum frameworks.
Innovation	Occasional	Internal initiative or pilot projects.	Trialling new teaching methods or AI-assisted teaching tools.
Transformation	Rare	Visionary leadership or crisis.	Rebuilding curriculum philosophy; creating new school models.

Table 10.1 - Comparison of drivers of change

In practice, most curriculum change within schools, colleges, and universities is driven by adaptation - reactively aligning curricular content and structures with government mandates, accountability systems, technological changes, updated curriculum frameworks, or new expectations around inclusion, digital literacy, and safeguarding (Crick, 2021). Such change is usually top-down, often requiring rapid compliance, as seen in the adoption of digital technologies; institutions frequently integrate these tools reactively, without long-term curriculum planning. The COVID-19 pandemic provided a stark example of this approach, with widespread rapid shifts to remote curriculum delivery, often without sufficient preparation (Crick, 2021).

Curriculum innovation, by contrast, is less frequent and often limited to specific areas or led by individual educators. Without concerted leadership or strategic investment, these innovations rarely gain traction across the whole curriculum.

Deep curriculum transformation involves reimagining fundamental aspects of educational values, aims, and structures. Such profound change is infrequent and typically arises in periods of major policy reform (especially following newly elected government) or systemic renewal within education systems. The Curriculum for Wales is a recent example, illustrating how national initiatives can drive comprehensive, foundational reforms, impacting curriculum design, delivery, and educational philosophy in institutions. (Evans, 2022).

Differences across educational contexts

While the fundamental process stages apply broadly, contextual factors influence curriculum change implementation. Primary schools often focus on whole-school development linked to statutory frameworks like the National Curriculum (DfE, 2014). Secondary schools may balance national exam requirements with school-based innovations. FE institutions typically deal with more complex modular programmes and diverse stakeholder groups, including employers and accrediting bodies. Change in HE is frequently subject to external quality standards such as the Quality Assurance Agency's UK Quality Code (QAA, 2024), requiring formal programme approval and periodic revalidation cycles.

Leaders of curriculum change

Effective curriculum change in education depends on purposeful, skilful leadership at every level. No matter the context, leaders of change are central in realising a relevant, coherent, and high-quality curriculum.

Core roles and responsibilities

Curriculum leadership involves fostering a clear vision, building consensus, and enabling staff to embrace ongoing improvement. Leaders - be they headteachers, subject or department leads, senior leadership teams (SLTs), or university faculty - drive the process by inspiring commitment, allocating resources, and modelling reflective practice. Crucially, they are responsible for creating a culture in which curriculum development is continuous rather than static (Gov.uk, 2025).

Clarity of purpose is widely recognised as fundamental to effective curriculum leadership. When leaders are explicit about what they intend to change - whether that is curriculum content, assessment practices, pedagogical methods, organisational structures, or overarching values - they can align stakeholders, build consensus, and drive coherent, purposeful action. Clear goals help to focus planning, resource allocation, and professional development, making it easier to communicate the rationale, anticipated benefits, and measures of success.

However, achieving such clarity is not always straightforward in practice. Leaders may face competing priorities, ambiguous policy mandates, or the need to balance national requirements with local needs. In complex educational environments, curriculum change can be iterative and responsive, requiring leaders to continually revisit and refine their aims as evidence emerges and stakeholder views evolve.

The literature (e.g. Fullan, 2016; Leithwood et al., 2020) emphasises that while clarity about the 'what' is essential, effective curriculum change also depends on clarity about the 'why' (purpose and values), the 'how' (strategies and processes), and the intended impact on learners. Without clear aims, curriculum change risks becoming fragmented, superficial, or misaligned with institutional vision and learner needs.

School leaders frequently serve as the main drivers behind curriculum review and development initiatives. In both primary and secondary education settings, they actively collect and analyse feedback from a wide range of sources, including teaching staff, pupils, parents, and external partners such as local businesses or educational authorities. This evidence is used to identify strengths, weaknesses, and emerging needs, which then inform the strategic direction for curriculum enhancements. Above all, their commitment to addressing the evolving needs of learners - shaped by shifting community demographics, new research insights, and ongoing professional development - remains the key catalyst for meaningful and sustainable change.

Shared leadership

Modern approaches emphasise shared leadership, where responsibility for curriculum development is shared among staff according to expertise and interest. This is especially powerful in large schools and multidisciplinary environments, where subject leads or heads of department become agents of innovation. Recent reforms in England, as well as international studies, confirm that delegating decision-making to those with curriculum and subject expertise leads to better progression, ownership, and specialist development.

Sharing leadership is not simply the division of tasks: it is an ethos where collaborative working, trust, and mutual respect underpin every stage of change. For example, subject leaders might manage progression planning or the introduction of research-informed practice, while senior leaders ensure coherence across the whole curriculum and support professional capacity. In HE, effective change leaders include department heads and academic committees, who are both stewards of existing standards and champions for innovation (Lattuca and Stark, 2009). The role requires balancing the need for coherence, regulatory alignment, and the encouragement of disciplinary distinctiveness.

Strategies and styles

Leaders of change are highly adaptive. They recognise when to employ visionary, participative, or coaching leadership styles, depending on the phase and context of change (Goleman, 2017). For example, implementing a new curriculum area in a primary school may involve co-design workshops, mentorship, and structured feedback loops to secure teacher buy-in and build ownership - a process shown to increase innovation and sustain improvements over time.

Successful curriculum change leaders also draw on external networks - partner schools, multi-academy trusts, or professional learning communities - enhancing their initiatives through shared expertise or benchmarking. In secondary, FE and HE, involving students in curriculum decisions can further democratise development, ensuring it resonates with learner aspirations and employer needs (DfE, 2025).

Professional learning and reflection

Across all sectors, leaders actively support staff through targeted professional development, coaching, and mentoring, recognising that change is most effective when teachers understand the rationale and feel included in the process. Building leadership capacity at all levels strengthens the institution's ability to manage future change, making improvements more likely to be sustained.

Cross-phase and contextual nuances

While the essential attributes of curriculum leaders are shared, context matters. In primary education, leadership is often collective and whole-school, focused on core curriculum areas and social development. In secondary schools, department leads act as mediators between national requirements and subject-based innovation. In FE and HE, leadership is distributed among module leaders, programme coordinators, directors, and quality assurance committees, who must also respond to stakeholder requirements and accreditation standards.

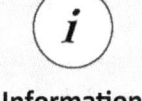

Information — The notion of distributing leadership tasks should not be confused with the principle of the model of *distributed leadership* which, despite the lack of an agreed definition, relates to the more general de-coupling of leadership from a central authority and sharing responsibilities and decision making with staff across the whole organisation.

Ultimately, the success of curriculum change relies less on particular structural models and more on the ability of leaders to build trust, encourage collaboration, and sustain a culture of ongoing review and improvement. Effective leadership ensures that, regardless of the educational context, meaningful and lasting change is achieved and maintained.

Curriculum management roles

Curriculum leadership involves the processes of designing, implementing, evaluating, and revising educational programmes to meet learner needs and institutional goals. It requires strategic thinking and collaborative decision-making.

Two dominant curriculum models guide curriculum leaders:

- **Product model** (Tyler, 1949): Emphasises defined learning objectives, outcomes, and assessment standards. It is linear, focusing on measurable end goals.
- **Process model** (Stenhouse, 1975): Centres on the learning experience and development of understanding, offering flexibility and adaptability in pedagogy and content delivery.

Effective curriculum leadership must often blend these models and align them with broader institutional missions. Leadership theories relevant to curriculum management include:

- **Transformational Leadership** (Leithwood & Jantzi, 2006): Inspires and motivates staff through vision and empowerment.
- **Instructional Leadership** (Hallinger & Murphy, 1985): Focuses on teaching and learning as core priorities.
- **Distributed Leadership** (Spillane, 2006): Involves multiple actors in leadership roles, sharing responsibility for curriculum outcomes.

The role of the principal

The principal's role in curriculum management is foundational. As strategic leaders, principals must articulate a clear vision, foster curriculum leadership at all levels, and balance accountability demands with innovation in pedagogy.

Vision-setting and aligning the curriculum with institutional goals

A compelling vision ensures curricular coherence and relevance by providing a clear and unifying framework for teaching and learning. As Harris (2011) notes, vision-setting is crucial because it shapes the direction, priorities, and implementation of the curriculum, aligning it with institutional aspirations. Principals who establish and communicate a well-defined strategic vision effectively create a roadmap that integrates subject content, pedagogical approaches, and assessment practices. This leadership role not only fosters shared understanding and motivation among staff and stakeholders but also secures a cohesive, outcome-focused curriculum that meets the evolving needs of learners and the wider community.

 "At Greenfield Academy, our vision is to deliver a dynamic and inclusive curriculum that nurtures both academic excellence and personal growth for all students. We strive to equip learners with the skills, knowledge, and values necessary to thrive in an ever-evolving global society. Our curriculum is thoughtfully designed to be challenging and engaging, ensuring accessibility for diverse learning needs and backgrounds. We place strong emphasis on fostering collaboration, critical thinking, creativity, and resilience to prepare students not only for immediate academic success but also for lifelong learning and responsible citizenship. Through sustained partnerships with local communities, industry, and higher education institutions, alongside comprehensive ongoing professional development for staff, we continually adapt and enhance our curriculum. This strategic approach ensures our provision remains relevant, forward-looking, and closely aligned to the needs and aspirations of our learners".

This vision underscores a strategic commitment to both excellence and innovation.

Supporting curriculum leadership across all levels

Principals play a critical role in nurturing leadership capacity within their teams, ensuring that responsibility for curriculum innovation and management is shared widely rather than concentrated at the top.
The nature and distribution of curriculum leadership roles varies according to educational phase and institutional context:

- *Primary schools:* Curriculum leadership is often highly collaborative, with subject coordinators or phase leaders (such as Key Stage or year group leads) taking responsibility for specific curriculum areas - e.g., literacy, mathematics, or science. These roles involve overseeing subject planning, supporting colleagues, monitoring standards, and liaising with senior leadership to ensure curriculum coherence across the school.

- *Secondary schools:* Curriculum leadership typically includes heads of department or subject leaders, who coordinate curriculum planning, teaching and assessment within their subject areas. These leaders play a pivotal role in driving subject-specific innovation, supporting departmental staff, ensuring standards, and facilitating cross-curricular projects. There may also be additional curriculum roles such as lead practitioners or whole-school curriculum coordinators overseeing aspects like assessment or personal development.

- *Further education (FE):* In colleges, curriculum leadership is frequently exercised by programme leaders, course coordinators, or heads of curriculum areas. These individuals are responsible for designing and updating vocational and academic programmes, overseeing quality assurance, engaging with employers or industry bodies, and supporting teaching teams in curriculum delivery and professional development.

- *Higher education (HE):* Curriculum leadership is typically exercised by module leaders or programme leaders in collaboration with a content development department. They oversee module design, content delivery, assessment strategies, and continuous review at both the module and programme levels. Heads of department and academic committees provide broader strategic leadership, ensuring alignment with institutional aims, subject benchmarks, and external quality standards.

By recognising and formalising such roles across all settings, school, college, and university leaders can foster a distributed approach to curriculum management. This ensures that expertise is developed at every level, staff are empowered to influence curricular decisions, and leadership capacity is sustained over time - making curriculum improvement a shared, dynamic, and institution-wide endeavour.

Table 10.2 presents practical strategies for fostering curriculum leadership, including ongoing professional development to enhance knowledge and skills, collaborative planning to promote collective ownership and shared expertise, and clearly defined leadership roles that establish accountability and clarity. These approaches help deepen staff engagement, distribute workload effectively, and strengthen the organisation's resilience to adapt to future challenges.

Strategy	Description	Examples/Actions
Evidence-based decision making	Use student performance data to inform curriculum decisions and leadership actions.	• Regularly analyse assessment data to adjust curriculum delivery. • Hold data meetings with teachers to discuss strategies based on student outcomes.
Clearly defined leadership roles	Establish specific roles for curriculum leaders at all levels to ensure clear ownership and accountability.	• Designate department heads, subject coordinators, or grade-level leads. • Create job descriptions outlining curriculum leadership responsibilities.

Collaborative planning	Encourage teachers and leaders to collaborate on curriculum development and refinement.	• Set up regular team meetings for curriculum review and planning. • Use collaborative tools (e.g., Google Docs, shared drives) for planning.
Mentorship and coaching	Pair experienced leaders with less experienced staff to guide and support curriculum leadership development.	• Assign senior teachers to mentor new teachers or middle leaders. • Provide instructional coaching to support curriculum leadership.
Shared leadership	Share leadership responsibilities across the staff to create a collective approach to curriculum management.	• Involve teachers in curriculum design and decision-making processes. • Empower middle leaders to take charge of key areas (e.g., assessment or pedagogy).
Professional development opportunities	Provide ongoing training to enhance leadership skills and curriculum knowledge across all levels of staff.	• Offer workshops on curriculum design and assessment methods. • Organise conferences and seminars with educational experts.
Regular feedback and reflection	Create a system for feedback and self-reflection to promote continuous improvement in curriculum leadership.	• Conduct regular staff surveys on curriculum effectiveness. • Hold reflection sessions after curriculum implementation to discuss challenges and successes.
Cross-institute collaboration	Encourage collaboration with other institutes or departments to expand ideas and approaches to curriculum leadership.	• Establish partnerships with neighbouring institutes for curriculum sharing. • Invite guest speakers or external educators for cross-institute discussions.
Recognition and incentives	Acknowledge and reward staff contributions to curriculum leadership and innovation.	• Implement staff awards for curriculum innovation. • Provide professional development grants or opportunities for outstanding leaders.

Table 10.2 - Practical strategies for fostering curriculum leadership

Balancing accountability with innovation

Accountability frameworks often prioritise measurable outcomes. However, fostering innovation requires flexibility. Harris (2011) identifies the principal as a mediator between these forces - upholding standards while enabling creative curriculum practices.

> **Case Study: Curriculum accountability**
>
> A secondary school implemented a cross-curricular project that integrated English, geography, and design technology to explore environmental sustainability. Students researched a local environmental issue, proposed solutions, and created physical or digital models to present their ideas. Through this approach, they developed critical skills such as research, collaboration, and creativity while meeting national curriculum standards for each subject.
>
> To maintain accountability, school leaders established clear objectives aligned with the curriculum. For instance, in English, students focused on persuasive writing to advocate for their solutions, while in geography, they analysed local data and proposed environmentally sound actions. In design technology, they applied principles of engineering and creativity to create prototypes. Traditional assessments such as written assignments and tests were complemented by innovative evaluations including group presentations, design reviews, and peer feedback sessions.
>
> The principal supported teachers in implementing this approach by providing professional development on interdisciplinary teaching methods, assessment strategies, and collaboration techniques. She also allocated time during planning periods for teachers from different departments to coordinate their lessons. Regular progress checks ensured that students met the required standards in all subjects while benefiting from a richer, more integrated learning experience.
>
> By encouraging innovation within the framework of national accountability systems, this secondary school principal has created opportunities for students to connect their learning across disciplines, preparing them for the complex, interconnected challenges of the modern world.

Strategies for building shared leadership

Shared leadership in curriculum development involves distributing leadership responsibilities across multiple roles and functions within the institution. This approach enhances curriculum relevance by incorporating diverse perspectives, fosters greater ownership among staff members, and creates an environment conducive to innovation and continuous improvement. It encourages collaborative decision-making and shared accountability.

Building leadership capacity at multiple levels

Spillane's (2006) distributed leadership model sees leadership as a collective endeavour. By identifying emerging leaders, principals can support professional growth through training, mentorship, and project-based leadership opportunities. Lambert (2002) advocates for teacher leadership as a foundation for shared responsibility in student achievement.

Enhancing ownership and engagement among staff

When staff contribute to curriculum design and review, they are more committed to its success. Participatory decision-making - highlighted by Fullan (2016) - improves both staff morale and curriculum quality.

A primary school implementing a new literacy programme organised co-design workshops where teachers collaboratively developed lesson plans and resources. This inclusive approach ensured that teacher insights shaped the programme, promoting practical relevance and buy-in. As a result, staff felt greater ownership of the curriculum, leading to more effective teaching and improved literacy outcomes for pupils.

Strategies for effective delegation and support

Bush & Glover (2003) emphasise that clear delineation of roles and responsibilities is fundamental to effective leadership. True delegation extends beyond merely distributing tasks; it requires leaders to provide access to relevant professional development opportunities, allocate sufficient time, and ensure availability of essential resources. Kotter (1996) further underscores that lasting and productive change depends on establishing a supportive organisational environment. This means creating a culture where team members feel valued, empowered, and equipped to fulfil their delegated responsibilities and contribute to sustained improvement.

Case Study: Shared curriculum leadership

Skeldale Primary, a large, multiple-entry primary school, implemented a collaborative approach to improve its science curriculum. Recognising the need for innovation, the head teacher established a curriculum leadership team comprising representatives from each year group.

> The leadership team was tasked with reviewing the existing science curriculum, identifying gaps, and proposing changes to align it with the school's vision of fostering inquiry-based learning. Members attended professional development workshops on curriculum design and collaborated during weekly meetings to draft new lesson plans and assessment strategies. Teachers were encouraged to trial these lessons and provide feedback, creating a dynamic process of refinement.
>
> To support the team, the head ensured access to resources such as science kits, training sessions, and dedicated planning time. Delegated responsibilities were clearly defined, with specific staff members leading on aspects like resource selection, lesson evaluation, and parent engagement. This collaborative effort resulted in a curriculum that not only met national standards but also sparked greater student interest in science.
>
> The success of this initiative highlights the importance of building leadership capacity, enhancing ownership, and providing effective support for staff involved in curriculum management.

Challenges and considerations

Navigating resistance and conflict

Resistance to change and overlapping responsibilities can significantly hinder effective shared leadership within educational settings. Principals and senior leaders must proactively establish clear communication channels, define roles and responsibilities precisely, and foster collaborative norms that support teamwork. Drawing on Kotter's (1996) change management principles, successful leaders cultivate trust, build a compelling shared vision, and engage stakeholders to overcome organisational inertia, ensuring smoother transitions and sustained commitment to curriculum and institutional improvements.

Time constraints and capacity

Balancing teaching and leadership requires time management and institutional support. Principals can allocate protected time for planning and coordination, ensuring staff capacity for curriculum engagement.

Recognising existing curriculum leadership

Curriculum leadership is often inherently shared in many institutions - led by programme managers, module leaders, subject heads, and coordinators. These individuals already ensure curriculum quality and innovation. While formal distributed leadership models can enhance practice, they are not always essential.

Many institutions achieve excellence without explicitly adopting such models. As Harris (2011) warns, poorly managed distributed leadership can lead to fragmentation. A context-sensitive approach is key: where staff leadership capacity is still growing or coherence is essential, a more centralised leadership model may be more effective.

Activity: Curriculum change leadership action plan

Select a curriculum change initiative relevant to your current or anticipated practice (in primary, secondary, FE, or HE). Drawing on the frameworks and strategies from this chapter, design a clear action plan outlining your vision, leadership approach, stakeholder engagement, implementation stages, data use, and methods for sustaining and reviewing the change.

1. **Diagnosis and vision**
   - What are the key drivers or needs prompting this curriculum change?
   - How will you articulate a clear, shared vision and goals to guide the process?

2. **Leadership and stakeholder engagement**
   - Who are the key leaders and stakeholders involved (e.g., principals, department heads, teachers, students, employers)?
   - How will you foster shared or distributed leadership to maximise ownership and expertise?
   - What strategies will you use to engage and communicate with stakeholders throughout the change?

3. **Implementation strategies**
   - What phased or collaborative approaches will you adopt to ensure effective rollout?
   - What professional development or resources will support staff during the change?
   - How will you anticipate and address potential barriers or resistance?

4. **Monitoring, evaluation, and sustainability**
   - How will you use data and evidence to monitor progress and impact?
   - What mechanisms will support regular reflection and responsive adaptation?
   - How will you embed the change to ensure it becomes a sustainable part of curriculum practice?

Prepare a report summarising your plan with reference to relevant models and literature from the chapter. Reflect on how this plan applies to your specific context and any challenges you foresee. If possible, discuss your plan with colleagues or mentors to gain feedback and identify areas for refinement.

Summary

Curriculum management is a driving force behind institutional success and positive learner outcomes. It encompasses the strategic planning, implementation, and continuous evaluation needed to keep the curriculum relevant, coherent, and ambitious. Strong leadership - whether exercised by principals, distributed among middle leaders and other staff, or embedded in collaborative teams - ensures that the curriculum reflects organisational priorities and adapts to changing educational contexts.

Effective management connects everyday teaching practices to the broader aims of the institution, promoting collective responsibility and consistency across subjects and phases. By fostering clear communication, shared vision, and a willingness to engage in reflective practice, curriculum leaders and teams can sustain high-quality provision and respond proactively to emerging challenges. Managing the curriculum thus becomes both a strategic and a relational endeavour, shaping every aspect of the educational experience for staff and students alike.

APPENDIX 1
ACTION VERBS FOR LEARNING OUTCOMES

Abstract	Collect	Develop	Implement
Activate	Combine	Differentiate	Improve
Acquire	Compare	Direct	Increase
Adjust	Compute	Discuss	Infer
Analyse	Contrast	Discover	Integrate
Appraise	Complete	Discriminate	Interpret
Arrange	Compose	Distinguish	Introduce
Articulate	Compute	Draw	Investigate
Assemble	Conduct	Dramatise	Judge
Assess	Construct	Employ	Limit
Assist	Convert	Establish	List
Associate	Coordinate	Estimate	Locate
Breakdown	Count	Evaluate	Maintain
Build	Criticise	Examine	Manage
Calculate	Critique	Explain	Modify
Carry out	Debate	Explore	Name
Catalogue	Decrease	Express	Observe
Categorise	Define	Extrapolate	Operate
Change	Demonstrate	Formulate	Order
Check	Describe	Generalise	Organise
Cite	Design	Identify	Perform
Classify	Detect	Illustrate	Plan
Point	Reflect	Separate	Trace
Predict	Relate	Sequence	Track
Prepare	Remove	Sing	Train
Prescribe	Reorganise	Sketch	Transfer
Produce	Repair	Simplify	Translate
Propose	Repeat	Skim	Update
Question	Replace	Solve	Use
Rank	Report	Specify	Utilise
Rate	Reproduce	State	Verbalise
Read	Research	Structure	Verify
Recall	Restate	Summarise	Visualise
Recommend	Restructure	Supervise	Write
Recognise	Revise	Survey	
Reconstruct	Rewrite	Systematise	
Record	Schedule	Tabulate	
Recruit	Score	Test	
Reduce	Select	Theorise	

APPENDIX 2
LEARNING TAXONOMIES

One of the most widely used ways of organising levels of expertise is according to *Bloom's Taxonomy of Educational Objectives*. Bloom's Taxonomy (Tables 1-3) uses a multi-tiered scale to express the level of expertise required to achieve each measurable student outcome. Organising measurable student outcomes in this way allows for the selection of appropriate classroom assessment techniques for a course.

There are three taxonomies. Which of the three to use for a given measurable student outcome depends upon the original goal to which the outcome is connected. There are knowledge-based goals, skills-based goals, and affective goals (values, attitudes, and interests); accordingly, there is a taxonomy for each. Within each taxonomy, levels of expertise are listed in order of increasing complexity. Measurable student outcomes that require the higher levels of expertise will require more sophisticated assessment techniques.

A knowledge-based goal requires that students learn certain facts and concepts. A skills-based goal requires that the students learn how to do something. An affective goal requires that the students' values, attitudes, or interests are affected by the course.

Table 1: Bloom's taxonomy of educational objectives for knowledge-based goals

LEVEL OF EXPERTISE	DESCRIPTION OF LEVEL / EXAMPLE OF MEASURABLE STUDENT OUTCOME
1. Knowledge	Recall/recognition of terms, ideas, procedure, theories, etc. *Example: When is the first day of Spring?*
2. Comprehension	Explain, translate, interpret, extrapolate, ... *Example: What does the summer solstice represent?*
3. Application	Apply abstractions, general principles, or methods to specific concrete situations. *Example: What would Earth's seasons be like if its orbit was perfectly circular?*
4. Analysis	Separation of a complex idea into its constituent parts and an understanding of organisation and relationship between the parts. Includes realising the distinction between hypothesis and fact as well as between relevant variables. *Example: Why are seasons reversed in the southern hemisphere?*

LEVEL OF EXPERTISE	DESCRIPTION OF LEVEL / EXAMPLE OF MEASURABLE STUDENT OUTCOME
5. Synthesis	Creative, mental construction of ideas and concepts from multiple sources to form complex ideas into a new, integrated, and meaningful pattern subject to given constraints. *Example: If the longest day of the year is in June, why is the northern hemisphere hottest in August?*
6. Evaluation	To make a judgment of ideas or methods using external evidence or self-selected criteria substantiated by observations or informed rationalisations. *Example: What would be the important variables for predicting seasons on a newly discovered planet?*

Table 2: Bloom's taxonomy of educational objectives for skills-based goals

LEVEL OF EXPERTISE	DESCRIPTION OF LEVEL / EXAMPLE OF MEASURABLE STUDENT OUTCOME
Perception	Uses sensory cues to guide actions. *Example: Some of the coloured samples you see will need dilution before you take their spectra. Using only observation, how will you decide which solutions might need to be diluted?*
Set	Demonstrates a readiness to take action to perform the task or objective. *Example: Describe how you would go about taking the absorbance spectra of a sample of pigments?*
Guided response	Knows steps required to complete the task or objective. *Example: Determine the density of a group of sample metals with regular and irregular shapes.*
Mechanism	Performs the task with developing confidence and proficiency, demonstrating correct technique with some consistency but occasional reliance on external guidance. *Example: Follow the given procedure to determine the quantity of copper in your ore sample. Ensure accurate measurement and basic data reporting, including the calculation of mean and standard deviation.*
Complex overt response	Performs the task with confidence and mastery, demonstrating fluency, independence, and consistency. Adapts techniques as needed to accommodate challenges. *Example: Independently design and conduct a titration to determine the Ka of an unknown weak acid, adjusting your approach as necessary to ensure accurate results.*

LEVEL OF EXPERTISE	DESCRIPTION OF LEVEL / EXAMPLE OF MEASURABLE STUDENT OUTCOME
Adaptation	Performs task or objective as above, but can also modify actions to account for new or problematic situations. *Example: You are performing titrations on a series of unknown acids and find a variety of problems with the resulting curves, e.g., only 3.0 ml of base is required for one acid while 75.0 ml is required in another. What can you do to get valid data for all the unknown acids?*
Organisation	Creates new tasks or objectives incorporating learned ones. *Example: Recall your plating and etching experiences with an aluminium substrate. Choose a different metal substrate and design a process to plate, mask, and etch so that a pattern of 4 different metals is created.*

Table 3: Bloom's taxonomy of educational objectives for affective goals

LEVEL OF EXPERTISE	DESCRIPTION OF LEVEL / EXAMPLE OF MEASURABLE STUDENT OUTCOME
Receiving	Demonstrates a willingness to participate in the activity. *Example: When I'm in class I am attentive to the instructor, take notes, etc. I do not read the newspaper instead.*
Responding	Shows interest in the objects, phenomena, or activity by seeking it out or pursuing it for pleasure. *Example: I complete my homework and participate in class discussions.*
Valuing	Internalises an appreciation for (values) the objectives, phenomena, or activity. *Example: I seek out information in popular media related to my class.*
Organisation	Begins to compare different values, and resolves conflicts between them to form an internally consistent system of values. *Example: Some of the ideas I've learned in my class differ from my previous beliefs. How do I resolve this?*
Characterisation by a value or value complex	Adopts a long-term value system that is "pervasive, consistent, and predictable". *Example: I've decided to take my family on a vacation to visit some of the places I learned about in my class.*

To determine the level of expertise required for each measurable student outcome, first decide which of these three broad categories (knowledge-based, skills-based, and affective) the corresponding course goal belongs to. Then, using the appropriate Bloom's Taxonomy, look over the descriptions of the various levels of expertise.

Determine which description most closely matches that measurable student outcome. As can be seen from the examples given in the three tables, there are different ways of representing measurable student outcomes, e.g., as statements about students, as questions to be asked of students, or as statements from the student's perspective.

Bloom's Taxonomy is a convenient way to describe the degree to which students are expected to understand and use concepts, to demonstrate particular skills, and to have their values, attitudes, and interests affected. It is critical that the levels of expertise that students are expected to achieve are determined because this will determine which classroom assessment techniques are most appropriate for the course. Though the most common form of assessment used in introductory college courses - multiple choice tests - might be quite adequate for assessing knowledge and comprehension, this type of assessment often falls short when we want to assess our student's knowledge at the higher levels of synthesis and evaluation.

Multiple-choice tests also rarely provide information about achievement of skills-based goals. Similarly, traditional course evaluations, a technique commonly used for affective assessment, do not generally provide useful information about changes in student values, attitudes, and interests. Thus, commonly used assessment techniques, while perhaps providing a means for assigning grades, often do not provide useful feedback for determining whether students are attaining course goals. Usually, this is due to a combination of not having formalised goals to begin with, not having translated those goals into outcomes that are measurable, and not using assessment techniques capable of measuring expected student outcomes given the levels of expertise required to achieve them.

Thus, Bloom's Taxonomy can be used in an iterative fashion to first state and then refine course goals. Bloom's Taxonomy can finally be used to identify which classroom assessment techniques are most appropriate for measuring these goals.

APPENDIX 3
SAMPLE PROGRAMME SPECIFICATION

Programme title

Level 3 Diploma in Hospitality (Food and Beverage Service)

Awarding body

Pearson BTEC / City & Guilds or equivalent awarding organisation

Programme purpose

To prepare learners for careers in the diverse hospitality industry by developing knowledge, skills, and behaviours essential for operational roles in hotels, restaurants, events, and related settings. The programme also supports progression to higher education and leadership training.

Programme aims

- Equip learners with practical and theoretical knowledge of hospitality operations.
- Develop interpersonal and customer service skills.
- Promote understanding of industry standards for health, safety, and food hygiene.
- Foster personal qualities such as teamwork, professionalism, and problem-solving.
- Encourage awareness of sustainability, diversity, and ethical practice in hospitality.

Entry requirements

- Four GCSEs at grade 4/C or above, including English and mathematics, or a Level 2 qualification in hospitality or related subject, or relevant work experience (subject to interview and initial assessment).

Intended learning outcomes

By the end of the programme, learners should be able to:

- Explain the structure and diversity of the hospitality sector.
- Demonstrate safe and effective food and beverage service skills.
- Apply customer service and communication skills in authentic scenarios.
- Maintain health, safety, and hygiene standards in line with legislation.
- Use industry-standard systems for reservations and front office functions.
- Plan and supervise a hospitality event, considering sustainability and customer needs.
- Reflect on practical work experience, identifying personal development goals.

Programme structure

Module/Unit Title	Level	Guided Learning Hours	Assessment Method
Introduction to the Hospitality Industry	3	60	Case Study, Presentation
Food and Beverage Service Skills	3	120	Practical Assessment
Front Office Operations	3	60	Portfolio, Observation
Food Safety and Hygiene	3	60	Online Test
Customer Service in Hospitality	3	90	Role Play, Report
Event Planning and Supervision	3	90	Project, Group Work
Hospitality Business Skills	3	60	Written Assignment
Work Experience/Industry Placement	3	60	Employer Appraisal

(Total guided learning hours: 600)

Teaching and learning strategies

- Interactive lectures and seminars.
- Practical workshops in realistic settings.
- Peer and group work.

- Industry visits and guest speakers.
- Blended and online learning activities.
- Supervised work placement.

Assessment methods

- Practical demonstrations and skills tests.
- Projects and coursework (written reports, portfolios).
- Presentations and role plays.
- Written assignments and tests.
- Reflective journals/logbooks.
- Employer evaluations (work placement).

Progression and career opportunities

- Direct entry into hospitality employment: hotels, restaurants, events, cruise lines, contract catering, etc.
- Progression to Level 4/5 Foundation Degree, HNC/D, or university.
- Specialist industry training programmes or apprenticeships.

Support and guidance

- Personal tutor assigned to each learner.
- Additional support for literacy, numeracy, and digital skills.
- Regular progress reviews.
- Careers advice and CV workshops.
- Wellbeing and safeguarding services.

Quality assurance and review

- Annual programme evaluation in line with college and awarding body requirements.
- Student and employer feedback sought for continuous improvement.
- External verification/moderation of assessments.

APPENDIX 4
SAMPLE MODULE SPECIFICATION

Module title	Leading Change in Education		Date of approval	2025
Module code	7AX243	Module level 7	Credit value	20
Module delivery mode	Online/Distance ✓	Blended/Face to Face ✓	Work-Based Learning X	
			Hours of work experience: NA	
Module description	In the context of frequent policy changes, rapid technological progress, and shifting societal expectations, educational organisations must continuously adapt. This module equips students with a critical understanding of change and the tools to drive innovation within varied educational environments. Through the study of core topics such as strategic leadership, organisational culture, stakeholder involvement, and frameworks for managing change, students will investigate how to intentionally foster and maintain innovation. Utilising up-to-date research and international case studies, the module highlights the ethical, adaptive, and transformative roles leaders play. Learners are encouraged to critically examine their own professional practice and to devise strategies that are contextually appropriate for leading effective and sustainable change.			
Module learning outcomes	On successful completion of the module, students will be able to: 1. Critically appraise change management drivers and strategies in an applied educational context. 2. Critically reflect on the utilisation of change management models and strategies responding to an area requiring effective improvement in an applied education context.			
Module Content	• Overview of innovation and change • Strategic leadership of change • Empowering staff to navigate change • Change management models			

	• Innovation in educational practice • Adapting to policy change • Transforming teaching and learning • Changing an organisation's culture • Sustaining educational reform	
Module Learning and Teaching	Scheduled Learning and Teaching Activities	15%
	Guided Independent Study	85%
	Placement Learning	0%
Module Assessment	**Component 1**: Coursework Summary of Assessment Method: Recorded presentation (3,500 words equivalent) Weighting: 100 % Assesses Learning Outcomes: 1 & 2	
Reading List	TBD	

Table 1 - Module specification
Adapted from a MA Education module, University of Derby

APPENDIX 5
SAMPLE SCHEME OF WORK

Secondary School - Design & Technology (Year 9, Term 1 of 2)

This scheme of work provides an overview for a 12-week first term (of two) for Year 9 Design & Technology. It covers core skills in design, research, planning, making, and evaluation, with a focus on practical progression and reflective learning.

Wk	Topic	Learning Outcomes	Activities	Resources	Assessment
1	Introduction to Design & Technology	Understand course structure, safety rules, and basic design process.	Course overview, health & safety briefing, intro tasks.	Course handbook, safety equipment.	Class discussion, safety quiz.
2	Design Brief and Specification	Write a design brief and specification to solve a simple problem.	Case studies, create and draft briefs for set scenario.	Sample briefs, worksheets.	Draft design brief/specification.
3	Research and Analysis	Conduct research and analyse existing products.	Product research task, group reflection, presentations.	Internet, real product samples.	Research report, group feedback.
4	Idea Generation	Generate varied design ideas using sketching and annotation.	Idea gathering, sketching workshop, peer review.	Sketchbooks, drawing tools.	Portfolio of initial ideas.
5	Modelling and Development	Develop ideas into refined designs (physical or CAD models).	Building prototypes/models, CAD basics, iterative review.	Modelling materials, CAD computers.	Model or CAD file submission.
6	Materials and Components	Identify and select suitable materials/components for design.	Material properties workshop, practical demos.	Material samples, reference charts.	Written report on choices.
7	Planning for Manufacture	Create a step-by-step manufacturing plan including tools and safety.	Develop plans, tool demonstration, peer assessment.	Planning sheets, workshop tools.	Completed manufacturing plan.
8	Safe Workshop Practice	Demonstrate application of safe workshop practices.	Safety drills, equipment checks, practice activities.	Workshop equipment, safety posters.	Practical safety test, reflections.
9	Skill Development Sessions	Build practical skills (cutting, joining, finishing techniques).	Hands-on skill workshops, guided task rotations.	Tools, consumable materials.	Demonstration of individual skills.
10	Project Work Start	Begin practical work on main project (guided by plan).	Start main project, supervised build, construction notes.	Materials, tools, project logbook.	Logbook entry, initial review.

| 11 | Project Work (Continued) | Refine and progress practical build, problem-solve as needed. | Continue project, peer/teacher feedback, adapt as needed. | Workshop, ongoing materials. | Logbook and verbal progress check. |
| 12 | Project Review and Evaluation | Evaluate product against brief/specification and suggest improvement. | Project presentations, self/peer assessment, feedback. | Presentation tools, evaluation forms. | Evaluation report, group feedback. |

Key Features

- **Progression:** Skills and knowledge deliberately sequenced - from initial safety and design principles to complex project work and evaluation.
- **Assessment:** Mix of formative and summative approaches - quizzes, practical demonstrations, portfolios, logbooks, and presentations.
- **Differentiation:** Activities adapted for varied abilities (e.g., extra support for sketching or CAD, peer tutoring in workshop skills).
- **Safety:** Regular emphasis on safe workshop conduct and equipment handling.
- **Reflective practice:** Evaluation and self-assessment embedded throughout to promote improvement and ownership.

Notes for Implementation

- Schemes of work should be reviewed and contextualised to address the needs of the specific student group and available resources.
- Opportunities should be built in for student choice, creativity, and collaborative learning.
- Industry links (e.g., guest speakers, materials donations, site visits) can enhance real-world relevance.
- Logbooks and evaluation forms should provide prompts to encourage meaningful reflection.

APPENDIX 6
SAMPLE LESSON PLAN

Lesson Plan: Year 4 Primary History

Topic
The Roman Invasion of Britain

Lesson title
Why did the Romans invade Britain?

Learning outcomes
By the end of this lesson, pupils will be able to:

- Identify key reasons for the Roman invasion of Britain.
- Describe how life in Britain changed as a result of the Roman arrival.
- Sequence major events related to the invasion on a simple timeline.
- Discuss at least one positive and one negative impact of Roman rule.

Curriculum links
- National Curriculum for History (Key Stage 2): "The Roman Empire and its impact on Britain".
- English: Listening, discussion, and presentation skills.

Resources
- Map of Europe and the Roman Empire.
- Timeline cards (events before, during, and after invasion).
- Worksheet: "Impacts of the Romans".
- Video clip (2-3 min): Introduction to the Romans in Britain.
- Access to coloured pencils and large paper for group work.

Key Vocabulary
- Empire
- Invade
- Conquer
- Resistance
- Settlement
- Legacy

Lesson Structure (60 min)

Section	Timing	Activities & Teacher Guidance
Starter	10 min	- Show map: Where was Rome? Where is Britain? - Ask: "What do you already know about the Romans?" - Elicit responses, record on whiteboard.
Introduction	10 min	- Watch short video about Roman invasion. - Teacher Q&A: "Why did the Romans travel to new lands?" - Clarify history vocabulary: invade, empire, conquer, resistance.
Main Activity	25 min	1. **Timeline relay** (Small groups): - Groups order cards showing events around the invasion. - Discuss and justify order. 2. **Why invade?** - Teacher-led discussion: Identify natural resources (tin, gold, fertile land), trade, and power. Pupils record three reasons on mini-whiteboards. 3. **Impact table** (Pairs): - Fill worksheet with ways life changed in Britain - positive (e.g., roads, new towns) and negative (e.g., resistance, loss of freedom).
Plenary	10 min	- Invite a few pairs to share key impacts. - Whole group reflection: "If you lived in Britain then, would you welcome or resist the Romans? Why?" - Recap main learning points.
Extension/Homework	—	- Research and illustrate a Roman invention or building that changed Britain (e.g., baths, roads). - Prepare to share findings next lesson.

Assessment

- Observation of group and class participation.
- Completion and quality of "Impacts of the Romans" worksheet.

- Verbal contributions during plenary reflect understanding of positive/negative consequences.

Differentiation

- **Support:** Sentence starters and vocabulary cards for EAL/SEND pupils; pairing with supportive peers.
- **Challenge:** Ask higher-attaining pupils to consider longer-term consequences of Roman rule or compare with another invasion (e.g., Vikings).

Notes

- Modify resources and timing depending on class needs.
- Ensure opportunities for active participation and oral feedback.

APPENDIX 7
STATEMENTS OF INTENT

Primary school statement of intent

At Brookfield Primary School, our curriculum is designed to nurture each child's individuality within a supportive, inclusive environment where respect, curiosity, and kindness are at the core of all learning experiences. Guided by the statutory requirements of the Early Years Foundation Stage and the Primary National Curriculum, our curriculum offers a rich and engaging learning journey that builds progressively in knowledge, skills, and personal development. We aim to inspire lifelong learners who are confident, compassionate, and ready to embrace future challenges.

The key goals driving our curriculum are to:

- Ensure every child learns to read fluently, establishing a lifelong love of books and language.

- Develop effective communication skills, including speaking, listening, and collaboration.

- Foster independence and resilience through exciting, hands-on learning opportunities.

- Cultivate empathy, respect, and an appreciation of diversity within our school and wider community.

- Expose children to a broad cultural perspective, promoting awareness of the world beyond their immediate environment.

- Inspire high aspirations grounded in perseverance and positive effort.

- Support every child to achieve or exceed national standards across all subjects by the end of primary education.

- Prepare pupils thoroughly for the curriculum demands and experiences awaiting them in secondary education and beyond.

Our vision is for every learner at Brookfield Primary to flourish as knowledgeable, responsible citizens who make a positive, lasting impact on their communities.

Secondary school statement of intent

At Regent Academy, our curriculum embodies our commitment to nurturing well-rounded, ambitious, and responsible young people equipped to thrive in a changing world. Grounded in our core values of respect, resilience, and aspiration, our curriculum is designed to provide a broad, balanced, and inclusive educational experience, meeting statutory requirements and reflecting our local community's needs. We believe education should cultivate not only academic excellence but also personal growth, social awareness, and lifelong learning skills.

Our curriculum aims to ensure that all students:

- Develop strong literacy and numeracy skills essential for success across all subjects and future pathways.

- Build knowledge and skills progressively through carefully sequenced learning experiences that challenge and engage.

- Grow in confidence, independence, and creativity, inspiring them to reach their full potential.

- Appreciate cultural diversity and global perspectives, fostering empathy and social responsibility.

- Are prepared for post-secondary education, apprenticeships, or employment with relevant academic and vocational skills.

- Are supported inclusively, with high expectations for all, including those with SEND and disadvantaged backgrounds.

Students follow a comprehensive curriculum including English, maths, science, languages, geography, history, and technology, alongside arts, PE, and PSHE. Targeted interventions ensure support for literacy and numeracy. Ability setting in core subjects supports tailored challenge and progression. Our intention is for every student at Regent Academy to be empowered to succeed and make a positive impact in their communities and beyond.

APPENDIX 8
SAMPLE ASSESSMENT RUBRIC

The following assessment rubric is taken from the assignment brief of an MA Education: Leadership & Management module. It links to the following assessment description and criteria:

Description of the assessment

A 3,500-word report that critically evaluates the effectiveness of leadership and management within own chosen educational context.

Assessment Content

The report should:
1. Critically evaluate the effectiveness of leadership and management within your own educational context (when compared and contrasted with theoretical models).
2. Cover a wide range of key LMS principles and concepts (in order to demonstrate your mastery of the subject).
3. Synthesise ideas into a critical, logical, coherent report.
4. Provide evidence of wider reading and supporting citations.
5. Be written in an academic style; clear, lucid, logical and coherent with good use of spelling, grammar and referencing that conforms to the Harvard system.

Assessment rubric

Exceptional: Distinction (90-100%)
The evaluation comprehensively analyses all aspects of leadership and management within the chosen context, guided entirely by theoretical models. It showcases exceptional ability, insight, and authoritative subject knowledge, demonstrating incisive original thinking, commendable originality, and the highest level of technical competence. The work is exceptionally well-researched and meticulously supported by evidence, potentially influencing the forefront of the subject and reaching publishable quality. It provides exhaustive coverage of key LMS principles and concepts (including substantial, significant insights from discussion forums), reflecting an exceptional depth of understanding and a very high level of engagement with relevant literature. The report is exceptionally well-written, exhibiting a scholarly style with outstanding presentation quality, clarity of ideas, coherence, logic, and flawless use of spelling, grammar, and language throughout. Referencing adheres precisely to the Harvard system, consistently accurate and complete without any errors.

Outstanding: Distinction (80-89%)

The evaluation comprehensively analyses and accurately gauges the effectiveness of all aspects of leadership and management within the chosen context, strongly informed by theoretical models. It demonstrates authoritative subject knowledge, showcasing a very high level of technical competence, incisive original thinking, and commendable originality. The work is exceptionally well-researched with extensive coverage of key LMS principles and concepts (including many significant insights from discussion forums), characterized by a high level of critical analysis and evaluation, positioning it near the forefront of the subject and approaching publishable quality. There is clear evidence of outstanding engagement with the literature, significantly enhancing the criticality of the piece. The report is exceptionally well-written in a scholarly style, featuring outstanding presentation quality, impressive clarity of ideas, excellent coherence and logic, and consistent use of correct spelling, grammar, and language throughout. Referencing adheres precisely to the Harvard system, consistently accurate, complete, with only trivial or very minor errors.

Excellent: Distinction (70-79%)

The evaluation comprehensively analyses the effectiveness of leadership and management within the chosen context, strongly influenced by theoretical models and demonstrating authoritative and current subject knowledge. It displays a high level of technical competence and accuracy, supported by balanced arguments and credible citations, showing exceptional critical analysis, evaluation, and originality. The evaluation covers a wide array of LMS principles and concepts (including significant insights from discussion forums), exhibiting excellent subject knowledge and extensive use of evidence, underscoring thorough research and deep understanding. The work showcases wide reading around the subject, enhancing its criticality and demonstrating a high level of engagement with relevant literature. It is exceptionally well-written in a scholarly style, presenting clear, lucid, logical, and coherent information with exemplary use of spelling, grammar, and language. The presentation is commendable, characterized by strong coherence and logic, reflecting thoughtful and effective communication. Referencing adheres precisely to the Harvard system, consistently accurate, complete, and excellent, with only minor errors or misunderstandings.

Very good: Merit (60-69%)

The evaluation comprehensively analyses the effectiveness of leadership and management within the chosen context, primarily influenced by theoretical models and demonstrating a well-developed and coherent analysis. It reflects sound and current subject knowledge with no significant errors in applying concepts or techniques. The evaluation is characterized by critical objectivity, featuring balanced arguments supported by credible citations, and displaying a very good level of critical analysis, evaluation, and some original thinking. It integrates numerous key LMS principles and concepts (including several insights from discussion forums), showcasing a very good level of subject knowledge and a solid understanding of the subject matter without significant errors. The work is extensively researched, indicating a high level of engagement with the literature, contributing significantly to the criticality of the piece. It is very well-written in a clear, lucid, logical, and coherent academic style, demonstrating good use of spelling, grammar, and language throughout, with a very good standard of presentation and generally clear and coherent ideas. Referencing adheres largely to the Harvard system, being very good with minor errors and misunderstandings, possibly with some deficiencies in presentation.

Good / Satisfactory: Pass (50-59%)

The evaluation analyses aspects of leadership and management within the chosen context, influenced by theoretical models with satisfactory subject knowledge demonstrated, albeit with possible conceptual gaps or limited use of techniques. It maintains a critical and objective approach, featuring balanced arguments supported by credible citations, and displaying a fair level of critical analysis and evaluation, leaning towards factual or derivative insights with minimal originality. The evaluation covers several key LMS principles and concepts (including some insights from discussion forums), indicating good subject knowledge and adequate research, reflecting a generally sound understanding. There is sufficient evidence of reading around the subject, contributing to the criticality of the piece, and showing a satisfactory level of engagement with relevant literature. The report is well-written in an academic style, conveying clear and logical information, though with minor errors in spelling, grammar, and language. Overall, the presentation is sound, with fairly clear and coherent ideas. Referencing adheres to the Harvard system, generally accurate with minor errors, and may exhibit some weaknesses in style or presentation.

Unsatisfactory: Marginal Fail (90-100%)

The evaluation exhibits a narrow scope and lacks theoretical underpinning, falling short of meeting the pass threshold despite showing some degree of merit. It demonstrates satisfactory subject knowledge but contains factual errors and conceptual gaps. The evaluation tends towards descriptive rather than analytical, with insufficient supporting citations, and lacks critical analysis, originality, and rigorous research. Coverage of key LMS principles and concepts, and insights from discussion forums, is limited, reflecting poor subject knowledge and inadequate use of appropriate techniques. Reading around the subject is insufficient for Masters level work, impacting the criticality of the piece and demonstrating inadequate engagement with the literature. The report lacks clarity and coherence, with a disorganized layout and numerous errors in spelling, grammar, and language. The presentation does not meet required standards, with unclear and incoherent ideas. Referencing does not adhere to the Harvard system, containing several errors that render it inadequate.

Very Poor: Fail (25-39%)

The evaluation lacks substantive content, both practical and theoretical, demonstrating inadequate subject knowledge with significant factual errors and conceptual gaps. It is predominantly descriptive, lacking supporting citations, and shows minimal awareness of relevant issues and theory, resulting in a weak critical analysis and evaluation. Coverage of key LMS principles and concepts, and insights from discussion forums, is severely limited, indicating very poor subject knowledge and a complete absence of appropriate techniques and rigorous research. Reading around the subject is grossly insufficient for Masters level work, with minimal engagement with relevant literature, severely impacting the criticality of the piece. The information conveyed is unclear and lacks coherence, with a disorganized layout and numerous errors in spelling, grammar, and language. The presentation standard is unacceptable, characterized by confused and incoherent ideas. Referencing does not conform to the Harvard system, containing numerous errors that render it inadequate and fail to meet the assignment requirements.

Nothing of Merit: Fail (0-24%)

The submitted work lacks any substantive value or relevance to the task. It presents information that is entirely irrelevant and disconnected from the required principles, theories, or evidence. There is no coverage of key LMS principles and concepts, demonstrating a complete absence of subject knowledge and meaningful content. Additionally, there is no evidence of reading around the subject, with no engagement with relevant literature or sources. The information presented is entirely unclear and devoid of meaning, compounded by an illogical layout and numerous errors in spelling, grammar, and language. The overall presentation is unacceptable, lacking coherence and logical structure. Referencing in the main body and reference list does not adhere to the Harvard system, with numerous errors indicating a fundamental misunderstanding of proper referencing techniques.

REFERENCES

ACARA (2024) The Australian Curriculum. Australian Curriculum, Assessment and Reporting Authority (online). Available at: www.australiancurriculum.edu.au (Accessed: 19/7/25).

Advance HE (2021) Inclusive Curriculum Design in Higher Education (online). Available at: www.advance-he.ac.uk (Accessed: 18/7/25).

Alexander, R. (2020) A dialogic teaching companion, Routledge.

Alexander, R. (2021) Education in spite of policy, Routledge.

Almond, N (2020) Curriculum Coherence: How best to do it?, in Sealy, C & Bennet [eds] (2020) The Curriculum: An evidence informed guide for teachers, John Catt.

Ambition Institute (2023) Curriculum design principles: A Guide for educators (online). Available at: www.ambition.org.uk (Accessed: 18/7/25).

Anderson, L. & Krathwohl, D. (2001) A taxonomy for learning, teaching, and assessing: A revision of Bloom's taxonomy of educational objectives, Longman.

Apple, M & Apple, M.W. (2004) Ideology and curriculum, Routledge.

Arnold, K. & Pistilli, M. (2012) Course signals at Purdue: Using learning analytics to increase student success, Proceedings of the 2nd International Conference on Learning Analytics and Knowledge, pp. 267-270.

Arnot, M. & Dillabough, J. (2000) Challenging democracy: International perspectives on gender, education and citizenship, Routledge.

Ashbee, R (2020) Why it's so important to understand school subjects - and how we might begin to do so in Sealy, C & Bennett, T (2020) The researchED Guide to The Curriculum: An evidence- informed guide for teachers, pp 31-40, John Catt Publishers.

Ausubel, D. (1968) Educational Psychology: A Cognitive View, Holt, Rinehart & Winston.

Ball, S. (2003) The teacher's soul and the terrors of performativity, Journal of Education Policy, 18(2), pp. 215-228.

Ball, S. (2008) The education debate, Bristol: The Policy Press.

Barber, M. (1997) The learning game: arguments for an education revolution, London: Gollancz.

Barnett, R. & Coate, K. (2005) Engaging the curriculum in higher education. Open University Press.

Bates, A. (2015) Teaching in a Digital Age, Open Educational Resources Collection, 6.

Beane, J. (1997) Curriculum integration: Designing the core of democratic education, Teachers College Press.

Bearman, M., Dawson, P., Boud, D., Hall, M., Bennett, S., Molloy, E. and Joughin, G. (2014) Guide to the assessment design decisions framework (online). Available at https://www.assessmentdecisions.org/wp-content/uploads/2014/09/Guide-to-the-Assessment-Design-Decisions-Framework.pdf (Accessed: 22/12/24).

Bernstein, B. (2004) The structuring of pedagogic discourse, Routledge.

Biesta, G. (2015) Good education in an age of measurement: Ethics, politics, democracy, Routledge.

Biggs, J. (2022) Teaching for quality learning at university: What the student does, 4th edn, Open University Press.

Black, P. & Wiliam, D. (1998) Inside the black box: Raising standards through classroom assessment, Phi Delta Kappan, 80(2), pp. 139-148.

Black, P. & Wiliam, D. (2009) Developing the theory of formative assessment, Educational Assessment, Evaluation and Accountability, 21(1), pp. 5-31.

Board of Education (1931) Report of the Consultative Committee on the Primary School (Hadow Report), London: HMSO.

Bobbitt, F. (1918) The curriculum, Houghton Mifflin.

Bond, M., Bedenlier, S., Marín, V. and Händel, M. (2021) Emergency remote teaching in higher education: Mapping the first global online semester, International journal of educational technology in higher education, 18(1), p.50.

Boud, D. & Falchikov, N. (2007) Rethinking Assessment in Higher Education: Learning for the Longer Term, Routledge.

Boud, D. & Molloy, E. (2013) Rethinking models of feedback for learning: the challenge of design, Assessment & Evaluation in Higher Education, 38(6), pp. 698-712.

Boud, D. & Soler, R. (2016) Sustainable assessment revisited, Assessment & Evaluation in Higher Education, 41(3), pp. 400-413.

Boud, D., Lawson, R., & Thompson, D. G. (2021). The calibration of student judgement through self-assessment: Disruptive effects of assessment patterns. Assessment & Evaluation in Higher Education, 46(1), 23-35.

Bromley, M. (2021) School & College Curriculum Design - Book three: Impact, Spark Education Books.

Brookhart, S. (2013) How to create and use rubrics for formative assessment and grading, ASCD.

Brown, M., Mhichil, M., Beirne, E. and Mac Lochlainn, C. (2021) The global micro-credential landscape: Charting a new credential ecology for lifelong learning, Journal of Learning for Development, 8(2), 228-254.

Brundrett, M. & Silcock, P. (2002) Achieving Competence, Success and Excellence in Teaching, Routledge.

Brundrett, M. & Rhodes, C. (2010) Leadership for quality and accountability in education, London: Routledge.

Bruner, J. (2009) The process of education, Harvard University Press.

Bryson, C. & Hand, L. (2007) The role of engagement in inspiring teaching and learning, Innovations in Education and Teaching International, 44(4), pp. 349-362.

Burnett, C. & Cremin, T. (2018) Learning to teach in the primary school, 4th edn. Routledge.

Bush, T. & Glover, D. (2003) School Leadership: Concepts and Evidence, London: SAGE Publications.

CACE (1967) Children and their Primary Schools (Plowden Report). Central Advisory Council for Education.

Calibr (2025) Top 11 instructional design models for eLearning in 2025 (online). Available at https://calibr.ai/blogs/11-most-popular-instructional-design-models-for-elearning (Accessed: 28/7/25).

Carless, D. & Boud, D. (2018) The development of student feedback literacy: enabling uptake of feedback, Assessment & Evaluation in Higher Education, 43(8), pp. 1315-1325.

Carless, D. (2020) Feedback loops and the longer-term: Towards feedback spirals, Assessment & Evaluation in Higher Education, 45(6), 885-895.

Chiriac, E. (2014) Group work as an incentive for learning - Students' experiences of group work, Frontiers in Psychology, 11, 534.

CITB (2025) Apprenticeship Standards and Frameworks, Construction Industry Training Board (online). Available at: www.citb.co.uk (Accessed: 19/7/25).

Cohen, E. (1994) Designing Groupwork: Strategies for the Heterogeneous Classroom, Teachers College Press.

Conati, C. & Kardan, S. (2013) Student modelling: Supporting personalized instruction, from problem solving to exploratory open-ended activities, AI Magazine, 34(3), pp. 13-26.

Conole, G. (2013) Designing for learning in an open world, New York: Springer.

Corbett, H. & Rossman, J. (1989) Three paths to implementing change: A research not Curriculum Inquiry, Vol 19, No. 2, pp.163-190.

Cordingley, P., Higgins, S., Greany, T., Buckler, N., Coles-Jordan, D., Crisp, B., Saunders, L. and Coe, R. (2015) Developing Great Teaching: Lessons from the international reviews into effective professional development, London: Teacher Development Trust.

Coughlan, S. (2014) Politicians' whims are harming schools, BBC News. [Online]. Available at: www.bbc.co.uk/news/education-29851020 (Accessed:22/7/25).

Crawford, J., Butler-Henderson, K., Rudolph, J., Malkawi, B., Glowatz, M., Burton, R., Magni, P. and Lam, S. (2020) COVID-19: 20 countries' higher education intra-period digital pedagogy responses, Journal of Applied Learning & Teaching, 3(1), 1-20.

Crick, T. (2021) Covid-19 and Digital Education: a Catalyst For Change?, ITNOW, 63(1), 16-17.

Crompton, H. & Burke, D. (2018) The use of mobile learning in higher education: A systematic review, Computers & Education, 123, pp. 53-64.

Cuban, L. (2010) Cutting through the hype: The essential guide to school reform, Harvard Education Press.

Dewey, J. (1938) Experience and education, Kappa Delta Pi.

Dewey, J. (1986) Experience and Education, Macmillan.

DfE (2014) The national curriculum in England: Framework for key stages 1 to 4. Department for Education.

DfE (2021) Skills for jobs: Lifelong learning for opportunity and growth, London: Department for Education.

DfE (2025) Curriculum and assessment review: Interim report (online). Available at https://assets.publishing.service.gov.uk/media/6821d69eced319d02c9060e3/Curriculum_and_Assessment_Review_interim_report.pdf (Accessed: 31/7/25).

Dichev, C. & Dicheva, D. (2017) Gamifying education: what is known, what is believed and what remains uncertain: a critical review, International Journal of Educational Technology in Higher Education, 14(1).

Digital Learning Institute (2023) The Big 5 eLearning Design Principles (online). Available at: https://www.digitallearninginstitute.com (Accessed: 28/7/25).

Donaldson, G. (2015) Successful futures: Independent review of curriculum and assessment arrangements in Wales, Cardiff: Welsh Government.

Drake, S. (2012) Creating Standards-Based Integrated Curriculum, 2nd edn. Thousand Oaks, CA: Corwin.

Duterte, J. (2024) Technology-enhanced learning environments: Improving engagement and learning, IJRISS, 8(10), pp.1305-1131.

Edge Education (2020) Five learning theories to consider in eLearning design (online). Available at https://edgeeducation.com/five-learning-theories-to-consider-in-elearning-design (Accessed@ 28/7/25).

Education Endowment Foundation (EEF) (2025) Teaching and learning toolkit (online). Available at: https://educationendowmentfoundation.org.uk/education-evidence/teaching-learning-toolkit (Accessed: 18/7/25).

Edwards, R. & Usher, R. (2008) Globalisation & pedagogy: Space, place and identity, Routledge.

Eisner, E. (1985) The educational imagination: On the design and evaluation of school programs, 2nd edn. Macmillan.

Eisner, E. (2017) The enlightened eye: Qualitative inquiry and the enhancement of educational practice, Teachers College Press.

eLearning Industry (2024) Branching scenarios: What you need to know (online). Available at elearningindustry.com/branching-scenarios-need-know (Accessed: 29/7/25).

Entwistle, N. (2017) Teaching for understanding at university: Deep approaches and distinctive ways of thinking, Bloomsbury Publishing.

European Centre for the Development of Vocational Training (ECDVT) (2009) European guidelines for validating non-formal and informal learning, Office for Official Publications of the European Union.

European Union (2015) ECTS Users' Guide (online). Available at https://op.europa.eu/en/publication-detail/-/publication/da7467e6-8450-11e5-b8b7-01aa75ed71a1 (Accessed: 20/7/25).

European Union (2022) European Skills Agenda: Working together to strengthen human capital (ONLINE). Available at https://employment-social-affairs.ec.europa.eu/policies-and-activities_en (Accessed: 21/7/25).

Evans, G. (2022) Back to the future? Reflections on three phases of education policy reform in Wales and their implications for teachers, Journal of Educational Change, 23, 371-396.

Expert Panel for the National Curriculum (2011) The Framework for the National Curriculum (online). Available at gov.uk/government/publications/framework-for-the-national-curriculum-a-report-by-the-expert-panel-for-the-national-curriculum-review (Accessed: 22/7/25).

Fieldwork Education (2024) International Primary Curriculum: Implementation Overview, London: Fieldwork Education.

Fixsen, D. (2005) Implementation research: A synthesis of the literature. University of South Florida, Louis de la Parte Florida Mental Health Research Institute, The National Implementation Research Network.

Fredricks, J., Blumenfeld, P. and Paris, A. (2004) School engagement: Potential of the concept, state of the evidence, Review of Educational Research, 74(1), pp. 59-109.

Freire, P. (1970) Pedagogy of the Oppressed, New York: Herder and Herder.

Fullan, M. (2016) The new meaning of educational change. 4th edn. New York: Teachers College Press.

Fuller, F. (1969) Concerns of teachers: A developmental conceptualization, American Educational Research Journal, 6(2), 207-226.

Gao, R., Merzdorf, H., Anwar, S., Hipwell, M. and Srinivasa, A. (2024) Automatic assessment of text-based responses in post-secondary education: A systematic review, Computers and Education: Artificial Intelligence, p.100206.

Garrison, D.R., Anderson, T. & Archer, W. (1999) 'Critical inquiry in a text-based environment: Computer conferencing in higher education', The Internet and Higher Education, 2(2-3), pp. 87-105.

Garrison, D., Anderson, T. & Archer, W. (2010) The community of inquiry framework: Ten years later, Internet and Higher Education, 13(1-2), pp. 5-9.

Gay, G. (2018) Culturally responsive teaching: Theory, research, and practice, 2nd edn. New York: Teachers College Press.

Gee, J. (2007) What video games have to teach us about learning and literacy, Palgrave.

Gershon, M. (2015) How to use Bloom's Taxonomy in the classroom: The complete guide: Vol 8, CreateSpace.

George, A., Hall, G. and Stiegelbauer, S. (2014) Measuring implementation in schools: The stages of concern questionnaire (online). Available at https://sedl.org/cbam/socq_manual_201410.pdf (Accessed: 25/7/25).

Gikandi, J., Morrow, D. and Davis, N. (2011) Online formative assessment in higher education: A review of the literature, Computers & Education, 57(4), pp. 2333-2351.

Gillard, D. (2011) Education in England: a brief history (online). Available at www.educationengland.org.uk/history (Accessed: 17/7/25).

Goleman, D. (2017) Leadership that gets results. In Leadership perspectives (pp. 85-96), Routledge.

Gredler, M. (2008) Learning and Instruction: Theory into Practice, 5th ed. Upper Saddle River, NJ: Pearson.

Greene, M. (2013) Curriculum and consciousness. In Curriculum Studies Reader E2 (pp. 140-152), Routledge.

GOV.UK (2019) Ofsted education: Busting the 'intent' myth (online). Available at https://educationinspection.blog.gov.uk/2019/07/01/busting-the-intent-myth (Accessed: 23/7/25).

GOV.UK (2025) Statutory framework for the early years foundation stage: Setting the standards for learning, development and care for children from birth to five (online). Available at https://www.gov.uk/government/publications/early-years-foundation-stage-framework--2 (Accessed: 17/7/25).

GOV.UK (2025) To what extent has curriculum quality changed in schools since the introduction of the Education Inspection Framework (online). Available at: https://www.gov.uk/government/publications/curriculum-quality-evaluating-the-impact-of-the-education-inspection-framework/to-what-extent-has-curriculum-quality-changed-in-schools-since-the-introduction-of-the-education-inspection-framework (Accessed 31 July 2025).

Greenhow, C., Graham, C. and Koehler, M. (2022) Foundations of online learning: Challenges and opportunities, Educational Psychologist, 57(3), pp.131-147.

Gronlund, N. (2000) How to write and use instructional objectives, 6th edn. Merrill/Prentice Hall.

Guri-Rosenblit, S. (2011) Digital technologies in higher education: Sweeping expectations and actual effects, New York: Routledge.

Guskey, T. (2002) Professional development and teacher change, Teachers and Teaching, 8(3), pp. 381-391.

Guskey, T. & Bailey, J. (2010) Developing Standards-Based Report Cards, Corwin Press.

Hall, G., Loucks, S., Rutherford, W. and Newlove, B. (1975) Levels of use of the innovation: A framework for analyzing innovation adoption, Journal of teacher education, 26(1), pp.52-56.

Hallinger, P. & Murphy, J. (1985) Assessing the instructional management behavior of principals, The elementary school journal, 86(2), pp.217-247.

Hamilton, D. (1999) The pedagogic paradox (or why no didactics in England?), Pedagogy, Culture & Society, 7(1), pp. 135-152.

Harden, R. (2002) Learning outcomes and instructional objectives: Is there a difference?, Medical Teacher, 24(2), pp. 151-155.

Hargreaves, A. & Fink, D. (2006) Sustainable leadership, San Francisco: Jossey-Bass.

Harris, A. (2011) Distributed leadership: Implications for the role of the principal, Journal of Management Development, 31, 7-17.

Hattie, J. & Clarke, S. (2019) Visible learning: Feedback, Routledge.

HEA (2013) Recognising prior learning in higher education: Challenges and opportunities, Higher Education Academy.

Hirsch, E. (2019) Why knowledge matters: Rescuing our children from failed educational theories, Cambridge, MA: Harvard Education Press.

Hockings, C. (2010) Inclusive learning and teaching in higher education: A synthesis of research, Higher Education Academy.

Hodges, C., Moore, S., Lockee, B., Trust, T., & Bond, A. (2020) The difference between emergency remote teaching and online learning, Educause Review, 27 March.

House, E. (1979) Technology versus craft: A ten-year perspective on innovation, Journal of curriculum studies, Vol 11, No.1, pp 1-16.

Hrastinski, S. (2008) Asynchronous and synchronous e-learning, Educause Quarterly, 31(4), pp. 51-55.

IBO (2024) Middle Years Programme - Curriculum framework (online). Available at https://www.ibo.org/programmes/middle-years-programme/curriculum (Accessed: 20/5/25).

Kentnor, H. (2015) Distance education and the evolution of online learning in the United States, Curriculum and Teaching Dialogue, 17(1-2), pp. 21-34.

Illeris, K. (2018) A comprehensive understanding of human learning. In Contemporary theories of learning (pp. 1-14), Routledge.

Institute for Apprenticeships & Technical Education (IFATE) (2025) Apprenticeship Standards. [Online]. Available at: https://www.instituteforapprenticeships.org/ (Accessed: 19/7/25).

Jaggars, S. & Xu, D. (2016) How do online course design features influence student performance?, Computers & Education, 95, pp. 270-284.

James, D. & Biesta, G. (2007) Improving learning cultures in further education, Routledge.

JISC (2023) Digital lifelong learning tools: Recognition and validation (online). Available at: https://www.jisc.ac.uk (Accessed: 21/7/25).

Jonassen, D., Spector, M., Driscoll, M., Merrill, M., van Merrienboer, J. and Driscoll, M. (2008) Handbook of research on educational communications and technology: a project of the association for educational communications and technology, Routledge.

Jonassen, D. (2010) Learning to solve problems: A handbook for designing problem-solving learning environments, Routledge.

Jonsson, A. & Svingby, G. (2007) The use of scoring rubrics: Reliability, validity and educational consequences, Educational Research Review, 2(2), pp. 130-144.

Kelly, A. (2009) The curriculum: Theory and practice, Sage.

Kentnor, H. (2015) Distance education and the evolution of online learning in the United States, Curriculum and Teaching Dialogue, 17(1-2), pp. 21-34.

Kerr, J. (1968) Changing the Curriculum, University of London Press.

Khan, R. & Jawaid, M. (2020) Technology enhanced assessment (TEA) in COVID 19 pandemic, Pakistan journal of medical sciences, 36(COVID19-S4), p.S108.

Kirkpatrick, D. & Kirkpatrick, J. (2016) Kirkpatrick's four levels of training evaluation, ATD Press.

Kirkwood, A. & Price, L. (2014) Technology-enhanced learning and teaching in higher education: what is 'enhanced' and how do we know? A critical literature review', Learning, Media and Technology, 39(1), pp. 6-36.

Knight, P. (2002) Being a teacher in higher education, Open University Press.

Knight, P. & Yorke, M. (2003) Assessment, learning and employability, McGraw-Hill Education, Maidenhead.

Knowles, M., Holton, E. and Swanson, R. (2014) The adult learner: The definitive classic in adult education and human resource development, 8th edn. Routledge.

Kolb, D.A. (2014) Experiential learning: Experience as the source of learning and development. FT press.

Kotter, J. (1996) Leading change, Harvard Business Review Press.

Krathwohl, D (2009) Methods of educational and social science research: The Logic of Methods, Waveland Pr Inc.

Laal, M. & Ghodsi, S. (2012) Benefits of collaborative learning, Procedia - Social and Behavioral Sciences, 31, pp. 486-490.

Ladson-Billings, G. (2021) Culturally relevant pedagogy: Asking a different question, Teachers College Record, 123(1), pp. 6-27.

Lambert, L. (2002) A Framework for shared leadership, Educational Leadership, 59(8), 37-40.

Lattuca, L. & Stark, J. (2009) Shaping the college curriculum: Academic plans in context, 2nd edn. San Francisco: Jossey-Bass.

Laurillard, D. (2012) Teaching as a design science: Building pedagogical patterns for learning and technology, Routledge.

Learn, H. (2000) Brain, mind, experience, and school, Committee on Developments in the Science of Learning, pp.14-15.

Leask, B. (2009) Using formal and informal curricula to improve interactions between home and international students, Journal of Studies in International Education, 13(2), pp. 205-221.

Leithwood, K. & Jantzi, D. (2006) Transformational school leadership for large-scale reform: Effects on students, teachers, and their classroom practices, School effectiveness and school improvement, 17(2), pp.201-227.

Leithwood, K., Harris, A. & Hopkins, D. (2008) Seven strong claims about successful school leadership, School Leadership & Management, 28(1), pp. 27-42.

Leithwood, K. & Louis, K. (2012) Linking leadership to student learning, 2nd edn. San Francisco: Jossey-Bass.

Lewin, K. (1947) Frontiers in group dynamics: concept, method and reality in social science; social equilibria and social change', Human Relations, 1(1), pp. 5-41.

Lumby, J. & Coleman, M. (2007) Leadership and diversity: Challenging theory and practice in education, Sage.

Major, C. (2015) Teaching Online: A Guide to Theory, Research, and Practice, Baltimore: Johns Hopkins University Press.

Marsh, C. (2009) Key concepts for understanding curriculum, 3rd edn. London: Routledge.

Marsh, C. & Willis, G. (2003) Curriculum: Alternative approaches, ongoing issues, Prentice Hall.

Martin, F. & Bolliger, D. (2018) Engagement matters: Student perceptions on the importance of engagement strategies in the online learning environment, Online Learning, 22(1), pp. 205-222.

McCulloch, G. (2011) The Struggle for the History of Education, Routledge.

McKinsey (2023) What higher education students want from online learning (online). Available at: https://www.mckinsey.com/industries/public-sector/our-insights/what-do-higher-education-students-want-from-online-learning (Accessed: 28/7/25).

Meyer, J. & Land, R. (2005) Threshold concepts and troublesome knowledge: Epistemological considerations and a conceptual framework for teaching and learning, Higher Education, 49(3), pp. 373-388.

Moon, J. (2013). A handbook of reflective and experiential learning: Theory and practice, Routledge.

Murchan, D. & Shiel, G. (2024) Assessment in Education: Policy and Practice, London: Routledge.

Newton, P. (2018) How common is commercial contract cheating in higher education and is it increasing? A systematic review, Studies in Higher Education, 43(4), pp. 634-650.

Nicol, D. (2014) From monologue to dialogue: improving written feedback processes in mass higher education. In Approaches to assessment that enhance learning in higher education (pp. 11-27), Routledge.

Nicol, D. & Macfarlane-Dick, D. (2006) Formative assessment and self-regulated learning: A model and seven principles of good feedback practice, Studies in Higher Education, 31(2), pp. 199-218.

Nicol, D. (2020) The power of internal feedback: Exploiting natural comparison processes, *Assessment & Evaluation in Higher Education*, *46*(5), 756-778.

Nicol, D., Thomson, A. and Breslin, C. (2014) Rethinking feedback practices in higher education: a peer review perspective, Assessment & Evaluation in Higher Education, 39(1), pp. 102-122.

Nieto, S. (2013) Finding joy in teaching students of diverse backgrounds: Culturally responsive and socially just practices in U. S. classrooms. Portsmouth, NH: Heinemann.

Nkomo, L., Daniel, B. and Butson, R. (2021) Synthesis of student engagement with digital technologies: a systematic review of the literature, International Journal of Educational Technology in Higher Education, 18, pp.1-26.

O'Flaherty, J. & Phillips, C. (2015) The use of flipped classrooms in higher education: A scoping review, Internet and Higher Education, 25, pp. 85-95.

Oates, T. (2011) Could do better: Using international comparisons to refine the National Curriculum in England, Curriculum journal, 22(2), pp.121-150.

OECD (2020) Trends shaping education 2020. OECD Publishing.

OECD (2023) PISA 2022 results (online). Available at oecd.org/en/about/programmes/pisa.html (Accessed: 21/7/25).

OECD (2025) Digital divide in education (online). Available at: https://www.oecd.org/en/topics/sub-issues/digital-divide-in-education.html (Accessed: 28/7/25).

Ofqual (2020) Regulated Qualifications Framework (online). Available from https://www.gov.uk/find-a-regulated-qualification (Accessed: 20/12/24).

Ofsted (2019) Education Inspection Framework: Overview of Research (online). Available at: www.gov.uk (Accessed: 18/7/25).

Ofsted (2021) School inspection handbook, Manchester: Ofsted.

Ofsted (2021) Remote education research (online). Available at gov.uk/government/publications/remote-education-research/remote-education-research (Accessed: 29/7/25).

Ornstein, A. & Hunkins, F. (2016) Curriculum: Foundations, principles, and issues, 7th edn, Boston: Pearson.

Ortiz, A., Gray, N., Kuborn, S. and Caldwell, J. (2022) Comparison of Course Learning Outcomes Online vs. Face-to-Face: A Case Study, Journal on Excellence in College Teaching, 33(3).

Patall, E., Cooper, H. & Robinson, J. (2008) The effects of choice on intrinsic motivation and related outcomes: A meta-analysis of research findings, Psychological Bulletin, 134(2), pp. 270-300.

Pea, R. (2018) The social and technological dimensions of scaffolding and related theoretical concepts for learning, education, and human activity. In Scaffolding (pp. 423-451). Psychology Press.

Pearson (2025) BTEC Nationals: Health and Social Care Specifications, Pearson Education Limited.

Pennsylvania Department of Education (PDE) (2025) Standards Aligned System (online). Available at https://www.pdesas.org (Accessed: 19/7/25).

Pinar, W. (2019) What is curriculum theory? 2nd edn. New York: Routledge.

Plowden Report (1967) Children and their primary schools: Report of the Central Advisory Council for Education (England), London: HMSO.

Popham, W. (2001) The truth about testing: An educator's call to action, ASCD.

Pressley, M. & McCormick, C. (2007) Child and Adolescent Development for Educators, 2nd edn. New York: Guilford.

Priestley, M. & Biesta, G. (2013) Reinventing the curriculum: New trends in curriculum policy and practice, Bloomsbury Academic.

Priestley, M., Biesta, G. and Robinson, S. (2015) Teacher agency: An ecological approach, London: Bloomsbury.

Pring, R. (2013) The life and death of secondary education for all, Routledge.

Print, M. (2021) Curriculum Development and Design, Routledge.

QAA (2024) UK quality code for higher education (online). Available at https://www.qaa.ac.uk/the-quality-code (Accessed: 18/7/25).

QAHE (2022) The evolution of online learning: A comprehensive overview (online). Available at qahe.org/article/the-evolution-of-online-learning-a-comprehensive-overview (Accessed: 28/7/25).

Quality Assurance Agency for Higher Education (QAA) (2024) Subject Benchmark Statements (online). Available at: www.qaa.ac.uk (Accessed: 19/7/25).

Quintana, C., Reiser, B., Davis, E., Krajcik, J., Fretz, E., Duncan, R., Kyza, E., Edelson, D. and Soloway, E. (2018) A scaffolding design framework for software to support science inquiry, In Scaffolding (pp. 337-386). Psychology Press.

Race, P. (2019) The Lecturer's Toolkit: A Practical Guide to Assessment, Learning and Teaching, Routledge.

Reay, D., Crozier, G. and Clayton, J. (2009) Strangers in paradise? Working-class students in elite universities, Sociology, 43(6), pp.1103-1121.

Richardson, J., Maeda, Y., Lv, J. and Caskurlu, S. (2017) Social presence in relation to students' satisfaction and learning in the online environment: A meta-analysis, Computers in Human Behavior, 71, pp. 402-417.

Rienties, B. & Toetenel, L. (2016) The impact of learning design on student behaviour, satisfaction and performance: A cross-institutional comparison across 151 modules, Computers in Human Behavior, 60, pp. 333-341.

Rivkin, S., Hanushek, E. and Kain, J. (2005) Teachers, schools, and academic achievement, Econometrica, 73(2), pp. 417-458.

Rogers, C. (1969) Freedom to learn, Merrill.

Rose, D. & Meyer, A. (2002) Teaching every student in the digital age: Universal Design for Learning, Alexandria, VA: ASCD.

Ryan, R. & Deci, E. (2000) Intrinsic and extrinsic motivations: Classic definitions and new directions, Contemporary Educational Psychology, 25(1), pp.54-67.

Sahlberg, P. (2021) Finnish lessons 3.0: What can the world learn from educational change in Finland?, Teachers College Press.

Schön, D.A. (2017) The reflective practitioner: How professionals think in action, Routledge.

Scriven, M. (1967) The methodology of evaluation. In Tyler, R.W. et al. Perspectives of curriculum evaluation: AERA Monograph Series on Curriculum Evaluation, No. 1.

Scriven, M. (1991) Evaluation thesaurus, Newbury Park, CA: Sage.

Selwyn, N. (2021) Education and technology: Key issues and debates, Bloomsbury Publishing.

Simmons, R. (2009) Entry to employment: Discourses of inclusion and employability in work-based learning for young people, Journal of Education and Work, 22(2), pp. 137-151.

Shermis, M. & Burstein, J. (2013) Handbook of Automated Essay Evaluation: Current Applications and New Directions, Routledge.

Sherrington, T. (2019) Rosenshine's principles in action, John Catt Educational.

Skelton, C. (2003) Boys and girls in the primary classroom, McGraw-Hill Education.

Spady, W. (1993) Outcome based education, Workshop report No 5, Canberra: ACSA.

Spillane, J. P. (2006). Distributed Leadership. San Francisco: Jossey-Bass.

SSAT (2023) Principled Curriculum Design (online). Available at: www.ssatuk.co.uk (Accessed: 18/7/25).

Stack, S. (2015) Learning outcomes in an online vs traditional course, International Journal for the Scholarship of Teaching and Learning, 9(1).

Stake, R. (1967) The countenance of educational evaluation, Teachers College Record, 68(7), 1-15.

Stavredes, T. & Herder, T. (2014) A Guide to Online Course Design: Strategies for Student Success, John Wiley & Sons.

Stenhouse, L. (1975) An introduction to curriculum research and development, Heinemann.

Stiggins, R. (2002) Assessment crisis: the absence of assessment for learning, Portland: ETS Assessment Training Institute.

Stufflebeam, D. & Shinkfield, A. (2014) Evaluation theory, models, & applications, San Francisco: Jossey-Bass.

Sweller, J. (2011) Cognitive Load Theory, Psychology of Learning and Motivation, 55, pp. 37-76.

Taba, H. (1962) Curriculum development: Theory and practice, Harcourt, Brace and World.

Taguma, M. & Frid, A. (2024) Curriculum frameworks and visualisations beyond national frameworks: Alignment with the OECD Learning Compass 2030.

Tai, J., Ajjawi, R., Boud, D., Dawson, P. and Panadero, E. (2018) Developing evaluative judgement: Enabling students to make decisions about the quality of work, Higher education, 76, pp.467-481.

Tan, C. & Deneen, C. (2015) Singapore's holistic curriculum: Beyond high-stakes testing, British Journal of Educational Studies, 63(3), pp. 263-286.

Tanner, D. & Tanner, L. (1995) Curriculum development: Theory into practice, 3rd edn, New York: Macmillan.

Third Space Learning (2024) A beginner's guide to curriculum development at primary (online). Available at: www.thirdspacelearning.com (Accessed: 18/7/25).

Tickell, C. (2011) The early years: Foundations for life, health and learning, HM Government.

Tomlinson, C. (2001) How to Differentiate Instruction in Mixed-Ability Classrooms, ASCD.

Topping, K. (2005) Trends in peer learning, Educational Psychology, 25(6), pp. 631-645.

Topping, K. (2009) Peer Assessment, Theory into Practice, 48(1), 20-27.

Topping, K. (2017) Peer assessment: Learning by judging and discussing the work of other learners, Interdisciplinary Education and Psychology, 1(1), pp.1-17.

Tyler, R.W. (1949) Basic principles of curriculum and instruction, University of Chicago Press.

Tyler, R. (2009) Basic principles of curriculum and instruction, The curriculum studies reader, pp.69-77.

Tyler, R. (2013) Basic Principles of curriculum and instruction, University of Chicago Press.

UK Government (2010) Equality Act, HMSO (online). Available at https://www.legislation.gov.uk/ukpga/2010/15/contents (Accessed: 19/12/24).

UNESCO (2022) Education for sustainable development: UK national implementation report (online). Available at unesco.org/en/sustainable-development/education (Accessed: 30/7/25).

Viscione, I., D'Elia, F., Vastola, R. and Sibilio, M. (2017) Psychomotor assessment in teaching and educational research, Athens Journal of Education, 4(2), pp.169-177.

Vorecol (2024) The Impact of AI on Test Validity and Reliability in Psychometric Assessments (online). Available at https://psico-smart.com (Accessed: 24/12/24).

Vygotsky, L. (1978) Mind in society: The development of higher psychological processes, Cambridge, MA: Harvard University Press.

W3C (2018) Web Content Accessibility Guidelines (WCAG) 2.1 (online). Available at: https://www.w3.org/TR/WCAG21 (Accessed: 28/7/25).

Waite, S. (2017) Children learning outside the classroom: From birth to eleven, Sage.

West, A. & Pennell, H. (2000) Publishing school examination results in England: Incentives and consequences, Educational Studies, 26(4), pp. 423-436.

Whalen, J. (2020) Should teachers be trained in emergency remote teaching? Lessons learned from the COVID-19 pandemic, Journal of technology and teacher education, 28(2), pp.189-199.

Whatfix (2024) Online Learning vs. Face-to-Face Learning: Which Is Best? (online). Available at: whatfix.com/blog/online-learning-vs-face-to-face-learning (Accessed: 28/7/25).

Wheeler, D. (1967) Curriculum Process, University of London Press.

Whitmore, E. (1998) Understanding and practicing participatory evaluation. New Directions for Evaluation, Summer 1998 (No. 80), pp. 19-31.

Whitty, G. (2010) Revisiting school knowledge: Curriculum and the state, in Whitty, G. & Furlong, J. (eds) Faith in education, Institute of Education.

Wiggins, G. & McTighe, J. (2011) The Understanding by Design Guide to Creating High-Quality Units, ASCD.

Wiliam, D. (2011) Embedded formative assessment, Solution Tree Press.

Williamson, B. (2021) Datafication and automation in education: Critical perspectives on AI and assessment, Big Data & Society, 8(1), 1-12.

Willingham, D.T. (2021) Why Don't Students Like School?, John Wiley & Sons.

Wing Institute (2024) Distributed Leadership (online). Available at: winginstitute.org/leadership-models-distributed (Accessed 31 July 2025).

Wood, D., Bruner, J. and Ross, G. (1976) The role of tutoring in problem solving, Journal of Child Psychology and Psychiatry, 17(2), pp. 89-100.

Young, M. (2008) Bringing knowledge back in: From social constructivism to social realism in the sociology of education, Routledge.

Young, M., Lambert, D., Roberts, C. and Roberts, M. (2014) Knowledge and the future school: Curriculum and social justice, Bloomsbury Publishing.

Young, M. & Muller, J. (2016) Curriculum and the specialisation of knowledge: Studies in the sociology of education, Routledge.

INDEX

Accreditation of Prior Experiential Learning 84-87, 236, 241
Action verbs 275
Adaptation 34, 36, 39, 46, 101, 112, 124, 149, 161, 261, 262, 278
ADDIE model 201
Affective domain 49, 239
Apprenticeships 40, 41, 42, 43, 92
AQA 92
Assessment 226-257
Assessment standards 6, 82, 205, 247, 266
Association for Science Education 92
Asynchronous assessments 210, 253
Authenticity 145, 211
Automated testing 253
Backward Design 34-36, 46, 53, 60, 123, 202
Behavioural model 14-15, 19
Behaviourism 17, 122, 200
Blended learning 20, 177, 197, 199, 214, 252, 253
Bloom's taxonomy 47, 50, 69, 70, 145, 239, 243, 276-279
Bobbit, Franklin 5, 14, 17
Branching scenarios 212, 214, 218
Bruner, Jerome 22, 34, 36, 53, 64, 66, 78, 123, 124, 206, 207
BTEC 15, 40, 42, 43, 81, 83
Canvas, 219, 222
Change leaders 264, 265, 273
Chunking content 206
City & Guilds 85, 92, 112, 280
Cognitive domain 49, 70, 239

Cognitive scaffolding 206-208
Cognitivism 200
Collaborative assignments 210
Community building 201, 203, 210
Community of Inquiry 201
Connectivism 201
Construct validity 247
Constructive alignment 17, 23, 30, 33, 48, 52, 69, 73, 202, 227
Constructivism 17, 122, 200
Content validity 247
Continuity 27, 63, 66, 88, 104, 113, 141, 156
Council for the Curriculum, Examinations and Assessment 91
CPD 151, 199, 260
Credit transfer 62, 79, 80-83, 86, 92
Criterion-related validity 248
Cumulative learning 47, 64, 231
Curriculum and Assessment Authority for Wales 91
Curriculum balance 94, 101, 103-105
Curriculum change 142, 258, 259, 261-265, 273
Curriculum coherence 45, 51, 54, 119, 134, 138, 154, 158, 159, 267
Curriculum components 6-10, 190
Curriculum definition 3
Curriculum design 26-30
Curriculum development agencies 90
Curriculum distortion 21
Curriculum frameworks 11, 15, 31, 38-43, 51, 58, 60, 90, 109, 136, 148, 227, 233, 261, 262

Curriculum instability 106
Curriculum organisation 62-88
Curriculum planning 2, 13, 21, 25, 26, 34-37, 78, 117, 132, 133, 230, 231
Curriculum Study Group 2
Dashboards 191, 219, 222
Department for Education 6, 91, 113, 132
Developmental model 15-16, 154
Differentiation 19, 21, 28, 46, 49, 52, 80, 84, 142, 146, 158, 161, 174, 177, 193, 227, 232, 239, 240, 286, 289
Digital Capabilities Framework 245
Digital games 245
Digital simulations 245
Distributed Leadership 265, 266, 271-273
Document analysis 154
Domains of learning 49, 70, 236, 239, 245
Drivers of change 260, 262, 264, 283
Early Years Foundation Stage (EYFS) 4, 40, 290
Education Reform Act 90, 105, 119
Education Scotland 91
Eisner's Connoisseurship 37, 53, 171, 181-187
Essays 220, 235, 237, 244, 245, 247, 248
European Union 87, 92
Evaluation 164-196
Evaluation documents 187-189
Evaluation instruments 189
Evaluation reports 189, 190, 191, 286
External influences 89-114
External reviews 41, 167, 171, 187, 189, 194, 250

Extra-curricular 8, 9, 12, 59, 101
Face to face learning 198, 204, 205, 218, 221, 283
Feedback 146, 154, 203, 218-222, 229, 230, 235, 252-253, 269
Focus group 57, 154, 179
Formal curriculum 10-14
Formative assessment 47, 218-220
Freire's Critical Pedagogy 37, 53, 123
Froebel 23
Grade descriptors 246, 247
Grading systems 246
Gradual release 208
Gronlund Approach 70-74, 88
Group assessment 236, 240, 241, 251
Hidden curriculum 4, 6, 9, 24, 46, 104, 150
Horizontal alignment 47, 63, 64
Horizontal relationships 63, 64, 67
Hybrid learning 78, 88, 113, 199, 200, 246, 251
Ideological bias 107
Impact 115-134, 164
Implementation 135-163
Individualisation 28, 240
Informal curriculum 11, 12, 13, 14, 25
Innovation 254, 261
Institute for Apprenticeships and Technical Education 40, 92
Instructional Leadership 266
Instructional objectives 49, 70
Instructor presence 197, 203, 209, 213, 221
Integration 67, 76
Interaction 10, 203, 210

Interactive content 197, 199, 212, 214-218
Interactive learning activities 253
International Baccalaureate 80, 250
Interviews 57, 154, 167, 189, 190, 192, 244
Journals 244
Kerr model 37
Kirkpatrick model 178, 184, 185
Kotter 272
Learned curriculum 8
Learner engagement 20, 184, 203, 209, 254, 256
Learning experience 5, 66, 144, 252, 266
Learning management system 198, 219, 222-225
Learning outcome 47, 204, 275
Learning taxonomies 70, 276-279
Lesson plan 48, 51, 60, 287-289
Level descriptor 63, 247
Lifelong learning 4, 23, 56, 87, 79, 80, 81, 84, 87, 88, 108, 120, 127, 236, 241, 255, 291
Log book 244
Managed learning environment 223
Marking scheme 247
Massive Open Online Course 198
Measuring implementation 152, 155, 157
Metacognitive scaffolding 208
Micro-credentials 198, 255
Moderation 219, 244, 247, 248, 249, 250, 252, 282
Modularisation 69, 79-83, 88
Module specification 51, 283-284

Moodle 219, 222
Multimedia 214
National Association for the Teaching of English 92
National Curriculum 40, 42, 50, 58, 83, 90, 93-100, 105, 109
National Curriculum Council 90
Navigation 207-209
NCFE 92, 95
Needs analysis 52-60
Null curriculum 6, 9
Objective model 14-15
Objectives 5, 47, 172,
OCR 92
Office for Students 92, 162
Official curriculum 6, 7, 14, 149
Ofqual 7, 91, 93, 95, 247
Ofsted 91, 125, 158, 191
Online learning 197-225
Oral assessment 244
Organising threads (strands) 68
Ornstein and Hunkins Framework 37, 53
Pedagogy 18-21, 37
Peer assessment 203, 234, 239, 245, 251, 252, 285, 286
Peer review 189, 210, 219, 222, 230, 249, 250, 251, 285
Piaget 18, 22, 27, 54
Plagiarism 219, 220
PLATO 198
Play-based learning 18, 22
Portfolios 244
Presentations 244
Problem-solving tasks 245

Process model 14-17, 34, 36, 60, 104, 116, 122, 132, 153, 237, 266
Process model 266
Product 3, 14-17, 119, 176, 266
Product and process assessment 237
Programme specification 33, 51, 72, 121, 124, 126, 127, 130, 173, 175, 280-282
Progressive model 15-16
Psychomotor domain 49, 239, 245
QAA Subject Benchmark Statements 41
Qualifications and Curriculum Authority 90
Quality assurance 160
Quality Assurance Agency 7, 15, 33, 41, 48, 92, 112, 162, 181, 187, 188, 194, 244, 250, 263
Questioning 149, 243
Quizzes 146, 179, 211, 217, 219
Re-contextualisation 110
Reflective practice 5, 8, 15, 86, 133, 150, 160, 162, 194, 258
Regulated Qualifications Framework 247
Reliability 190, 219, 229, 233, 236, 242, 244, 245, 247-251, 254
Reporting 186, 226, 244
Resistance to change 139, 143, 156, 272
Responsive orientation 175
Review panel 250
Role-play 245
Rousseau 23
Rubric 189, 203, 219, 221, 228, 229, 235, 236, 242-251, 292-295
Scheme of work 44, 51, 149, 285-286

School Curriculum and Assessment Authority 90
School Examinations and Assessment Council 90
SCORM 224, 225
Secondary Schools Examination Council 2
Self-assessment 154, 189, 219, 245
Self-evaluation 188, 189, 194
Seminar 244
Sequencing 47, 66, 128
Shared group grades 251
Shared leadership 264, 269, 270, 272
Simulation 217, 245
Situated learning 200
Skinner 18
Social scaffolding 208
Spiral curricula 22, 28, 32, 34, 36, 53, 60, 78, 123, 124, 206
Stages of Concern 154-156
Stake's Countenance Model 173, 175, 184, 185
Stake's judgmental matrix 174
Standardisation 249
Standards 47-50
Statement of intent 121, 290-291
Stenhouse, Lawrence 15, 125
Stenhouse's Process Model 17, 34, 36, 53, 60, 123, 237, 266
Student feedback 20, 30, 56, 65, 154, 158, 168, 174, 194
Stufflebeam's CIPP model 176-178, 184, 185
Subject-based curriculum 74
Summative assessment 153, 219, 220-233, 244

Synchronous activities 210

Synchronous assessments 253

Taba, Hilda 18, 20, 34, 35, 52, 53, 60, 148, 149

Taught curriculum 7, 8

Taxonomic levels 69, 73

Teach to the test 9, 19, 33, 45, 100, 103, 107, 119, 141

Teacher agency 20-22, 141, 149

Teacher importance 148

Teacher leadership 150, 271

Technical scaffolding 208

Technology-Enhanced Assessment 226, 245, 252-254, 257

Tested curriculum 6, 8, 9

Tests 244

Total curriculum 6

Transformation 261, 262

Transformational Leadership 266

Tyler, Ralph 14, 52, 60

Tyler rationale 17, 26, 30-35, 38, 115, 119, 122, 165, 237, 266

Tyler's objectives model 172, 184

Validity 84, 229, 247, 248, 254

Vertical alignment 45, 63, 65

Virtual learning environment 198, 222

Vygotsky 18, 22, 54, 64, 124, 146, 231

Wheeler model 36, 53

Wiggins & McTigh's UbD 34, 35, 43, 45, 46, 123, 172, 202

www.ingramcontent.com/pod-product-compliance
Lightning Source LLC
Chambersburg PA
CBHW051400070526
44584CB00023B/3229